ENCOUNTERS WITH ALBION
BRITAIN AND THE BRITISH IN TEXTS BY
JEWISH REFUGEES FROM NAZISM

LEGENDA

LEGENDA is the Modern Humanities Research Association's book imprint for new research in the Humanities. Founded in 1995 by Malcolm Bowie and others within the University of Oxford, Legenda has always been a collaborative publishing enterprise, directly governed by scholars. The Modern Humanities Research Association (MHRA) joined this collaboration in 1998, became half-owner in 2004, in partnership with Maney Publishing and then Routledge, and has since 2016 been sole owner. Titles range from medieval texts to contemporary cinema and form a widely comparative view of the modern humanities, including works on Arabic, Catalan, English, French, German, Greek, Italian, Portuguese, Russian, Spanish, and Yiddish literature. Editorial boards and committees of more than 60 leading academic specialists work in collaboration with bodies such as the Society for French Studies, the British Comparative Literature Association and the Association of Hispanists of Great Britain & Ireland.

The MHRA encourages and promotes advanced study and research in the field of the modern humanities, especially modern European languages and literature, including English, and also cinema. It aims to break down the barriers between scholars working in different disciplines and to maintain the unity of humanistic scholarship. The Association fulfils this purpose through the publication of journals, bibliographies, monographs, critical editions, and the MHRA Style Guide, and by making grants in support of research. Membership is open to all who work in the Humanities, whether independent or in a University post, and the participation of younger colleagues entering the field is especially welcomed.

ALSO PUBLISHED BY THE ASSOCIATION

Critical Texts
Tudor and Stuart Translations • *New Translations* • *European Translations*
MHRA Library of Medieval Welsh Literature

MHRA Bibliographies
Publications of the Modern Humanities Research Association

The Annual Bibliography of English Language & Literature
Austrian Studies
Modern Language Review
Portuguese Studies
The Slavonic and East European Review
Working Papers in the Humanities
The Yearbook of English Studies

www.mhra.org.uk
www.legendabooks.com

GERMANIC LITERATURES

Editorial Committee
Chair: Professor Ritchie Robertson (University of Oxford)
Dr Barbara Burns (Glasgow University)
Professor Jane Fenoulhet (University College London)
Professor Anne Fuchs (University College Dublin)
Dr Jakob Stougaard-Nielsen (University College London)
Professor Annette Volfing (University of Oxford)
Professor Susanne Kord (University College London)
Professor John Zilcosky (University of Toronto)

Germanic Literatures includes monographs and essay collections on literature originally written not only in German, but also in Dutch and the Scandinavian languages. Within the German-speaking area, it seeks also to publish studies of other national literatures such as those of Austria and Switzerland. The chronological scope of the series extends from the early Middle Ages down to the present day.

APPEARING IN THIS SERIES

1. *Yvan Goll: The Thwarted Pursuit of the Whole*, by Robert Vilain
2. *Sebald's Bachelors: Queer Resistance and the Unconforming Life*, by Helen Finch
3. *Goethe's Visual World*, by Pamela Currie
4. *German Narratives of Belonging: Writing Generation and Place in the Twenty-First Century*, by Linda Shortt
5. *The Very Late Goethe: Self-Consciousness and the Art of Ageing*, by Charlotte Lee
6. *Women, Emancipation and the German Novel 1871-1910: Protest Fiction in its Cultural Context*, by Charlotte Woodford
7. *Goethe's Poetry and the Philosophy of Nature: Gott und Welt 1798–1827*, by Regina Sachers
8. *Fontane and Cultural Mediation: Translation and Reception in Nineteenth-Century German Literature*, edited by Ritchie Robertson and Michael White
9. *Metamorphosis in Modern German Literature: Transforming Bodies, Identities and Affects*, by Tara Beaney
10. *Comedy and Trauma in Germany and Austria after 1945: The Inner Side of Mourning*, by Stephanie Bird
11. *E.T.A. Hoffmann's Orient: Romantic Aesthetics and the German Imagination*, by Joanna Neilly
12. *Structures of Subjugation in Dutch Literature*, by Judit Gera

Managing Editor
Dr Graham Nelson, 41 Wellington Square, Oxford OX1 2JF, UK
www.legendabooks.com

Encounters with Albion

*Britain and the British in
Texts by Jewish Refugees from Nazism*

Anthony Grenville

Germanic Literatures 17
Modern Humanities Research Association
2018

*Published by Legenda
an imprint of the Modern Humanities Research Association
Salisbury House, Station Road, Cambridge CB1 2LA*

*ISBN 978-1-78188-707-3 (HB)
ISBN 978-1-78188-408-9 (PB)*

First published 2018

All rights reserved. No part of this publication may be reproduced or disseminated or transmitted in any form or by any means, electronic, mechanical, photocopying, recording or otherwise, or stored in any retrieval system, or otherwise used in any manner whatsoever without written permission of the copyright owner, except in accordance with the provisions of the Copyright, Designs and Patents Act 1988, or under the terms of a licence permitting restricted copying issued in the UK by the Copyright Licensing Agency Ltd, Saffron House, 6–10 Kirby Street, London EC1N 8TS, England, or in the USA by the Copyright Clearance Center, 222 Rosewood Drive, Danvers MA 01923. Application for the written permission of the copyright owner to reproduce any part of this publication must be made by email to legenda@mhra.org.uk.

Disclaimer: Statements of fact and opinion contained in this book are those of the author and not of the editors or the Modern Humanities Research Association. The publisher makes no representation, express or implied, in respect of the accuracy of the material in this book and cannot accept any legal responsibility or liability for any errors or omissions that may be made.

Trademark notice: Product or corporate names may be trademarks or registered trademarks, and are used only for identification and explanation without intent to infringe.

© *Modern Humanities Research Association 2018*

Copy-Editor: Alastair Matthews

CONTENTS

	Acknowledgements	ix
	Introduction	1
1	Arrival and Early Years in Britain	5
2	Internment	34
3	Memories of Wartime Service and Combat	65
4	The Years of Settlement, 1945–60	91
5	Established Refugee Writers	110
6	The Child Refugee's Perspective	130
7	A Wealth of Memoirs: Autobiographies of the 1990s and 2000s	149
	Afterword	176
	Bibliography	177
	Index	181

To my wife, Eva

ACKNOWLEDGEMENTS

It is a pleasure to acknowledge my gratitude to the people and institutions that have assisted me in writing this book. I must first thank the Association of Jewish Refugees (AJR) for its generous financial support for my research and for the many years over which it has supported my work generally. I have enjoyed working with Michael Newman, now the AJR's Chief Executive, for more years than I care to count. I have also gained enormously from my participation in the activities of the Research Centre for German and Austrian Exile Studies at the Institute of Modern Languages Research, School of Advanced Study, University of London. My colleagues on the committee of the Research Centre have been a pleasure to work with for twenty years now, as well as a constant source of new material, fresh ideas, and friendship. My thanks go also to Legenda, for publishing *Encounters with Albion*, and to Graham Nelson in particular. Last but not least, I thank my wife, Eva Urbach-Grenville, who has supported me while I worked on this book and has had to put up with the long periods during which I was carrying out the research for the book and writing it.

A.G., London, April 2018

INTRODUCTION

The refugees from Nazi persecution who arrived in Britain after 1933 from Germany and, later, from Austria and Czechoslovakia long rated little more than a footnote in the historical record as it was written in Britain in the years after 1945. But that changed in the 1980s and 1990s, as the Holocaust came to be seen as a defining event in the history of the twentieth century, and as interest in the victims of Nazi persecution among both academics and the general public increased correspondingly. Over the past twenty-five years, the refugees from Hitler, mostly Jewish, have come to occupy an increasingly important place in British public consciousness: the trains that brought some ten thousand Jewish children to Britain in 1938–39, known as Kindertransports, have impinged to a significant degree on public awareness; names like that of Sir Nicholas Winton are now recognized widely; and the wealth of culture, learning, and scholarly and scientific expertise that the refugees brought with them to their adopted homeland is more generally appreciated. The United Kingdom is even planning its own Holocaust Memorial.

In parallel with these developments, academic studies of the refugees have also proliferated over the past three decades. However, it is noticeable that many of these studies focus on British attitudes towards and reactions to the refugees, most obviously in the case of the major histories of the refugees in Britain by A. J. Sherman, Bernard Wasserstein, and Louise London;[1] these, of necessity, rely heavily on official government records in documenting the evolution of British policy towards the refugees, who in large measure play the part of passive objects of it. The numerous studies of anti-Semitism and hostility towards the refugees are also written predominantly from a British perspective, with the refugees again appearing primarily as the victims of British prejudice and intolerance. Studies of individual events such as the internment of many thousands of Jewish refugees in summer 1940 as 'enemy aliens' are also primarily written as records of, and judgements on, British policy in that sphere. One volume that merits special mention is *Second Chance: Two Centuries of German-Speaking Jews in the United Kingdom*, edited by Werner Mosse; published in 1991, this is a unique collection of essays by experts, including refugee scholars, on Jewish immigrants in Britain during the nineteenth and twentieth centuries.[2] There are, of course, also innumerable studies devoted to individual refugees or groups of refugees which are written from what one might call the refugee perspective. But it remains true that studies that range more broadly and attempt an overview of the refugee experience tend to adopt the British perspective, viewing the refugees through the prism of British attitudes, policies, or actions.

This book attempts to reverse that tendency — to view matters through the opposite end of the telescope, as it were — by consciously adopting the refugee perspective and focusing on the refugees' view of the British. *Encounters with Albion* seeks to document the evolution of the refugees' image of Britain and British society as it appears in some fifty texts by refugee authors written between 1933 and 2012: autobiographies, memoirs, diaries, letters, and works of fiction. The study aims to provide for the first time a comprehensive account of refugee attitudes and reactions to Britain by analysing a substantial number of relevant texts. It is also the first study to examine so many texts by refugees, as there is to date no comparable large-scale survey of refugee literature, though there are, of course, many studies of individual refugee writers and groups of writers. Foremost among them is Richard Dove's masterly account of five refugee writers from Germany and Austria in Britain in the 1930s and 1940s, *Journey of No Return*.[3]

Encounters with Albion consists of seven chapters, the first four of which are arranged chronologically, covering the refugees' arrival in Britain, the internment of 'enemy aliens' in 1940, the war, and the initial period of settlement after 1945; the last three chapters are devoted to important groupings of texts: those by established refugee writers, those written from the point of view of the child refugee, and finally a selection from the many autobiographies and memoirs that have appeared since 1990. I hope that this arrangement will help to clarify the difficult question of periodization by distinguishing between texts written at different stages in the history of the settlement of the refugees in Britain and showing how their image of the British developed over the decades. In the interests of academic rigour, I have adopted strict criteria for the selection of texts: the texts chosen for each chapter were all written contemporaneously, or very nearly so, with the period of time and the events described. The only exception is Chapter 3, which deals with the war: since published wartime diaries by refugees fighting in the British forces are hard to find, I have used the seven wartime memoirs and autobiographies selected in it to trace the differing paths taken by refugees who fought in the war as they integrated into British society, or turned away from it. On account of the relative shortage of texts by refugees published in the very early years of settlement, I have included among the nine texts analysed in Chapter 1 two texts available only as unpublished manuscripts; otherwise, I have used only published texts, so that readers may have easy access to them and can check my findings against the full original texts. Most of the texts are written in English; where they are in German, the translations of quotations are all mine.

My analysis of the literary and autobiographical texts studied relies on close reading and detailed textual interpretation. Consequently, my book contains numerous quotations; to avoid an undesirable proliferation of endnotes, I have given the full details of publication only in the initial reference to each text, and thereafter just the page number in parentheses after each quotation; any emphasis in quotations is also present in the original. By means of this close analysis of the texts as documents and by building up a detailed picture of my subject, I have sought to write a historical study of the evolution of refugee attitudes towards the society that took them in, not always very willingly. As all the texts have literary qualities, however modest, I have adopted an approach that combines literary and historical analysis. In the absence of any other substantial body of documents recording the refugee experience in Britain, literary and autobiographical works are almost certainly the best and most informative sources available to us in this area.

I have approached these works in full awareness of the care needed when treating literary texts as source material for a primarily historical study, and in the hope that I have achieved an appropriate balance between literary and historical analysis; the distinction between the two has in any case been greatly blurred by theoretical developments in recent decades, which tend to regard all documents as 'texts'. Using literary texts for historical purposes creates its own problems, which can, however, be resolved if approached rigorously and methodically, and with an awareness of the factors that may cause sections of a text to be less reliable as historical evidence. That is the case with memoirs written long after the experiences described; when I use such texts, in Chapters 3 and 7, I do not treat them as sources that reflect the surface detail of a given historical situation, but rather as a means of revealing the longer-term developments in the relationship between the refugee author and British society. Particular care must be taken when using fictionalized narratives as documentary material; when analysing the internment novels of Leo Kahn and Richard Friedenthal in Chapter 2 or Zvi Jagendorf's *Wolfy and the Strudelbakers* in Chapter 6, I take into account that these are set in a realm of the imagination, albeit one that draws directly on lived reality.

In exploring the image of Britain and the British that emerges from these texts by Jewish refugees from Hitler, I have gone beyond merely depicting such features as the initial reception accorded them, the material conditions that they encountered in Britain, the customs, practices, and values that governed British life, and the relations between individual refugees and the British people with whom they interacted, important though all those are. My reading of the texts has led me to focus on two important themes that run through them. The first is agency, the degree to which conditions in Britain allowed the refugees to assume control over their own lives and to build a secure and stable new existence for themselves — a process that was also influenced in each individual case by such factors as age, gender, upbringing, education, and personal temperament, as well as sheer chance. The second is identity, the degree to which the refugees adopted elements of a British identity, which, combining with both the German, Austrian, or Czech identity and the Jewish identity that they had developed before emigration, created a new synthesis in which these differing elements merged, often over a long period of time and with considerable conflict and friction. That process was again strongly influenced by the particular character and the individual experiences of each refugee writer. *Encounters with Albion* draws on a volume of material sufficient to give a comprehensive account of its subject, the image of Britain as portrayed by the refugees, and also to give weight to the conclusions that it reaches in relation to these key themes that are fundamental to the relationship between the refugees and the host society.

Notes to the Introduction

1. A. J. Sherman, *Island Refuge: Britain and Refugees from the Third Reich 1933–1939* (London: Cass, 1994; original edn London: Elek, 1973); Bernard Wasserstein, *Britain and the Jews of Europe, 1939–1945* (Oxford: Oxford University Press, 1988; original edn London: Institute of Jewish Affairs, 1979); Louise London, *Whitehall and the Jews, 1933–1948: British Immigration Policy, Jewish Refugees and the Holocaust* (Cambridge: Cambridge University Press, 2000).
2. *Second Chance: Two Centuries of German-Speaking Jews in the United Kingdom*, ed. by Werner E. Mosse (Tübingen: Mohr, 1991).
3. Richard Dove, *Journey of No Return: Five German-Speaking Literary Exiles in Britain, 1933–1945* (London: Libris, 2000).

CHAPTER 1

Arrival and Early Years in Britain

The period of the arrival of the Jewish refugees from Nazism in Britain after 1933 and the initial phase of their settlement was above all one of struggle and insecurity, though it was also marked by relief at having escaped the far worse conditions confronting Jews in the Third Reich. The refugees were affected by changes in material conditions: many had lost their main sources of income and had to live in much reduced circumstances, while almost all found it difficult to adapt to such aspects of daily life in Britain as food or housing. The problem of language, which beset most refugees during these early years, loomed particularly large for refugee writers, who were dependent on German for their livelihood and their chosen vocation. That prevailing sense of unfamiliarity is arguably the most prominent factor determining the portrayal of Britain and British society in texts by refugees written in the pre-war period of the 1930s. The refugees in turn appeared as an unfamiliar, alien group to the British, who almost universally designated them as outsiders, even when well disposed towards them. Refugee writers conveyed in novels, autobiographies, memoirs, and diaries their consciousness of the identity imposed on them as a marginalized, sometimes stigmatized group that struggled to gain acceptance in British society or to integrate into it to any significant extent. In this important respect, pre-war British society differed from the post-war Britain where many refugees opted to settle and assimilate.

Discourses of Disempowerment

Among the groups of refugees from Nazism in Britain most severely disadvantaged by enforced emigration were the elderly, less well able to adapt to their new environment, and those whose professional skills and abilities could not be transferred to that environment in order to earn both livelihood and status. This was the case with Stefan Zweig, born in 1881, and Alfred Kerr (originally Kempner), born in 1867, both of whom wrote in German and whose readership was primarily — in Kerr's case almost entirely — German-speaking and versed in German-language culture. Both were sharply aware of the loss of status that their emigration to Britain entailed, and both suffered from their abrupt demotion from acknowledged literary celebrity to the rank of outsider; although Zweig did receive some recognition, he was never accepted into the British literary establishment.[1]

Of all literary texts, perhaps only Joseph Roth's *Radetzkymarsch* [The Radetzky March] is as closely associated with the swansong of imperial Vienna in the late nineteenth and early twentieth centuries as is Stefan Zweig's *Die Welt von gestern* [The World of Yesterday].[2] Yet the book was written in emigration, and Britain forms the backdrop to a substantial part of it: the sections covering the six years that Zweig spent in this country from 1934 until his departure for America in 1940. Zweig's reaction to the country of his emigration, first voluntary, then, after March 1938, enforced, is consequently central to a full understanding of the text.

The sections of *Die Welt von gestern* depicting Zweig's years in Britain can be understood as recording a seemingly relentless process of disempowerment. Advancing by stages, that process saw him first visiting Britain in November 1933 with the full rights both of a citizen in his home country and of a foreigner abroad; then in February 1934 as a voluntary exile unwilling to live under the Dollfuß-Schuschnigg dictatorship, after the arbitrary violation of his civil rights by the police who had undertaken a search of his house in Salzburg; then, after the annexation of Austria by Nazi Germany in March 1938, as a refugee unable to return to his native land and reduced in Britain to the supplicant status of statelessness; and finally, after the outbreak of war, as an 'enemy alien' threatened with internment and the suspension of his most fundamental rights and liberties. The result is a compelling study in the psychology of the refugee, deprived in stages of his free agency, his ability to control and determine the course of his life.

Yet Zweig was an internationally acclaimed writer whose work had been translated across the world, including in Britain. He was by any standard one of the most fortunate and privileged refugees, continuing to write and have published in Britain such works as his studies of Mary Stuart and Erasmus of Rotterdam. Zweig, however, perceived himself as the victim of menacing, impersonal historical and political forces operating at a level far beyond the control of the individual; as a writer, he was capable at most of acting as a 'wehrloser, machtloser Zeuge' [defenceless, powerless observer] (4) of events. Following the end of the golden age of security in 1914, these forces had become increasingly evil and destructive, fuelled by nationalism, expressed in totalitarian mass ideologies, and pressed into the service of ever more authoritarian apparatuses of state. The extent of Zweig's sense of disempowerment is apparent in the preface to *Die Welt von gestern*, entire sections of which are dominated by images of individual powerlessness. Historical events are repeatedly likened to natural catastrophes that irrupt into individual lives, to volcanic eruptions or to earthquakes, the epicentre of which is the Central Europe where Zweig's earlier life had unfolded. In Zweig's preface, individuals are no longer active subjects capable at least in part of determining their own fate, but have become the passive objects of irresistible, inescapable, impenetrably malign forces. This is mirrored in the very syntax: when Zweig describes the relationship of individuals to the forces of history, he uses those forces and events as the subjects of his sentences, while the human beings on whom they operate are the objects. Human beings do not act, but are acted on.

When Zweig left Salzburg in autumn 1933 and went to London, he did so freely, deliberately deciding not to travel to his beloved Paris but to stay in London, which he had not visited for thirty years. At this stage, his decision-making still had the appearance of freedom. When he arrived at Victoria Station on a foggy November day, he was essentially a stranger to the culture and society of Britain, having, as he expressly states, no friends in Britain and little in the way of literary connections or contacts. He was to remain an outsider in Britain. Yet within a few days, he could declare that he felt indescribably well in London, where, instead of the tensions that disfigured Austrian public life, he encountered again a civil — one might say civilized — and polite way of life, a society in which a higher measure of legality and decency held sway than amidst the hatred and inflamed excitability of Salzburg in 1933 (396). Zweig returned to Austria in early 1934, only to experience the brief but bloody civil war of February 1934 that saw the consolidation of Dollfuß's authoritarian regime. Once the police had searched his house, he felt compelled to leave Austria and returned to London.

Zweig was now an exile; his freedom to determine the course of his life had been restricted, if only partially. On the one hand, he had intended to return to London, to complete work on his biography of Mary Stuart; but on the other hand, the time and the manner of his departure from Salzburg had been dictated by developments in Austria. At first, Zweig states, he hardly considered himself in exile in Britain (405). Yet his return to London in late February 1934 was undoubtedly very different from his arrival in 1933, for then he had been a visitor, free to come and go as he pleased, whereas now he was resolved to stay in Britain indefinitely and could not return to Austria at will. This new, provisional status was reflected in his desire to avoid commitment and any appearance of permanence: he decided to rent a small flat with sufficient space only for his writing.

In Britain, he felt surrounded by a foreign culture, deeply unsettled by the uncertainties of his situation as a foreigner, and unable for the first time in his professional life to take any part in the public life of his country of residence. He had exchanged the status of a visitor to Britain for that of a resident outsider, a distinction keenly felt. When he attended a debate between George Bernard Shaw and H. G. Wells, his pleasure at the brilliance of the exchanges was marred by his inability to understand the sources of the unspoken tension between the two men, and indeed the entire cultural context within which the event was played out. Yet Zweig stresses repeatedly that he found Britain a pleasant country in which to live, calling it 'diese gute Insel' [this good island] (407). He admired the civility of English public life, what he saw as its tolerance and essential decency, the way in which political conflicts were settled by reasoned debate, a practice anchored in a long tradition of democracy and respect for the law. He went so far as to seek to excuse the Munich Agreement, which he considered an appalling mistake, by arguing that it was the very decency and honesty of the British and their long schooling in legality that had led them to trust a leader like Hitler and to believe, as in a gentleman's agreement, that he would keep his word (434–35). When he attended the funeral of his revered friend Sigmund Freud, Zweig pronounced himself content that the best of his homeland had been laid to rest in English earth

(440). Even when, just after the outbreak of war, he decided to get married, he found the officials at the registry office willing to be as helpful to an 'enemy alien' as regulations permitted.

Zweig's situation in Britain deteriorated radically with the annexation of Austria by Germany in March 1938. At a blow, he lost what security remained to him when he was deprived of his Austrian citizenship and his Austrian passport became invalid. From that point on, he was a stateless refugee, dependent on documents issued to him by a foreign country, Britain; he was not entitled as of right to those documents and the (inferior) status they accorded him, being instead dependent on the grace and favour of his hosts. Zweig came to see himself as a supplicant, whose rights could be withdrawn at any time. He felt very acutely his degradation in status from that of a foreign citizen and 'gewissermaßen Gentleman' [to some extent, gentleman] (425) to the status of refugee: viewed with suspicion, liable to deportation, and subjected to the endless, humiliating process of queuing for visas, registration, and any number of other bureaucratic requirements designed to turn a free-born human being into the dependent object of arbitrary officialdom. From the day that he had to live with foreign papers, Zweig wrote, he lost his sense of secure, integrated individuality: as he put it, something of his natural identity with his original and essential self had been destroyed forever (428).

As war threatened, Zweig withdrew from London to Bath, where his sense of disempowerment plumbed new depths. He depicted in graphic terms the utter impotence of ordinary people whose fate was determined by the decisions of remote and powerful elites (446–48); he compared himself to a fly trapped defencelessly in a spider's web, to a condemned man in his cell, chained and immured in endless, pointless waiting, and, in an image of utter despair, saw his entire existence as dependent on the fickle roll of a roulette wheel. Never in his life, he wrote, had he felt the impotence of the individual in the face of the events of world history more cruelly. The outbreak of war, at which point the narrative concludes, brought Zweig to the lowest point in his years in Britain, when he became an 'enemy alien'. For Zweig, the Austrian Jew who had been expelled from Germany on account of his race and his convictions, the bureaucratic decree that classed him among the Nazi enemies of Britain represented the ultimate absurdity. At the very juncture when he would most have wished to rally to the British cause, this sudden act of exclusion made him feel alone and useless as never before. One could speculate that this feeling of disempowered isolation accompanied him across the Atlantic and ultimately played its part in his decision to end his life.

The image of Alfred Kerr as a refugee in Britain has largely been shaped by his daughter Judith's description of him in her two semi-autobiographical volumes *When Hitler Stole Pink Rabbit* and *The Other Way Round*, recently reissued under the title *Bombs on Aunt Dainty*.[3] 'Papa', as she calls him, appears as an elderly, careworn figure, ground down by the pressures of emigration in an unfamiliar and uncomprehending environment, which contribute to the heart disease that will kill him a few years later, and as increasingly impoverished and dependent on the meagre income that his wife earns through secretarial work. In his rented room, first in a shabby-genteel hotel in the Bloomsbury area of London, then, after being bombed out, in another establishment for rootless and aimless refugees in Putney, the erstwhile doyen of Berlin's theatre critics continues to write, but fails to find a publisher, let alone to reach a reading public. 'Papa's' situation epitomizes the drastic loss of status suffered by refugee writers and intellectuals in Britain, where their professional skills, dependent on a foreign culture and language, are belittled or ignored.[4]

Kerr's diaries covering the period from his arrival in Britain from France in November 1935 until the early part of the war were published only in 1979, over thirty years after his death in October 1948, under the title *Ich kam nach England* [I Came to England].[5] Although the conditions that Kerr endured in emigration arguably rendered his situation substantially worse than Zweig's, his diaries adopt a very different and notably more positive attitude to life as a refugee in Britain. His text is, as he himself put it, very friendly to England,[6] though, like Zweig, Kerr was an ardent Francophile and had had little relationship to Britain before 1935. The stance he assumes towards his country of refuge largely lacks Zweig's sense of anguished helplessness — though of the two, Kerr was far more the disempowered outsider — and it enables him to adopt the role of impartial observer, on a footing almost equal to British society, the object of his observation. Kerr adds that his friendly view of Britain was mixed with criticism, using the phrase 'Nicht ohne heitere Kritik zwischendurch' [Not without light-hearted criticism on the side] (200); the word *heiter*, usually translated as 'cheerful' or 'serene', conveys a sense of unconstrained freedom to approve or criticize from a position of even-handed neutrality. The diaries are written from the perspective of a free and sovereign witness to British customs and conditions, who, though not part of British society, can observe and comment on it with wit and independence of spirit.

Without being blind to its faults, Kerr describes Britain with affection and admiration. At the outset, in the section entitled 'Gruß an die Insel' [A Greeting to the Island] (25–26), he expresses his gratitude to Britain, where he feels sheltered, stating that the longer one lives there, the more grateful one feels; soon after his arrival in November 1935, he writes that it is impossible not to like the British, not only because they are friendly, helpful, polite, and dependable, but also because they have the gift of performing ethical actions with a particular aesthetic charm; and the final section, 'Dank an England' [Thanks to England] (197–98), closes the main diaries with a powerful reaffirmation of gratitude.

Like Zweig, Kerr was impressed by the quality of British public life, which he saw as characterized by decency, order, and maturity, adding: 'Die große fairness ist hier' [The great fairness is here] (29). Quoting a note written by a German woman before she committed suicide to escape the Gestapo, in which she states that there is no kinder, more helpful, considerate, polite, well-mannered, and honourable people than the English, he declares that all refugees should remember these words and that they form 'der Kerninhalt unserer eignen seelischen Beziehung zu England' [the essence of our own spiritual relation to England] (31). As such titles of sections as 'Unerforschliches England' [Unfathomable England] (31–32) and 'Unwirkliches

England' [Unreal England] (37–40) show, Kerr finds much that is puzzling, eccentric, and inexplicable to a foreigner. He is not sparing in his criticism of British customs, practices, and institutions, but when he makes personal contact with them, as in the case of the public schools to which he sent his two children, he comes to admire them (unlike his daughter, who loathed her time at boarding school).

Kerr's portrayal of Britain and British society is frequently humorous, in marked contrast to Zweig's. A note of comedy frequently pervades the vignettes of often mundane and apparently trivial aspects of British life that make up much of the book, as in his reflections on the English weekend, on the ubiquity of lamb, a food he abhorred, or on the police at the coronation of King George VI conducting themselves like sheepdogs of the people (75). Kerr describes a variety of frivolous and superficial details of British life with great gusto and in an inimitable style, combining sympathetic understanding with criticism, and bewildered amusement at English eccentricities with a kind of activist reflective observation, which prevents him from falling prey to a sense of impotence and irrelevance, as did Zweig.

When it came to British foreign policy, however, Kerr was acutely aware of his total inability to influence events. Like many refugees who were familiar with Hitler and National Socialism, he was in the agonizing situation of understanding the reality of Nazi Germany's aggressive, expansionist intentions while being unable to awaken the British, blindly committed to the policy of appeasement, to the falsity of the assumptions on which that policy was based. Kerr felt very deeply the pain and frustration of the refugee from Germany who knew what the future held but as a foreigner was condemned to remain silent. This pessimistic mood of impotence reached its low point with the Munich Agreement of autumn 1938, but was replaced with a growing belief in the British will to resist Hitler as the nation belatedly came to recognize that war was unavoidable. The experience of Britain in 1940, under the full force of war, vindicated Kerr's underlying faith in the British people, as he makes clear in the praise that he lavishes on the British in his epilogue (198–99). The most significant effect of the war on Kerr's relationship to Britain was, however, the way in which he perceived it as having transformed his situation from that of an outsider and German refugee to a member of a community united in its resistance to Nazi Germany. When he was bombed out of his hotel, narrowly escaping serious injury, he felt a sense of pride, as if, by sharing in the suffering inflicted by the bombing, he and his fellow refugees had joined the collective of Londoners who refused to be cowed by the Luftwaffe, becoming 'Schicksalsgefährten Englands' [England's comrades in fate] (198), liberated from the painful constraints of their refugee status by a new degree of acceptance into the community around them. Significantly, the diaries close with a postscript in memory of Johnny Fleetwood-May, whom Kerr had met on holiday in France in 1939 and who had been killed in action aged twenty, serving as a pilot in the RAF. In writing this epitaph to one of 'the Few', Kerr was arguably signalling that he had, in his sense of solidarity with the British people at war, gained an added measure of agency over his own life in Britain through his writing.

Activist Strategies

Among the refugees who embarked on a course of action designed both to counteract their own sense of purposelessness and disempowerment and to alleviate the plight of their fellow immigrants was Lily Wagner, an energetic middle-aged woman who arrived in Britain from Berlin on 2 February 1938 with her younger daughter, Inge. Her elder daughter, Irene, known as Puck, had come over earlier on a domestic service permit; it was Irene Bloomfield, as she was by then, who in 2002 gave me her mother's account of the boarding house that she had set up in 1938 for demoralized and deracinated refugees.[7] Lily Wagner was a highly educated and cultured woman with a doctorate. She had worked as a writer and freelance journalist in Germany and had visions of continuing her researches in the British Museum. Recognizing, however, that this was impossible, she rejected the option of lapsing into depression and inaction and decided instead to work for the good of the near-destitute, marginalized, isolated refugees, many of whom were trapped in enforced idleness by their inability to work or were reduced to menial domestic labour.

Lily Wagner's arrival in Britain was typical of that of many refugees. Fearful of being turned back by the immigration officer, anxious about her uncertain future in a foreign land, tormented by memories of the homeland that she had been forced to leave, she experienced in full the emotional and psychological anguish of emigration. She was also almost penniless. 'No one', she wrote, 'could call it a promising start' (1). Nevertheless, her refusal to allow herself to become the passive object of emigration was at once evident. She rapidly overcame her initial disgust at the conditions in her first shared accommodation and accepted the reality of her new existence:

> This little room had brought it home to me that we all had to renounce quite consciously our former mode of living, all our small comforts and luxuries. A new life had to be begun, a hard life, without snugness and bourgeois respectability. (2)

It was in that spirit of positive purpose that she reacted to the influx of Austrian Jews that commenced in March 1938 with the *Anschluss* and the anti-Semitic excesses accompanying it. In the face of the horrors that these people had endured, Wagner laid her plans for writing aside:

> I had to find something more closely connected with life, as it now was, and above all, to try and help those poor refugees, who arrived here homeless and desperate. Was there no possibility of opening a home for them? Of giving them an atmosphere that would make them forget their misery, their sufferings, if only for a time? (3)

The project of the boarding house took shape; it was to be

> a real home for those emigrants, who had lost everything at one single blow, an intellectual and social centre where they would not feel lonely, and where companionship with their fellow-countrymen would be a consolation, where their personal fate and suffering could be borne more easily, because it had become the fate of them all. (3)

Wagner was fortunate in finding British people who helped her to realize her project. A young Englishwoman, Judith Wilson, who was committed to improving the lot of the refugees from Nazism, became the home's manager, working for a meagre wage under spartan conditions. They found 'the house of our dreams' at 30 Frognal Lane, Hampstead, ideally situated in a quiet location that backed onto a small park (5–6). Armed only with the sum of fifty pounds lent to her by fellow ex-Berliners, Wagner could not have afforded to rent a property in such a prime district of London without the understanding and generosity of the owners, Mr and Mrs Challen.

Wagner describes her first encounter with Mrs Challen in terms that encapsulate both the relationship between the refugees and the British at this early stage and the divide between the supplicant, insecure newcomers and the settled, self-confident host population:

> The lady smiled, obviously aware of the strange difference in her position and ours: She belonging to one of the most respected nations in the world, a rich, beautiful woman, living in her own house in her own country, had little to fear regarding her future. While we must have seemed to her like gipsies, nomads in search of a safe tenting place. (6)

The Challens proceeded to offer the house to Wagner on very favourable financial terms; Mr Challen accepted her as a tenant even though she could not produce a bank reference, not having a bank account. With a flow of inmates provided by Bloomsbury House, seat of many of the committees dealing with refugees, she subsequently opened three more homes. In late 1939, she turned two of them into a hostel for domestic servants, a particularly isolated and exploited group, many of whom had lost their jobs when war broke out; by early 1940, when Wagner's account was written, the hostel accommodated nearly fifty women.[8]

Judith Wilson and the Challens were far from representative of the British in their behaviour towards the refugees. The number of British people that appear in early texts by refugees like Lily Wagner is small, since much of British society held aloof from the refugees and left them to their own social interaction. Those that came into contact with refugees frequently treated them with some condescension, aware of their own supposedly superior situation as 'benefactors', to use Wagner's term; others, especially those who employed refugees as domestic servants, sometimes exploited them shamefully, as in the case of the woman in Cambridge who drove a friend of Wagner's to a breakdown. Wagner represents British society above all as distant from the refugees, especially in its emotional reserve and coolness:

> I had not long been in England and still had a good deal of natural, exuberant feeling and warm readiness for friendship. In the meantime the English climate and mentality which demand a certain reserve have changed and to some extent subdued me too.

The awareness of a loss in warmth and spontaneity of feeling is evident here:

> We feel that our English hosts do not appreciate extravagance or passion and prefer a distant friendliness, which is none the less sincere. And so we try to

> control our overwhelming feelings and keep in check our too warm hearts, however hard this enforced reserve may seem. (18)

Wagner defines the predominant response of the refugees to life in Britain in enforced emigration as an acute sense of loss and disorientation. In addition to loss of professional status and financial security, she identifies the lack of language skills as a prime factor in the corrosive demoralization and lack of self-worth that paralyses the energy and sense of initiative of many refugees:

> Especially older people, who could not get used to the strange English surroundings, were terribly unhappy, and cried their eyes out, if sometimes for days they could not understand anything except 'yes' or 'no' or 'isn't it a lovely day'. They did not understand the English mentality, and could hardly be expected to do so. But they had no chance to learn to understand it, and did not know what to do, as they could not even grasp the simplest phrases. (4)

Such barriers to communication with an unfamiliar environment lead to shattered lives, as in the cases of men who cannot resume their professions or women whose hopes of marriage are dashed.

This inability to adapt to life in Britain and to undertake any productive activity causes a debilitating sense of uselessness in many refugees, inducing in them the lethargy and lack of energy that Wagner identifies as salient features of refugee life. She recognizes that many refugees lack a purpose in life and are consequently beset by feelings of aimlessness, hopelessness, and futility that only productive activity can overcome: 'the only really important thing for the refugees', she writes, is 'that they are accepted as potential workers and helpers, that they do not need any more to feel outside the gate, entirely useless, a nuisance to everybody' (19). The outbreak of war, however, marks a decisive change in the situation of the refugees in this respect. By early 1940, Wagner notes the increasing numbers of refugees joining the forces or receiving permission to work in response to the demand for labour created by the war effort. She cites her daughter Inge's husband as an example of the psychological transformation evident in those who join up, thereby becoming a valued part of the war effort, members of a community united against the common enemy:

> He seemed a different man. All that weakness, that lack of courage, the weariness and feeling of uselessness has gone. He is no longer the foreigner, the outsider, who is only suffered and does not belong. Now he is a man who has a duty to do, a task to fulfil, he is again part of the community, and has a place in the world. (19)

Another refugee who made a notable contribution to his community was Werner Rosenstock, born in Berlin in 1908, who served as General Secretary of the Association of Jewish Refugees (AJR) from its foundation in 1941 until 1982, and as editor of its monthly journal, *AJR Information*, from 1946 until 1982. Rosenstock, who had trained as a lawyer and worked for the representative organization of the Jews in Germany until his emigration in August 1939, was actively involved from the outset in the creation of an organization to represent the Jewish refugees

FIG. 1.1. Werner Rosenstock, General Secretary of the Association of Jewish Refugees, 1941–82. Courtesy of Michael Rosenstock.

from Nazism in Britain.[9] He was the key figure in the establishment and, for four decades, the running of the AJR, arguably the most important and enduring institution founded by the Jewish refugees in Britain after 1933, and one of the most important such organizations anywhere. Rosenstock left two volumes of memoirs, the first written in 1945 and the second in 1986.[10] His position in the refugee community allowed him special insight into the development of the Jewish refugees' relationship to Britain. That relationship turned on three separate but interrelated decisions taken individually and collectively by the refugees: how to relate to their German or Austrian past; how to relate to Anglo-Jewry, the existing Jewish community in Britain composed in the majority of immigrants from Eastern Europe; and how to relate to the British. These were, one might say, the strategic decisions that defined the broad parameters of refugee life in Britain and the sense of refugee identity that emerged there; not all refugees responded in the same way, but Rosenstock's insights hold true, broadly speaking, for very many of them.

Rosenstock was firmly opposed to those who rejected the German-Jewish past out of hand and in its entirety. Even allowing for the trauma of the Nazi years, he remained able to take pride in that past and the culture to which it had given rise. While condemning without reservation the atrocities committed by the Nazis, Rosenstock held firm in his belief in the value of the traditions and the cultural achievements of German Jewry. For Rosenstock, no shame attached to the German-language culture and society developed by the assimilated, secularized Jews of Germany. He maintained his belief in what is now known as the German-Jewish symbiosis, denying that his continuing attachment to the German component in it represented a betrayal of his Jewishness.

As an assimilated German Jew, Rosenstock was also unwilling to adopt the path of total integration into British society and to abandon the German language and German culture completely for their British equivalents. When some younger refugees protested at the use of German at a meeting held in early 1940, Rosenstock was incensed, as his memoirs revealed:

> I also resented the overdoing of certain people who behaved as if they had arrived with William the Conqueror and had forgotten their origin from Germany. I resented this less because after all German Jews had been formed by German culture and had no reason to be ashamed of it, but because I considered it as a new tendency of exaggerated Jewish assimilation. (I, 80)

On the one hand, Rosenstock stood for those German Jews who had assimilated into German society and for whom, once the Nazis had put a halt to that, measured integration into British society was the natural alternative. On the other hand, he attached the utmost importance to his German-Jewish identity and would not allow it to be erased by an over-hasty integration into British life, language, and values. He was secure in his German-Jewish heritage, and equally secure in his belief that he and his family could, within the limits set out above, assimilate in Britain.

When the refugees from Nazism arrived in Britain, it was widely assumed that they would be absorbed into Anglo-Jewry. But in the event, the refugees maintained their own distinct and discrete communal identity, separate from Anglo-Jewry, created their own institutions (such as the AJR, Belsize Square Synagogue, and the Wiener Library), and established themselves as an independent, readily recognizable community in their areas of settlement, principally north-west London. Although the refugees were grateful for the financial and organizational support provided to them by Anglo-Jewry, relations between the two groups remained somewhat distant, principally because the assimilated, German-speaking Jews had undergone a process of social development in Central Europe very different from that of the Anglo-Jewish community, the majority of which had its origins in Eastern Europe. The differences between the two groups in part re-enacted the tensions from the pre-1933 era between the assimilated, secularized, middle-class Jews of the German-speaking cities, who had adopted a westernized way of life, venerated German high culture, and had abandoned strict religious observance, and the Eastern Jews, Yiddish-speaking, proletarian or lower middle class, orthodox by religion, and faithful to traditional customs and practices.

The unfamiliarity of each group with the values, aspirations, and social self-image of the other was made clear to Rosenstock when he met an Anglo-Jewish family from the East End during the war. They had taken in a refugee child after the Kristallnacht pogroms of November 1938, only to discover, to their outrage, that the girl was not, as they expected, 'a downtrodden impoverished child', but came laden with expensive clothes; to make matters worse, when the family sat down for the Friday evening meal, 'the girl had never heard the Sabbath blessings' (II, 7–8). They considered that they had been deceived. Such incidents, frequent as they were, if not necessarily typical of either party, revealed the differences in social culture and the lack of mutual understanding that divided the refugees from Anglo-Jewry.

The refugees opted broadly for the path of integrating into British society, while preserving their Continental identity as German-speaking Jews. Indeed, as Rosenstock pointed out, one of the main reasons for the foundation of the AJR in 1941 was precisely that the most active refugee organizations then in existence, the Free German League of Culture and the Austrian Centre, were both urging their members to return to Germany or Austria after the war, thereby leaving unrepresented the bulk of the Jewish refugees who 'did not intend to return to Germany but to strike roots in England and, above all, wanted their children to integrate into the country which had given them refuge' (II, 1). The AJR took a strongly integrationist line on behalf of its members: Rosenstock deliberately gave pride of place on the very first page of *AJR Information* in January 1946 to the Home Secretary's announcements about the naturalization of refugees, regarding the acquisition of British citizenship as the first key step towards their integration. Rosenstock himself decided to stay in Britain, leaving unused the visas that would have enabled him and his family to settle in the United States (I, 90).

Like many refugees, Rosenstock's view of Britain was crucially influenced by his wartime experiences, and especially by his admiration for the behaviour of the civilian population in London during the Blitz, which shines through the somewhat awkward prose of the first volume of his memoirs:

> I myself was greatly impressed by the state of nerves and the discipline of the population. On the morning after a grave attack you could see the workmen clearing [up] the mess with cigarettes in their mouths as if it was quite an ordinary job.

Even the emotional reserve of the British became a matter for praise here: 'This was not lack of emotion on their side but the typical self-discipline achieved during the long history of the nation' (1, 88). Even when it came to the highly contentious issue of the mass internment of refugees in 1940, arguably the darkest chapter in the history of the refugees from Nazism, Rosenstock sought to present a partial exculpation of the British authorities, though he had himself been interned for some six weeks. Like many refugees, he was prepared to countenance criticism of the inefficient implementation of the policy of internment, but not of the policy itself. He dwelt instead on the positive aspects of the internment period: the stout defence of the liberty of the individual by critics of internment like Eleanor Rathbone, MP, and the holding of a debate on the matter in the House of Commons despite the imminent threat of Nazi invasion, which he saw as the historic merit of the British people. Such attitudes indicate that activists like Rosenstock would turn their energies towards the integration of the Jewish refugees into British society, while preserving their particular communal identity.

Voices from the Periphery

In the early years, marginalization and isolation were frequently the hallmarks of refugee life, markedly so in the case of some groups of female refugees — domestic servants working in unfamiliar households, for example, or married women confined at home with small children. The title of Ruth Borchard's *We Are Strangers Here* tellingly encapsulates this aspect of the refugee experience in Britain. Ruth Borchard, née Berendsohn, born in 1910 in Hamburg, had arrived in Britain with her husband Kurt Borchard in 1938; she wrote *We Are Strangers Here* during the war, after her release from internment on the Isle of Man in 1941, but it was only published in full in 2008, with the subtitle *An 'Enemy Alien' in Prison in 1940*.[11]

The first chapters of the book depict the life of Anna Silver, a non-Jewish refugee from Germany who has fled to Britain with her Jewish husband, Bert, covering the period immediately before her arrest in May 1940, while the later chapters describe her detention in a London prison, drawing directly on the author's own experience of Holloway Prison in summer 1940. Anna's prison experiences, which will be covered in Chapter 2, should not be allowed to overshadow the compelling picture in the book's opening sections of a young refugee woman struggling to come to terms with an alien environment. Significantly, Anna experiences these difficulties despite being, by refugee standards, in a relatively favourable situation: she is financially secure, since her husband has a good job, to the extent that they can afford a cleaning lady; she has a house with a garden where her baby daughter Nele can play; she lives in the pleasant university town of L., small enough for its university's German department to invite local refugees to social events. Anna's fluent use of colloquial English slang — 'pinched' (for 'stolen'; 48), 'peeved' (44), 'wangled' (105) — and her familiarity with English children's rhymes (98) denote a degree of integration into everyday British life as well as a good command of the language.

Yet Anna is beset by her inability to understand the British, who in turn do not understand (or in many cases wish to understand) the refugees; as her mother-in-law tells her: 'We are strangers here in this country, and they cannot look beneath our skins' (49). These intangible barriers to communication mean that Anna is reduced to dependence on the narrow confines of domestic life, on her daughter, and especially on her husband; her growing anxiety that he is conducting an extramarital affair is thereby rendered yet more acute. Beyond her small circle, the British appear as an anonymous, incalculable, and unfamiliar collective, whose social codes, customs, and practices she has not yet internalized. A few individuals stand out, like Anna's two friends in L., Molly and Gwen, or her cleaning lady, Mrs Morgan, but even they continually surprise her with their behaviour, attitudes, reactions, and choices of courses of action. When Anna is threatened with internment, Molly, unstintingly supportive, is appalled at the prospect of the internment of a woman with a baby, whereas Gwen, influenced by the press campaign portraying the refugees as potential enemy agents, refuses to speak on Anna's behalf before the tribunal that will decide on her case.

Anna's uncertainty in her dealings with the British contrasts with the assurance that she displays in her exchanges with her fellow refugees, from her dignified mother-in-law, Ida Silver, to the frivolous young Viennese women that she meets in prison, and from the fussily self-important Miss Hochfeld to the mercurially attractive Hilde Gottschalk; these people she can understand and predict, as she can locate them accurately in terms of their background, attitudes, and likely responses to events. After the tribunal has ruled that both Anna and Bert are to be detained, though separately, she again fails to gauge the reactions of the British people around her. It comes as a complete surprise to her when Mrs Morgan offers to take Nele into her family — an offer of great generosity, considering that the Morgans are poor and can barely provide for their own children — as does the unexpected decency of Mr King, the prospective tenant to whom Anna lets the family's house, and who offers to pay her more than the agreed sum in rent so as to avoid taking advantage of her situation.

Anna also finds the British authorities bafflingly unpredictable. At first, she is naively convinced that the British, with their long tradition of justice and democracy, will never intern women and children. When that hope proves false, she attributes the tribunal's decision to English cant and hypocrisy (47), but is forced to recognize during her two interviews with the local chief constable that the situation is more complex. She is impressed that the man who bears responsibility for a whole city at a time when the country is threatened by invasion and when tens of thousands of 'aliens' are being removed from their homes — L. is in a 'protected area' where 'enemy aliens' are not permitted to reside — can yet take a sympathetic interest in the case of 'one foreign old lady' (61), Anna's mother-in-law. Ultimately, even the chief constable is unable to bend the rules of government policy, though his disapproval of the treatment of Anna and her family is made very clear to the reader. In the course of the events leading up to her detention, Anna encounters a bewildering combination of humane sympathy with impersonal bureaucracy, of bumbling inefficiency with the cold-hearted inhumanity that separates her from her husband at the stroke of a pen. Her capacity to cope with British institutional bureaucracies and their treatment of foreign refugees will be tested further when she is incarcerated with Nele in Holmdale (Holloway) Prison.

Some refugees were consigned from the outset to isolation and to an existence on the margins of British society. The diaries of Sophie Roth, covering the years 1940 to 1944, furnish a moving record of an extreme case.[12] Sophie Roth, née Landau, arrived in Britain from Vienna on 29 August 1939 with her husband Norbert and their younger son Richard Georg, known as Schurli, who was terminally ill with cancer and died in Manchester on 28 October 1939, just short of his eleventh birthday; their elder son Erwin (later Edwin) was already in Britain. The diaries are dominated by the mother's overwhelming grief, reflecting the extent to which other aspects of life — the family's desperate flight from Vienna, the hardships of emigration, the war, the aerial bombardment of Manchester, and even the internment of her husband and elder son in 1940 — are overshadowed by the loss of her younger son. Roth's sense of loss creates an emotional barrier between her and her surroundings that reduces her involvement with British society to a purely functional minimum.

The diaries' intense focus on grief and loss has a distancing effect on their depiction of other events, and can also be said to render that depiction more objective, since the experience of emigration, however distressing, is for the diarist merely the background against which her desperate attempts to save her son's life are played out. After a harrowing journey across Europe on the eve of war, the family arrives at Harwich, where Sophie Roth, already fearful of facing the immigration authorities, is greatly alarmed by the announcement that they will all be subject to a medical examination. But far from refusing them entry, the duty doctor is primarily concerned with the sick child's health, insisting that they must seek medical advice at the earliest opportunity. Indeed, the medical care extended to Schurli is consistently excellent. In London, he is admitted to St Bartholomew's Hospital, where the facilities are far superior to those available to a Jewish child in Vienna, and he is then transferred to the Christie Hospital in Manchester, one of the leading centres for cancer care in Europe, with special expertise in childhood cancers.

The family's status as 'enemy aliens' appears to have been completely disregarded. Schurli receives the best and most modern treatment, while his mother is greatly affected by the kindness of the medical staff: a year after his admission, on 3 October 1940, she records that she visited the ward sister responsible for his care, adding that it was a year ago that they came to know Sister Malqueen 'in all ihrer Güte' [in all her kindness] (36). From the hotel owner in London who offers to take them into her own home (32) to the staff who remove the crucifix from the hospital chapel to which Schurli's body is taken after his death (56), the family meet with acts of kindness and consideration from the British people they encounter; the diaries record no instances of hostility or anti-Semitism towards them. However, the internment of Norbert and Erwin Roth, which leaves the grieving Sophie Roth bereft, destitute, and utterly alone in a foreign city, comes across as an act of gross and callous inhumanity on the part of the British authorities. The dispersal of Sophie Roth's extended family from their home city, the separation from all that was familiar in her life, and her acute isolation in Britain are principal themes in the diaries, as they are fundamental to the experience of forced emigration.

The Roths arrive in Britain with no money, no accommodation, and none of the support system necessary for a family with a sick child; they are accordingly very dependent on others for assistance and support. Their frequent and disruptive changes of accommodation and the poverty that makes it hard for them to afford five shillings (twenty-five pence) to send a telegram to Tel Aviv are additional barriers to their participation in British society, from which they are effectively excluded; they move almost entirely in a small circle of fellow refugees, often friends and acquaintances from Vienna. Consequently, a profound sense of isolation from her surroundings pervades Sophie Roth's writings. On the anniversary of her departure from Vienna, she describes herself lying in bed completely alone, with her husband and elder son interned and with only her yearning for Vienna and the prospect of visiting her younger son's grave to occupy her thoughts (17). The internment of Norbert and Erwin Roth is a particularly cruel blow, depriving Sophie of all her immediate family members and providing a fresh source of anxiety for her; one of the most grimly depressing passages in the diaries is her description of her visit to the internment camp at Huyton on Merseyside and her return journey to Manchester in the dark, unaccompanied and exposed to air raids (45–46).

The air raids add to the desolation surrounding Roth: on 9 October 1940, a heavy raid that killed nine people in her vicinity provides the background to her description of herself as 'mutterseelenallein' [utterly alone] (50) in a house of strangers, while on 31 December 1940, New Year's Eve, she surveys the bombed buildings and shattered windows left in the aftermath of the 'Manchester Blitz' of 22–24 December, and reflects that she has been separated from her husband for almost half a year (64). There is nothing here of the defiant sense of community evoked in other recollections of wartime Britain, only grief and loneliness that are intensified by emigration. 'Es ist alles so traurig' [It is all so sad], Roth concludes on 11 March 1941: 'Emigrantenleben! Wird sich das jemals noch ändern? [...] Das Leben ist *so* schwer!' [Life as an emigrant! Will things ever change? [...] Life is *so* hard!] (66). The experience of emigration appears in Roth's diary as a chronicle of loss, separation, isolation, and marginalization that leaves the refugees, powerless to determine their own lives, at the mercy of the disruption and violence of war.

Among the groups of refugees who were most isolated and subject to exploitation were young women who came to Britain on domestic service permits; many of them, coming from comfortable middle-class families, were totally unprepared for the demeaning drudgery that they were required to perform in the households of strangers. An early account of such a refugee is to be found in Ruth Feiner's novel *Fires in May*, published in 1936.[13] Feiner, born in 1909, left Germany soon after the Nazi assumption of power and set about establishing herself as an author in Britain;

she wrote thirteen novels before her early death in 1954, successfully switching from her native German to English.[14] Feiner's best-known novel, *Young Woman of Europe* (1942), contains a detailed and critical description of British society and of the treatment afforded by Britain to the refugees from Nazism.[15]

Fires in May fictionalizes the experiences of the early wave of young female refugees through the story of Vera Hansen, a student of twenty-two forced to flee Germany in 1933 because her elder brother Hans has accidentally killed a Nazi while defending a friend in a brawl; unlike the novel's author, Hansen is non-Jewish. The text contains a detailed picture of the conditions of life and the particular psychology of a refugee, but is set in a narrative framework more akin to romantic fiction — the boy-meets-girl love story of Hansen and John Ashley, the wealthy upper-class English heir to a large electrical manufacturing firm with whom she falls in love but whom she has to leave, to marry another man. The novel is heavily plot-driven. It begins with Hansen's arrival in Britain, where on the train from Harwich to London she encounters Edward March, a senior executive at Ashley's, and through him meets John Ashley. Through a welfare organization, Hansen finds employment as a domestic with the Pottles, a sterile and dreary household of three unmarried women and their elderly, senile father. Although the workload is light and the Pottles are concerned in their limited way for her well-being, Hansen finds her situation unbearable; the stifling routine, the narrow-minded prejudices, and the restricted horizons of the shut-away house in Notting Hill, symbolized by its walled garden and permanently locked gate, are lifeless and deadening to her.

Predictably, Hansen falls prey to an unscrupulous married man who abandons her when she becomes pregnant. She loses her job and has to go Paris to procure an abortion. But at this low point in her life, Hansen undergoes a transformation, from a naive and cosseted young student, the passive victim of events and the actions of others, to a more mature and independent woman who begins to take control of her own life. Hansen's story is in this sense an exploration of the gender-based roles that are open to women in emigration, though vitiated in part by the narrative of romantic fiction in which it is set. On her return to Britain, already confronting the rigours of the Channel crossing with new confidence, Hansen is determined to cope by means of her own resources: she finds work at an expensive hotel as a secretary doing correspondence for German-speaking guests.

As a result of this initiative, she meets Herr Hoffmann, a Viennese theatre producer, and through him Mr Silverbotham, a theatrical agent; she then writes a play, which thanks to her new contacts is a West End hit, a turn of events whose improbability is only somewhat mitigated by the fact that she had been about to embark on a doctorate in theatre studies in Germany. Although John Ashley and Vera Hansen fall deeply in love, she realizes that his family will never accept her (on account of her refugee status and the scandal of her abortion in approximately equal measure); she also realizes that she has to care for her brother Hans, now due for release from the concentration camp in which he has been incarcerated. She decides to enter into a marriage of convenience with Silverbotham in order to obtain British nationality,[16] which enables her to effect Hans's unhindered departure from

Germany to safety in Vienna. The novel ends with John taking Vera to Dover, on her way to meet Hans; the prospect of their future reunion remains open. The novel's plot relies heavily on contrivance and chance encounters. Its often acute observation of British society sits uneasily with the romantic stereotype of the poor, outcast young woman who, despite all obstacles of wealth and status, wins the love of her Prince Charming — notwithstanding the fact that here she displays her new-found autonomy by choosing to marry another.

The depiction of Britain and the emotions it evokes in the newly arrived refugee is developed in considerable psychological depth. Hansen's feelings towards Britain are complex and mixed, though her attraction to her country of refuge is expressed repeatedly. At the beginning, Britain appears both unfamiliar and reassuring (9–22). Hansen arrives in Harwich 'utterly miserable' (9), green with seasickness and full of foreboding; the complete outsider, no one has spoken to her throughout the crossing. Everything, from the language to the name and aroma of the local cigarettes, is strange to her, as if to prove the truth of the novel's motto: 'the distance from the Continent to England is greater by thousands of miles than the distance from one end of the world to the other ....'. She is further marginalized and disadvantaged by her precarious status as a refugee with permission to stay in Britain only for a limited period: 'A person's life in a land where one does not happen to have been born endures only so long as is allowed by the immigration officer's stamp. What happens after is just as vague as existence after death' (10). On the train to London, however, with solid British earth under her, she recovers 'that look of courage and relief' (9), and the prospect of London causes her mood of depression to give way to 'excitement and expectation' (11). Even her preconception that Englishmen are 'unapproachable and cold' (12) is proved wrong when, to her delight, Edward March addresses her in English and she understands him. But the exchange goes only so far; although March is moved by Hansen's evident distress, his conversation dries up and he buries himself in his newspaper.

The same combination of distance and kindness is evident in the English ladies from the welfare organization who provide her with temporary accommodation. Her room is small, functionally furnished, and above all unfamiliar: 'Everything is so different here, she thought. The windows, the beds, the taxis, the heating' (21). But the greatest surprise is the open fire which, still burning in the month of May, gives the novel its title. The fire becomes the principal symbol of Britain and British life, in stark contrast to the fires that burnt in Germany in May 1933, when thousands of allegedly un-German books were consigned to the flames. To Hansen, who has never seen an open fire before, it seems 'fairy-like': 'It seemed to speak of comfort, it was friendly' (21). The warm tone of the housekeeper who accompanies her to her room persuades her of the helpfulness and friendliness of the British: 'She suddenly felt wonderfully secure and safe. Here there were no storm-troopers and no political murders' (22). Hansen duly discovers much that is less friendly in British life, from her predatory lover to her narrow-minded, emotionally desiccated employers, but by comparison with Nazi Germany her initial impression of the solid comfort of Britain ultimately proves well founded.

The open fire recurs at key points in the narrative, reflecting Hansen's relationship to Britain. At the lowest point in her trajectory, pregnant, about to lose her job, and facing the prospect of travelling to Paris for an abortion, Hansen stares into the Pottles' fire and forms the resolve to return to Britain: 'And suddenly at the thought of leaving England she felt a curious homesickness for England, a country she had known such a short time. She would come back! She must!' (189). The fire even provides the name for the anti-fascist publishing house, Fires in May, that John and Vera plan to help 'the phoenix of intellectual freedom' (260) to rise again from the Nazi bonfires by republishing burned books. When, near the end of the novel, Hansen demonstrates her new-found self-confidence by burning her German passport — and with it, her bridges, as she knows that the German authorities will never issue her with another — she does so by throwing it into the open fire in her apartment.

Throughout the novel, the image of Britain as perceived by Hansen remains ambiguous. She is disconcerted and disorientated by the differences between Britain and Germany: the food, the weights and measures, the English Sunday. But she also finds London exhilarating and exciting. When she walks through the city, she is surprised and gratified by the helpfulness and good humour of the police, by the easy-going freedom of the people, who casually walk on the grass in the parks, by their orderliness in queues, and by their good-humoured tolerance in political matters. Yet at the same time she concludes that she has never felt lonelier than among the crowds thronging the West End (75). Loneliness is the defining feature of Hansen's early months in Britain; it makes her vulnerable to sexual exploitation, driving her into the arms of a practised seducer. Even much later in the novel, the loneliness of the outsider is vividly evoked in the description of Hansen's first New Year's Eve in Britain, completely alone in a miserable rented room with nothing but a gas fire for company (231).

Towards the end of the novel, Hansen has grown to love England:

> On this cool, quiet, sunny morning, with its hint of the coming spring, she realized that no matter where she might go in the world she would always long to be back in England [...]. The customs and habits which she had at first found so impossible and strange seemed to be part of her. (279)

But even here she remains conscious of a barrier to her full integration. When declaring her love of England to John Ashley, Hansen compares it to 'an unhappy and unrequited love': 'I shall never really belong here [...]. D'you know, John, in some way England has a closed door against the "bloody foreigner" [...]. You see, my whole attitude towards life, my mentality is so different from yours!' (271). Even the refugee who has learnt to love Britain can never expect to be fully accepted, to overcome all obstacles to integration.

The external conditions of refugee life are sketched in rather more briefly than is its emotional and psychological dimension. The regulations imposed by the British authorities are a constant influence on Hansen's life: her immigration status means that she has to report to Bow Street Police Station; the Ministry of Labour restricts her to employment as a domestic, though its rules can be circumvented relatively easily; the Home Office, on the other hand, has the power to deport her, just as it deports her friends Dr and Mrs Moses, who are refused permission to extend their stay in Britain. The conditions under which Hansen lives and works as a domestic are also described in some detail: she earns fifteen shillings per week, has a room to herself (albeit with the bed in which the Pottle sisters' mother had died), and her duties consist of light household work such as dusting. But the bulk of the sections depicting Hansen's stint as a domestic (40–47, 64–71) concentrate on its psychological impact on her: the mind-numbing routine of household chores that empties her days of life and interest; the deadening quiet of the household that denies her any mental or intellectual stimulus; the lack of physical exercise that saps her energy; the absence of human contact and warmth that leaves her lonely and vulnerable; and the knowledge that she is at the beck and call of strangers, undermining her self-confidence as an autonomous individual.

The external face of British society around Hansen is in considerable measure defined in terms of its class structure. The working classes, represented by figures like the Pottles' warm-hearted charlady Mrs McCarthy, are presented as generous and naturally kind, despite their abject poverty and squalid living conditions. By contrast, the lower middle classes, represented by the Pottles, are small-minded, prejudiced, and ungenerous in spirit: when Hansen is invited to a tea party by an unknown young man, the Pottles are shocked, but rapidly change their minds when the name Ashley is mentioned, thus combining outdated prudishness with instinctive deference to their supposed superiors in the class system. The English upper class, as represented by John Ashley's parents, is solidly prejudiced against refugees like Hansen, while the younger generation is absorbed by trivialities and superficial social pursuits; the young women also display an unpleasant liking for malicious gossip, as in the case of Adeline Harrison, who spreads a rumour implying that Hansen is accepting money from the theatre producer Hoffmann in return for sexual favours.

Overt hostility to the refugees only occurs in rare cases, like Edward March's housekeeper, who dislikes all foreigners on principle. As a German, Hansen is made to feel very aware of her difference from the British, for British attitudes to the refugees are defined by a combination of condescension and ignorance: 'Several thousand people had arrived, hopeless, penniless, homeless, from a country of which it was mostly known that it had lost the last war and possessed an impossibly difficult grammar' (55). Partly as a result of this ignorance, some elements in the upper classes, like John Ashley's father, are predisposed to sympathize with Hitler and his regime. In Feiner's later novels, such views are seen as gravely weakening Britain's stance towards the threat posed by Nazi Germany.

Identity and Integration

The issues of integration into British society and the concomitant need to construct a new identity affected the younger refugees most acutely. Whereas the older refugees came to Britain with their socialization largely complete and their identity largely established, refugees who arrived as children or teenagers completed their education in British academic institutions and grew up in a predominantly English-speaking environment, to which they had to adapt their German- or Austrian-Jewish identity and lifestyle. The majority made the adjustment to British society, sometimes problematically and painfully, but others did not. Among the latter were those who stayed in Britain only temporarily and who saw little need to adopt a British identity, even though, after their expulsion from their native countries, it was no longer possible for them to perceive themselves as Germans or Austrians.

One such refugee was Sibylle Ortmann, born on 5 January 1918, who arrived in Britain on 31 October 1933, aged fifteen. She was the daughter of Eva Ortmann, née Löwenfeld, and a non-Jewish father, who had left his family when Sibylle was four. Ortmann's two stays in Britain, the first lasting some eight months and the second, following almost two years back in Germany, some sixteen months, ended with her departure to the United States in September 1937; they are documented in the voluminous correspondence between mother and daughter that has been collected by Peter Crane, Sibylle's son.[17] In the letters, Sibylle Ortmann appears as exceptionally mature, independent, and self-reliant for her age, coping with the difficulties and unexpected contingencies of forced emigration with remarkable coolness and resilience. The Ortmanns were under threat both as Jews and as communists, known opponents of the Nazi regime. When it became clear that she could not continue her education in Berlin, Sibylle left Germany in the hope of gaining the qualifications that would enable her to build a new life outside Germany; she came to Britain only because a close friend of her mother's, a Quaker, put her in contact with the Bishop family in the London suburb of Blackheath, with whom Sibylle could stay as a paying guest while studying.

Ortmann remained resolutely a foreigner and an outsider in Britain whose observations on British society were sometimes critical but mostly not unfriendly. Her initial encounter with British officialdom on arrival at Dover set an instructive precedent. She pretended to be entering Britain as a tourist, for a short stay only, knowing that she lacked the means to support herself and would not be granted permission to stay longer. The immigration officer was not deceived by her tourist pose, since she had little money and no return ticket to Germany. Faced with the prospect of being returned to Germany, Ortmann invented another story, which the official, though aware that it was a fiction, could accept; to the applause of her fellow passengers on the train to London, she was admitted. This set the tone for her dealings with the British authorities, who always issued her with residence permits, and later a work permit, though sometimes after considerable effort on her part. Once she became a student, at Pitman's Secretarial College, she obtained extensions to her residence permit without difficulty.

Ortmann's reports to her mother focus on such aspects of life in Britain as language, food, domestic arrangements, and the weather, the standard preoccupations of newly arrived refugees. Language was an important initial concern, as she feared that her imperfect command of English would affect her ability to communicate with those around her and to undertake an educational or vocational course of study. That concern diminished as her English improved, though this also allowed her to appreciate the difficulty of overcoming the subtle barriers of upbringing, custom, and convention that divided the refugees from mainstream society. On arrival, Ortmann assured her mother that her first meal was copious and palatable (101), though this may have formed part of her strategy of reassuring Eva and assuaging her anxieties. In February 1934, however, she declared forthrightly that English food was extremely unhealthy, with fish for breakfast, barely credible amounts of meat at every meal, and tasteless boiled vegetables (204). Among Ortmann's first impressions of the Bishops' house was the lack of heating; the abysmal cold prevalent in British households caused her to value her hot-water bottle (205). She complained bitterly about the damp, fog, and grime of the London environment, and about the colds and chilblains from which she suffered (155–56). Like other refugees, she was struck by the sheer size of London, and by the thronging masses of people in the West End, the volume of traffic, and the capital's apparently inexhaustible energy and vitality.

Ortmann initially found the Bishops charming, with the courtesy that she at first attributed to the English in general, and was touched by the motherly way in which Mrs Bishop treated her. She liked the house, the view, and the area, despite the time-consuming journey from Blackheath to the areas in west and north-west London where her fellow refugees lived. But by early 1934 Ortmann had grown dissatisfied with what she perceived as an uncultured domestic environment. As the granddaughter of Raphael Löwenfeld, the translator of Tolstoy and founder of the Schiller-Theater in Berlin, high culture was an integral part of her life. She lamented what she saw as a complete lack of intellectual culture, of any interests beyond knitting stockings, patience, and crossword puzzles, and declared that 'das Spießig-Konservative' [the philistine conservatism] (170) of the Bishops was gradually driving her mad. This problem was resolved when she went to live with the Rubinsteins, a secularized, assimilated Anglo-Jewish family, in Ealing; she developed a lifelong friendship with Cambridge-educated Mary Rubinstein, with whom she could discuss matters of shared interest. But the lack of culture in Britain — the poverty of its musical life, the poor taste manifested in clothes, furniture, and decoration, and the sentimental kitsch popular in the cinema — remained a constant theme in her letters.

Ortmann adapted rapidly to life in Britain; from her letters, it appears that the time she spent in the country was for the most part happy, even allowing for the disruption and difficulties inherent in emigration. But she remained aware of the gulf separating her from the British: 'Nur das ist sicher, daß man sich das "Akklimatisieren" und "Assimilieren" ungeheuer viel leichter vorstellt und als Faktor unwesentlicher, als es, wenn man es dann erlebt, ist' [Only one thing is certain, that one imagines 'acclimatization' and 'assimilation' as vastly easier and as a less significant factor than it is once one experiences it in reality] (195). In any country other than Germany, she concluded, refugees like her would always remain foreigners. As she never intended to stay in Britain and adopt elements of a British identity, she was thrown back on her existing identity. She remained deeply attached to Germany, often expressing her homesickness for Berlin, and envious of her friend Evi Jessner (daughter of the famous theatre director Leopold Jessner) when she made a return visit (201). Indeed, Ortmann returned to Germany in 1934 for almost two years, staying until her employer, the American commercial attaché, could no longer guarantee her safety. Refugees like Ortmann still saw Germany as the land of poets and thinkers (the *Land der Dichter und Denker*) even after 1933, and her attachment to its culture was of overriding importance to her. As the German Jews had been especially prominent in the cultural sphere, it was possible for refugees like her to carry this dimension of their German-Jewish identity into emigration with them and to preserve it, even in face of the new regime in Germany.

One important factor in Ortmann's preservation of the identity of a German Jew was the distance that separated her from British Jews. The tensions that had existed in Germany between the westernized, assimilated Jews and the orthodox Jews from Eastern Europe (known pejoratively as *Ostjuden*) appear in Ortmann's letters — in her description of a gathering of orthodox Jews at a funeral, when she claimed that she did not believe that such people still existed (328), and in her remark that it was cruel to place an assimilated refugee girl in an Eastern European, Polish, house (230). She found the tendency among some British Jews deliberately to create distance between themselves and British society both incomprehensible and undesirable. But the principal cause of the friction between Ortmann and Anglo-Jewry was her treatment by the Jewish relief committees based at Woburn House. Here again, the issue of culture played a key role.

On her first visit to the Jewish Refugees Committee, Ortmann was dismayed by the cold and patronizing treatment she received from the Hon. Lily Montagu (109–10); her interview later in November 1933 with Mrs Model, another senior member of Anglo-Jewry, reduced her to tears, so dismissive was Model of Ortmann's aspirations to education (132–33). Worse still was Model's treatment of family friends of Ortmann's, whose daughter wished to study for the English matriculation examination. This received short shrift from the '76jährige Hexe' [76-year-old witch], who delivered another tirade against German-Jewish intellectual aspirations: 'Immer noch dieser akademische Dünkel? Das hat aufgehört, dafür sind wir Hitler dankbar! Ein Glück, daß er gekommen ist' [Still the same academic pretensions? That's over now, for that we are grateful to Hitler! It's a good thing he's appeared] (239). This gulf in attitudes towards intellectual and cultural matters was a major barrier to the integration of many — though of course not all — refugees from Germany and Austria into Anglo-Jewry. Refugees like Ortmann remained true to the values and identity of German Jewry in exile and even when their community was on the brink of destruction.

By contrast, Ingrid Jacoby, who was born in Vienna on 9 March 1927 and arrived in Britain on a Kindertransport in June 1939 with her elder sister Lieselotte, stayed in Britain, where she experienced her schooling and her working and married life.

Fig. 1.2. Refugees at Woburn House, where the Jewish relief committees were based. Courtesy of the Wiener Library.

Her father escaped to Britain from France in 1940, but her mother was unable to leave Austria and died in the Holocaust. Jacoby lived in Falmouth, Cornwall, from June 1939 until September 1944, when, after leaving school, she went to study at a secretarial college in Oxford. The first of the three volumes of her diaries, collectively entitled *My Darling Diary*, covers her time as a schoolgirl in wartime Falmouth.[18] *My Darling Diary* is one of the most important diaries produced by a Jewish refugee from Nazism in Britain, not only for its vivid and detailed picture of life in wartime and post-war Britain and for the insight it provides into the emotional development of a young woman, but also for the quality of its writing. Jacoby displays exceptional literary sophistication for a girl of her age, playing with the form of the diary so as to render more complex and multilayered the relationship between author, text, and reader.

In Falmouth, far from the centres of refugee settlement, Jacoby lived in an almost entirely English environment; even her sister, her main link to her Viennese past, was determined to integrate and as far as possible to adopt an English identity, allowing her English friends to anglicize her name from Lieselotte to Lizzy (159). The sisters were first taken in by a middle-aged couple, Mr and Mrs Robins, but Ingrid was delighted to go and live with Miss Davis, who, with her younger sister, Miss Kitty, taught English and took in children at her house, St Joseph's. She stayed there for the rest of her time in Falmouth, except for a period in 1942–43 when she stayed in a boarding house owned by Mr and Mrs Tamblyn, from which she was again delighted to return to St Joseph's. As a child refugee wrenched from a happy and secure family home, Jacoby experienced in full the pain and disruption of forced emigration; she lost her much-loved mother, while her relations with her father, who lived in distant London, were strained.

Initially, Jacoby struggled to adapt to the utterly unfamiliar surroundings of a small Cornish town and suffered acutely from homesickness, as she wrote on 3 July 1939, shortly after her arrival: 'How I envy English children! They are able to live at home with their parents. I'm sure there are many in Austria who envy *me*, but they needn't. Homesickness is terrible' (28; the diary entries before October 1940, originally written in German, have been published in English translation). But once she moved to St Joseph's, where she formed close relationships with the Misses Davis and with the other children, and once she had started at Falmouth Girls' High School, where she was rapidly accepted into a circle of schoolfriends and classmates, her unhappiness and sense of inferiority abated:

> And so my misery and homesickness were gradually overlaid by an enjoyment of new friends and, ultimately, even by a superficial feeling of belonging. After more than half a century I look back on those five years in Falmouth as being among the happiest of my life. ('Introduction', unnumbered page)

As she was only twelve when she arrived, Jacoby's perceptions of Britain and the British were largely determined by those with whom she came into daily contact, initially Mr and Mrs Robins. Jacoby was at first thoroughly miserable in Falmouth, struggling with a strange language, and bent on portraying herself as an outsider whose otherness defined her identity:

> I'm in a foreign country and no longer at home. If someone corrects me I immediately think the worst: they want to annoy me, they hate me. Then I tell myself: 'These people are strangers. What have they got to do with you? This is not your country. You weren't born here and consequently you don't belong here.' (28)

But her initial dislike of England clearly owed much to her dislike of Mr and Mrs Robins. As soon as she went to live with Miss Davis at St Joseph's, her emotional condition changed completely. Surrounded by warmth and understanding, she began to adapt to life in Falmouth and to enjoy it. There are still outbursts against England, but these were almost always triggered by specific conditions and correspondingly brief in duration, as when the failure of her plan to go and live in Portsmouth with a friend from Vienna prompted her to pour out her feelings to her diary:

> Although I've tried, and often thought I'd succeeded, an inner voice tells me repeatedly: You will never be English! You will never be English! You will never be English! YOU HAVE FOREIGN BLOOD IN YOU! You don't know what an inferiority complex is, do you, so I will tell you: it's dreadful. I may enjoy art, writing and music but I'm no good at any of them, in fact I'm no good at anything. I'm a failure, one of God's feeble creatures only here to make up numbers. (201)

However, this attack of insecurity soon passes, to be replaced by a sense of relief at remaining at St Joseph's.

After the difficult phase of her early months in Falmouth, Jacoby's perception of Britain changes markedly as she comes to regard the country and its inhabitants with genuine affection. In September 1942, after listing the numerous aspects of life in Britain that she likes, she declares: 'I love England and English people' (139). In July 1943, she gives eloquent expression to these feelings:

> I may never actually have put it into words but you must know by now how much I love England. People say to me: 'Never mind, dearie, soon everything will be over and you can go back to your own country again.' But I don't want to go back to my own country! Can't they understand that? I want to be English. I want to do things for England. It has done a lot for *me*, after all. I love everything English — the language, the towns and countryside, the sea, the shops, and above all the people — their polite good manners, their reserve, their sense of humour, everything. (187)

One can detect in such passages an underlying sense of insecurity, a desire to compensate for perceived inferiority and otherness by embracing all things English and thus creating a new identity that will overlay the Austrian past. Jacoby goes on to articulate her discomfort with anything foreign, presumably because it reminds her of her own foreign origins:

> I'm often taken for English and I love that. I can't get on with foreigners, except of course with Lieselotte, who's so English herself. The other day I was listening to my father and my aunt talking — they were listing all the things they didn't like about England! I was quietly fuming. (187).

The conflicted sense of identity underlying this arguably excessive embrace of a British identity finds powerful expression when she is introduced to a fellow refugee from Austria in September 1944: 'He's an elderly man and had a very strong accent. We went for a walk together. I didn't want anyone to see me with him. How could I have anything in common with someone so un-English?' (268). The vehemence of the rejection of anything foreign, and especially Austrian, points to tensions as yet unresolved in Jacoby's sense of her own identity and in her relationship to her country of refuge.

For the most part, however, the diary consists of daily entries detailing the thorough integration of a young girl into English life. This is particularly evident in Jacoby's description of her experiences at Falmouth Girls' High School, where her initial anxieties about her foreign name and accent were rapidly resolved by her admission into a circle of close friends and her participation in the usual round of tennis and netball, seaside walks, and excursions to local resorts, as well as numerous invitations to other girls' houses. After passing the entrance examination to the High School in April 1940, she was delighted to be able to wear the typical uniform of an English schoolgirl, navy blue knickers and all (59). Like any other schoolgirl, she acquired a nickname, 'Inky' (for Ingrid), or 'Inky Polly' (for Ingrid Pollak, her original name). As presented in the diary, Jacoby's interactions with her schoolmates were typical for a girl of her age — friendships and enmities, adolescent crushes and tiffs, all the usual give-and-take of life in a school community. Although she felt herself to be different, there is never any evidence of her being treated differently by her schoolmates; despite her accent, they accepted her as one of their number and never singled her out, either as a target for abuse and discrimination or as requiring special assistance and support.

Jacoby's acculturation took place through the medium of the English language, which she mastered rapidly: by spring 1940, she was able to pass the entrance examination for her school, which proved too difficult for Miss Davis's niece Connie, and by autumn 1940 she was writing her diary in English, displaying a command of the language across its registers. She immersed herself in English literature, as her reading shows: among her favourites were Shakespeare, the Brontë sisters, Oliver Goldsmith, Kipling, and George Bernard Shaw, while she also cites such perennial favourites as *Little Women*, *Anne of Green Gables*, *Lorna Doone*, and *The Prisoner of Zenda*, and displays a thorough familiarity with popular contemporary novelists like Daphne Du Maurier, Howard Spring, Margaret Kennedy (*The Constant Nymph*), and Hugh Walpole. Her adoption of English popular culture also proceeded apace. She was an avid cinema-goer, listing *Wuthering Heights*, *The Hunchback of Notre Dame*, *The Thief of Baghdad*, *Gone with the Wind*, *The Life and Death of Colonel Blimp*, *Bitter Sweet*, and *Lady Hamilton* among the films she saw; visits to 'the flicks' formed part of her social routine, as they did for countless British teenagers, complete with the fixation on film stars that led her to solicit autographs from such figures as Anna Neagle, Anton Walbrook, and Laurence Olivier and his wife Vivien Leigh when they were staying in Cornwall.

Daily life at St Joseph's also contributed to Jacoby's acculturation, since she was surrounded there by a quintessentially British environment. Indeed, much of the diary consists of accounts of the round of activities of a typical teenage girl of the time. At St Joseph's, she learned to play games like Monopoly, Tiddlywinks and Rummy; to enjoy the English manner of celebrating birthdays, Christmas, and New Year's Eve with parties; and to sing the popular songs of the day, like the novelty song 'Mairzy Doats' and an anti-Nazi version of 'Whistle While You Work' (from the film *Snow White and the Seven Dwarfs*). She also acquired, it must be said, some of the less attractive, class-based attitudes prevalent among the British middle class, as in her rejection of boys from the local grammar school as 'common' or in her dismissal of the American soldiers who came to Falmouth in advance of the D-Day landings as 'Yanks', uncultured and uncouth. Overall, the diary provides abundant evidence of her familiarity with the everyday paraphernalia of British life, from Poppy Day to her Post Office savings book, from Christmas carol services to the Helston Floral Dance, signifiers of her initiation into a new way of life and a new identity.

As previously indicated, however, Jacoby always remained aware of her status as a refugee and foreigner — sometimes uncomfortably so — and could never assume an entirely British identity, however much she became integrated into British society. That integration was made easier by her lack of a pronounced Jewish identity; her family had already been thoroughly assimilated in Vienna, and had abandoned all Jewish observance in Britain. Jacoby converted to Christianity in 1944, as an Anglican, and was later to marry a Catholic Pole. Initially, she was reluctant to abandon Judaism; she confided her disapproval of her sister's baptism to her diary (99), and at first could only go to church with a certain sense of transgression. But as Miss Davis was a devout churchgoer, albeit a Catholic, and as there was no synagogue in Falmouth, Jacoby became accustomed to church services. She helped on occasion to decorate the church and became familiar with Anglican practices through school prayers, stating in July 1943 that 'Onward Christian Soldiers', that anthem of muscular Victorian Christianity, was her favourite hymn (187).

Yet her awareness of her Jewish origins remained a partially hidden source of insecurity to her: she reproached herself bitterly for failing to confront the boarding-house owner Mrs Tamblyn when the latter spoke disparagingly about Jews (194–95), one of the very rare occasions when Jacoby encountered anti-Semitism. That Jacoby lacked the courage to tell Mrs Tamblyn that she was herself Jewish can be attributed to her feelings of inferiority as a Jew and a foreigner, feelings that underlay the confident familiarity with British life that had otherwise allowed her to develop a new identity as an English schoolgirl growing into adulthood far from her native Vienna.

The reception extended to the Jewish refugees from Nazism in Britain largely determined the way in which their country of refuge is depicted in the texts analysed in this chapter, though that depiction varies according to such factors as age on arrival or gender. Incidents of outright hostility, xenophobia, or anti-Semitic prejudice were not common, but even those authors who enjoyed a mostly benign reception were conscious of the distance that separated them from the British, who tended to treat them with a certain aloof indifference. British society was above all unfamiliar terrain, leading most refugees to interact predominantly with other refugees, except for cases like Ingrid Jacoby in Cornwall, where there were few refugees to mix with. Refugee authors record in their texts the experience of being cast as outsiders, an experience common to all those who have undergone a forced emigration to a foreign country. The conditions prevailing in Britain determined the particular manner in which that identity of the outsider was imposed on the refugees from Nazism; but at the same time the character and temperament of the individual refugees, their pre-existing attitudes and propensities, shaped their reaction to their new situation and the degree to which they were able, or willing, to create a new identity in response to British conditions. The texts discussed in this chapter record these processes in the period before the caesura of the outbreak of war.

Notes to Chapter 1

1. For a masterly account of Zweig's years in Britain, see Dove, *Journey of No Return*, esp. pp. 43–63.
2. Stefan Zweig, *Die Welt von gestern: Erinnerungen eines Europäers* (London: Hamilton; Stockholm: Bermann-Fischer, 1941).
3. See Chapter 6 for a fuller discussion of these texts.
4. See Dove, *Journey of No Return*, pp. 118–26, for Kerr's vain efforts to publish in Britain.
5. Alfred Kerr, *Ich kam nach England: Ein Tagebuch aus dem Nachlaß*, ed. by Walter Huder and Thomas Koebner (Bonn: Bouvier, 1979).
6. As quoted in Thomas Koebner, 'Bemerkungen zu dieser Ausgabe', in Alfred Kerr, pp. 200–02 (p. 200).
7. Lily Wagner, 'Emigrants' Daily Life', unpublished typescript (1940).
8. On the under-researched subject of refugee boarding houses, see Anthony Grenville, *Jewish Refugees from Germany and Austria in Britain, 1933–1970: Their Image in 'AJR Information'* (London: Vallentine Mitchell, 2010), pp. 230–33.
9. On Rosenstock, see Anthony Grenville, 'Guardians of a Heritage: The Editors of the *Association of Jewish Refugees Journal*', in *Voices from Exile: Essays in Memory of Hamish Ritchie*, ed. by Ian Wallace (Leiden: Brill Rodopi, 2015), pp. 162–77.
10. Werner Rosenstock, memoirs 1941–86, unpublished typescript, 2 vols (1945, 1986), in my possession, kindly supplied to me by Michael Rosenstock, Werner Rosenstock's son. I have preserved the slightly faulty English of the earlier volume.
11. Ruth Borchard, *We Are Strangers Here: An 'Enemy Alien' in Prison in 1940*, intro. by Charmian Brinson (London: Vallentine Mitchell, 2008).
12. Sophie Roth, *Für mein Schurlikind: Tagebuch 1940–1944*, ed. by Evelyn Adunka (Vienna: Theodor Kramer Gesellschaft, 2012).
13. Ruth Feiner, *Fires in May*, trans. by Norman Alexander (Philadelphia: Lippincott, 1936).
14. See the obituary by L[eon] Z[eitlin], *AJR Information*, September 1954, p. 4.
15. See Nicole Brunnhuber, *The Faces of Janus: English-Language Fiction by German-Speaking Exiles in Great Britain, 1933–1945* (Berne: Lang, 2005).
16. On refugees entering into marriages of convenience, among them the novelist Sybille Bedford, see Irene Messinger, 'Marriages of Convenience as a Strategy for Escape and Survival', *AJR Journal*, November 2014, pp. 1–2.
17. Peter Crane, *'Wir leben nun mal auf einem Vulkan'* (Bonn: Weidle, 2005).
18. Ingrid Jacoby, *My Darling Diary*, 3 vols (Penzance: United Writers Publications, 1998–2009), I: *A Wartime Journal — Vienna 1937–39, Falmouth 1939–44* (1998). The subsequent two volumes, continuing up to 1955, will be discussed in Chapter 4.

CHAPTER 2

Internment

The internment of many thousands of mostly Jewish refugees as 'enemy aliens' in summer 1940 represented the low point in relations between the Jews from Germany and Austria and the British; it is without doubt the most contentious period in the history of the refugees from Nazism in Britain. Internment is also the issue over which accounts written by refugee authors differ most strikingly from those written by historians and other academics. The latter are unanimous in their highly critical attitude to internment, which they see as an unjust and senseless measure, as the result of xenophobic prejudice and hysteria whipped up by right-wing political interests and the right-wing press, and as causing unnecessary suffering and loss of life. This holds true across the decades: from scholarly publications at the time, like François Lafitte's stinging denunciation of the policy of internment and its implementation, published in 1940, to the standard studies by Peter and Leni Gillman and by Ronald Stent, both published in 1980 after the relevant official papers had been made public, to the volumes containing articles by experts published in the 1990s and 2000s, to the most recent comparative study of wartime internment in Britain and the United States.[1]

By contrast, the refugee authors, though they also denounce the injustice, inhumanity, and sheer stupidity of internment, take a markedly more conciliatory line; their depiction of the British and their treatment of the refugees lacks much of the bite and severity of Lafitte's study. Arguably, this is because summer 1940 showed Britain both at its worst, at least on the home front, in the detention of 'enemy aliens', and at its best, in its lone resistance to Hitler; internment played out against the background of the Battle of Britain, which administered the first major defeat to Hitler's previously all-conquering forces. The evident fondness and admiration that the authors covered here developed for Britain led them to adopt narrative strategies that allowed them to present the British in a milder light than they perhaps deserved.

Men behind Barbed Wire

The outbreak of war in September 1939 was a major turning point for the refugees, though they, like the rest of the civilian population, did not come face-to-face with war's full reality until May–June 1940, when the Nazis overran the Low Countries and France and prepared to invade Britain. The British government initially wished to avoid interning enemy aliens en masse, as it had in World War I. It set up tribunals before which all German and Austrian nationals, now classed as 'enemy aliens', had to appear and which assigned them to one of three categories. Only a tiny minority, mostly those with Nazi sympathies, were assigned to Category A and interned. The great majority of refugees were classed as victims of Nazi oppression and included among those assigned to Category C, which left them at liberty. Those whose cases the tribunals judged unclear were assigned to the intermediate Category B and were subject to certain restrictions.[2]

In the early summer of 1940, after the collapse of France and under pressure from the right-wing press, the government gave way to those who argued that the refugees posed a threat to national security as potential spies and fifth columnists. In May 1940, the newly installed coalition government under Winston Churchill first decreed the internment of male enemy aliens between sixteen and sixty living in 'protected areas' on the threatened sectors of the coast, then issued the notorious order to 'collar the lot'. Male refugees in Category B were interned, as were Category B women; the detention of male refugees in Category C, ordered in June, was under way when the policy of internment was halted the next month, following the sinking by a German submarine of the *Arandora Star*, one of five ships transporting internees to Canada and Australia. This measure, to some extent a panic response to the situation of national emergency prevailing in May–June 1940, ultimately caused the internment of some twenty-seven thousand enemy aliens, including some four thousand women, most of whom were Jews who plainly posed no security risk whatsoever.

The mass internment of 'enemy aliens' was the darkest chapter in the history of relations between the British and the Jewish refugees from Hitler, a 'bespattered page', as Victor Cazalet, MP, put it in a debate in the House of Commons on 22 August 1940. This is reflected in diaries written during the period of internment and in recollections composed immediately afterwards, three of which will be considered in this section. Together, they trace the itineraries of the detainees from their arrest, via a variety of holding camps, to the permanent camps on the Isle of Man. Paul Bondy, aged thirty-five, who was living with his wife and small daughter on Cheyne Walk, London SW3, recorded the initial shock of his arrest on 16 June 1940 in his diary.[3] As was often the case, Bondy was arrested early in the morning, when two policemen rang the bell of his house and ordered him to be ready in half an hour. In the event, they 'waited quite decently' for about an hour while Bondy packed in haste (he was allowed one suitcase) and attempted to make arrangements for his wife in his absence. He was then taken by bus to Chelsea Police Station, already reflecting on the stupidity and pointlessness of the detention of harmless refugees: 'All the time I could think of nothing except the waste and frustration of effort' (16). The police behaved in a friendly and humane way to Bondy and his fellow detainees, but nevertheless transported them like common criminals by Black Maria to an improvised barracks, located in a girls' school on Sydney Street. There, the presence of soldiers to guard them showed that they were entering the realm of the military, which would assume custody of them fully once they arrived at their next destination, Kempton Park racecourse.

Professor Paul Jacobsthal, a distinguished classicist aged fifty-eight who had left Germany in 1935 and secured a position at Christ Church, Oxford, conveyed the shock of his arrest, the irruption of the wartime emergency into the measured rhythms of scholarly work, in terms the more telling for their coolly factual tone: 'On Friday July 5 1940 in the morning when I was peacefully writing on Celtic Geometric Ornament a knock came at my door in Christ Church and a plain clothes policeman entered producing a warrant of arrest' (198).[4] Jacobsthal experienced his arrest as an arbitrary violation of the fundamental rights and freedoms of a resident of the United Kingdom, and as a betrayal of the faith placed by the refugees from Hitler in the British regard for legality and justice. Like Bondy, he was transported to his home in a Black Maria, packed his case, and bade his wife farewell. At Oxford Police Station, he joined an array of eminent academics, men whose contribution to their disciplines and, in some cases, to the war effort was temporarily nullified by their internment. Although the police officers were friendly, Jacobsthal's razor was impounded, a typically obtuse administrative measure — as he remarked drily, 'in other places they took more interest in boot-laces' (198). Before their transfer to Cowley Barracks, Professor (later Sir) John Beazley came to give Jacobsthal his treasured copy of the *Odyssey*, one of many acts of kindness on the part of British civilians recorded by the detained refugees. At Cowley Barracks, the detainees were guarded by sentries with fixed bayonets and could only gaze out at the surrounding countryside through the barbed wire that was to dominate their visual impressions of camp life over the coming months.

The composer and musicologist Hans Gál, born in Vienna in 1890, had fled to Britain in March 1939 and found a friendly haven in Edinburgh, where he and his family lodged with Sir Herbert Grierson, Emeritus Professor of English. Gál was arrested on 12 May 1940 and held for six days with about a hundred other internees at the Donaldson Hospital, which had housed deaf-and-dumb children. The antiquated building was ill-suited to the purpose, and the preparations undertaken for the detainees were wholly inadequate. Gál's reaction was one of fury, as the tone of incandescent anger in the opening pages of his internment diary indicates: 'Und wie unsagbar abscheulich alles ist, was da an die fünf Sinne dringt. Dieser scheußliche, schale, aus menschlicher Ausdünstung, Abtrittdüften, Lysol, schlechtem Essen gemischte Kaserngeruch im ganzen Haus, auf allen Gängen und Stiegen! Wie ich dieses Haus hasse!' [And how unspeakably repulsive is everything that impinges on one's five senses here. The disgusting, stale reek of the barracks, a mixture of human body odour, the stench of the latrines, disinfectant, and bad food, throughout the entire building, in all the corridors and on all the staircases! How I hate this building!] (7).[5] Gál complained about the food, the cramped accommodation, the inadequate sleeping arrangements, and the degrading, semi-public routine imposed on those needing to relieve themselves at night.

But it was less the poor physical conditions than the psychological effect of detention in the ugly, forbidding institution that caused Gál to feel such outrage, mixed with nervous foreboding and an overwhelming sense of powerlessness. The windows set too high in the walls to allow any view of the outside world became

FIG. 2.1. Hans Gál and friends in internment on the Isle of Man.
From left to right: Willi Gross, Max Sugar, Hans Gál, and Hugo Schneider.
Courtesy of Eva Fox-Gál.

for him an image of incarceration and restriction in a confined space, while the building's maze of corridors became a metaphor for the labyrinthine bureaucracy of internment, an unseen and arbitrary higher power that was now controlling his life. Like his fellow authors, Gál railed against the British because of the sheer stupidity of internment, the absurdities of its procedures, 'diese sinnloseste aller Sinnlosigkeiten' [this most senseless of all senselessnesses] (4), and the inefficiency of its implementation, sometimes amounting to gross negligence.

On 14 May 1940, two days after his arrest, Gál gave vent at length to his sense of injustice at being treated like a common criminal. He was deeply affected by the abrupt change in British attitudes towards the refugees from Nazi Germany:

> Und *wer bestraft uns?* Sind das unsere Freunde, dieselben Briten, die uns freundlich aufgenommen, unsere Arbeit anerkannt, unseren Kindern Gastfreundschaft geboten, uns das Gefühl einer neuen Heimat gegeben haben? [...] Und nun kommt der Freund, mit verändertem, kalt-unzugänglichem Gesicht, sagt 'sorry' und behandelt dich, den vertrauenden, dankbaren Gast, wie den ärgsten Feind und Verbrecher!

> [And *who is punishing us?* Are these our friends, the same British people who received us in friendly fashion, recognized our work, offered our children their hospitality, gave us the feeling of a new homeland? [...] And now the friend comes with a changed, coldly unapproachable face, says 'sorry' and treats you, the trusting, grateful guest, like the worst enemy and criminal!]

Utterly depressed by the widespread satisfaction in British press reports at the internment of 'enemy aliens', he concluded: 'Ich habe das Gefühl, daß unsere Lage hoffnungslos ist' [I have the feeling that our situation is hopeless] (8). For Gál, the greatest blow was arguably not the inefficiency, the senselessness, or even the injustice of internment, but the shock to his psychological and emotional security and his very sense of identity. After being welcomed as a refugee from Nazi oppression by men like Sir Herbert Grierson and the composer Sir Donald Tovey, Gál could not reconcile himself to the change in status being forced on the Jewish internees, who, deprived of their status as loyal adherents to the Allied cause, were suddenly treated like the Nazis, their persecutors. Having lost his identity as a loyal Austrian in 1938, Gál now faced the potential loss of his identity as a refugee from Nazism and a loyal friend of Britain.

Like a large number of internees from the London area initially held at racecourses, Paul Bondy was detained at Kempton Park. His reception there was, as he put it, 'rather strongly military' (19): by way of a welcome, the new arrivals were barked at by a sergeant major, subjected to a rigorous search and the confiscation of an apparently random selection of their possessions, and then allocated a space on a concrete floor with mattresses to sleep on. The food was execrable and sometimes appeared only irregularly:

> The meal was an exasperating sticky mess of rather hard burned rice, with an occasional prune thrown in, and though we were quite hungry, having spent all day in the open, many of us were unable to touch that kind of food. (33)

Some of the British officers were courteous and helpful, but one took a malicious pleasure in harassing the detainees: 'Though in a less violent form, he behaved meanly enough to become in our eyes quite the picture of an SS officer in a concentration camp.' Bondy immediately qualified this judgement with reference to the received image of the British officer: 'Nevertheless, I continue to hope that he was quite an exceptional case and entirely out of step with the splendid tradition of the British officer and gentleman' (30).

As with Gál, it was the psychological effect of internment that Bondy felt most keenly. It threatened to rob the internees not only of the new material basis that they had begun to build up, but also of the sense of hard-won security felt by refugees who had been uprooted, sometimes more than once. British policy was undermining the stable core of their identity by placing their loyalty in question and treating them as potential traitors: 'That this loss should occur through the inconsiderate action of a country all admired and whose cause was their own, was very hard and bitter for these internees' (26). Bondy became aware of the altered reality of their existence behind barbed wire, cut off from their families 'whom we had left behind in that other real world' (32). The barbed wire that bounded their lives became the prime symbol of internment, as the detainees gazed out across it to the vista of freedom and serenity beyond. Confined in a restricted area, the men milling aimlessly around on the racecourse were deprived by the barbed wire of their liberty and of their firm grasp on reality itself.

Paul Jacobsthal was sent from Oxford first to the far south-west, to Seaton in Devon, then to the north-west, to the notorious detention centre at Warth Mill in Bury, near Manchester. Conditions in Warth Mill, a disused cotton mill, were atrocious. The building was indescribably filthy, littered with pieces of antiquated factory machinery, and by any civilized standard uninhabitable; the primitive facilities available, especially the sanitary facilities, were totally inadequate for the numbers of men detained. Jacobsthal, unlike Gál, described the conditions he endured with distanced detachment: 'But I have not to criticize or to accuse, but to describe' (202). One can see this measured tone as a defensive reaction against the transformation of the ordered life of an Oxford don into the disorder of detention. Jacobsthal's recollections of the week that he spent at Warth Mill, from 9 July to 16 July 1940, depict in detail his arrival, the reception procedures so lengthy that they caused some of the tightly packed men to faint, the decrepit and dangerous interior of the building, the filth, the stench, the absence of basic hygiene, adequate food or bedding, and medical and recreational facilities — and the evident incapacity of the British authorities to remedy the situation.

Jacobsthal stated that 'the smallest details' of this 'hellish labyrinth' were forever imprinted on his memory, as if it were modelled on the imagined prisons of Piranesi (201). In his case, too, life in detention took on the quality of a nightmare, of an altered reality that formed a distorted counterpart to the reassuring certainty of the world outside:

> When later on, in the Isle of Man, I went through my notes, I realized that I had seen all through a mist. These figures moved and talked in an atmosphere of haunted unreality, vision and sound were distorted, the men were hardly themselves, nor was I myself. (207)

Jacobsthal was psychologically destabilized by internment, to the extent that he felt that his own identity had become fluid and insecure. Conditions on the journey from Liverpool to the Isle of Man aboard the aged *Tynwald of Douglas* were equally bad: seven hundred men were crowded below decks 'like cattle or slaves' as they waited fifteen hours for the ship to weigh anchor for the five-hour crossing, during which time Jacobsthal survived on a piece of chocolate. Knowing that the *Tynwald of Douglas* had brought men back from Dunkirk, he forbore to complain beyond drawing a contrast between the heroism of Dunkirk and the senselessness of internment: 'But I also thought that they had done it for a good cause and that I was a victim of a very stupid measure, of no avail to the country' (208).

For many internees, the last temporary camp was a newly built council estate at Huyton, on the eastern outskirts of Liverpool, from where they were shipped to the Isle of Man. As is evident from Hans Gál's account and from Paul Bondy's fragmentary notes, Huyton had the great advantage of consisting of houses, alongside the disadvantage of being merely a transit camp not designed for permanent residence. The accommodation was new, but not ready for habitation, lacking basic amenities like furniture and hot water. Consequently, conditions were at first bad, with inadequate food and overcrowding so severe that some men had to live in tents. Under the first commandant, the outgoing post did not leave the camp, and the resulting lack of communication with the outside world caused a sharp fall in the morale of the detainees; however, this improved with the arrival of a new commandant, Lieutenant Colonel Slatter, under whose regime conditions improved markedly. The detainees were in large measure responsible for the day-to-day administration of the camp, through a system common throughout the internment camps. Each house or hut elected a representative. These representatives were known as 'house leaders' or 'house fathers'; from them, men were elected to represent each street or row, and from them in turn, a 'camp leader' or 'camp father' was elected. The British administration thus remained to some extent at arm's length from the detainees, a practice that Paul Jacobsthal saw as deriving from the British experience of colonial administration (214).

After his traumatic experience of the Donaldson Hospital, Hans Gál's first impression of Huyton on the morning of 19 May 1940, the day after his arrival, was pleasant enough: white, tidy-looking, two-storey houses in bright sunshine on a clean, well-paved street in a brand-new housing estate. Gál could take a bath in a proper bathtub, though only with cold water; for the time being he still had to sleep on a palliasse, as the houses were entirely unfurnished. But he was able to share his new accommodation with three friends, who were an important boost to his morale, as well as a ready source of support and congenial company. On the other hand, the arrangements for feeding the men initially failed to function: Gál called the food 'pigs' feed', and the canteen block became known as 'Starvation Hall' (18). The image of the unshaven, ill-clad inmates, whose neglected appearance mirrored the primitive conditions under which they were forced to live, would haunt Gál long after his release, remaining as a nightmare image in his memory (17). He spent four weeks at Huyton; there he began to suffer from an acute skin problem on his face that eventually affected his eyes, but also to compose his hauntingly beautiful *Huyton Suite*, written for the instruments available in internment.

Gál found the British soldiers pleasant enough, but the behaviour of the officers continued to arouse his anger, as in the case of the captain who welcomed them with a speech but felt unable to use the word 'victory', as if it would be tactless to speak to the refugees of a German defeat. The inability of the British to understand the difference between Germans and refugees, especially Jewish refugees, was one of the greatest sources of bitterness for the internees. The principal hallmark of the British administration was its abysmal inefficiency, apparent at the daily roll-call, in the disorder that accompanied the drawing up of lists of men to be transferred to the Isle of Man, and in the postal system — at least until the detainees took it over. The commandant was rarely seen, other than when the inmates were on parade, when he expressed surprise at the number of refugees in the camp (22). In the absence of this ineffectual figure, day-to-day responsibility rested with his adjutant, Captain Tanner, a bully and, Gál suspected, a drunk, who was given to exercising his powers in such arbitrary actions as confiscating all musical instruments. Gál referred dismissively to such authority figures using the German terms 'die Herren' [these gentlemen] or simply 'man', the impersonal pronoun approximating to the amorphous English 'they'.

The internees' horizon was determined both physically and psychologically by the barbed wire that circumscribed the area within which they were free to move. Behind the wire, as Gál saw it, the men were held as if inside a cage (17). The visual image of internment is now subjectively defined by the interplay between the freedom of the open world beyond the wire fence and the caged confinement of the men inside it. This in turn corresponds to the two conflicting aspects of the detainees' perception of their internment — as innocent men aware of their right to freedom but at the same time as prisoners unjustly deprived of their liberty. The disjunction between rightful liberty and wrongful detention conditions the entire area of Huyton; every free space in the detainees' small world is bounded by the barbed wire, reinforced by a watchtower and armed sentries.

Most of the inmates at Huyton were soon transferred to permanent camps on the Isle of Man. Gál left for Central Promenade Camp on 14 June 1940, where he was detained until 27 September, while Jacobsthal arrived at Hutchinson Camp on 16 July 1940 and was held there until 30 September. On the Isle of Man, the men were mostly accommodated in requisitioned boarding houses and hotels; they were now lodged in rooms purpose-built for residence, even though two men often had to share a bed and the blocks of houses were encircled by barbed wire. Gál's initial impression of Central Promenade Camp (43–44) was depressing, but in view of its manifold advantages over Huyton he resolved to concentrate on its positive aspects — its view out across the sea, and the charm of the curving bay of Douglas and the green hill rising behind it. Jacobsthal described Hutchinson Camp as consisting of about forty boarding houses forming two rows around Hutchinson Square, 'these built of yellow brick in a style of timeless undateable ugliness', with a third parallel row of 'more pretentious grey houses' (214). Each house had a small front garden, some with a palm tree; the houses overlooked the bay and the islet of Conister, and from the top floor one could see the distant hills inland. But always present was the double barbed-wire fence that enclosed the camp, a feature that led Gál to compare Central Promenade Camp to a human zoo.

Both Gál and Jacobsthal shared their accommodation with friends of their choice, in the latter's case the eminent musicologist Egon Wellesz, and both were able to establish something of a settled routine, knowing that they would not be transferred again (provided they avoided deportation overseas). But the likelihood of a lengthy period of detention on the Isle of Man was also a deeply depressing prospect for the internees, exacerbated in the early days by the fear that, in the event of a German invasion, they would be trapped on the island with no way of escape, and later by fear for the well-being of loved ones at risk from the German bombing of British cities. After the initial inadequacies had been remedied, conditions in the internment camps improved: Gál noted the immense pleasure felt when the men were first allowed out of Central Promenade Camp for walks, albeit under guard. The regular arrival of mail and newspapers was particularly welcome, as the unconscionable delays in the post had had a severe effect on the morale of the internees, especially when they suspected, sometimes with justification, that the British authorities were holding their letters up, either out of inertia or because it suited their convenience.

Both men welcomed the cultural activities that became a prominent feature of their camps, reflecting the wealth of creative, intellectual, and academic talent confined there. Gál threw himself into the musical life of Central Promenade Camp, whose inmates organized concerts and musical performances; the high point of his internment came when he directed the musical revue *What a Life!*, which turned out to be a such a success at its dress rehearsal that he voluntarily delayed his release from internment by a day to attend the first performance. Jacobsthal noted with approval the establishment of a camp university in Hutchinson Camp, though he was critical of the quality of some of the lecturers. He was, however, unstinting in his praise of the camp's musical life. Both men were able to resume activities closely connected with their professional life in the outside world, which re-established the sense of identity that derived from their occupations in the realm of high culture and academia respectively. Gál was delighted to absorb himself in *What a Life!*, a congenial project where his energy and expertise were readily acknowledged by his peers, while Jacobsthal became again the classicist, carrying his copy of the *Odyssey* like a badge of his status. It is perhaps not surprising that he portrayed his release as a happy return to Oxford, in whose university world he could immerse himself, secure again in his identity as a respected academic.

Relations with the British authorities improved somewhat in the relative stability of the camps on the Isle of Man. Even Gál, who never became reconciled to those responsible for his internment, noted the improvements in the food, the canteen, and the banking system set up to administer what money they had (57). But he continued to complain repeatedly about the inertia and inefficiency of the camp authorities, reflected in the disorder that reigned in the commandant's office (69) and which obstructed the implementation of simple measures that would have alleviated the suffering and anxieties of the detainees. His tone of sarcasm when describing the British authorities remained constant, as in his account of the visit by the senior officer on the island and his staff to one of Gál's musical performances (52).

The manner in which the British organized the deportation of internees to Canada and Australia attracted Gál's most severe criticism: in the case of the first of the three transports that he listed, which departed for Canada on 1 July 1940, administrative failures left those to be deported to sleep on the floor of the Palace Hotel, seat of the camp administration, unfed and in unnecessary discomfort. The method of selection for transport overseas also aroused his suspicions: the authorities first sought to list those whose loyalty to Britain was questionable, but then switched abruptly to ordering the deportation of young and unmarried men. The chicanery that lay behind the drawing up of these lists, by the camp leaders under instructions from the British command, would later be laid bare in fictional form by Leo Kahn in the penultimate chapter of *Obliging Fellow* (1946).[6] Gál was particularly incensed by the underhand methods employed by the British, as in the official statement that only prisoners of war and Category A internees had been aboard the torpedoed liner *Arandora Star*. This deceit reached its low point when the adjutant, Major Daniels, persuaded twenty-three married men to volunteer for the third transport, bound for Australia, by promising them that their wives would follow, an assurance that proved to be cynically dishonest (71–72, 87–88).

In the concluding pages of his account, Paul Jacobsthal reflected on the unreality of the experience of internment on the Isle of Man:

> Slowly and imperceptibly we lost every feeling of the fantastic irreality of this life, of its absurd rhythm and *nomos* [laws], and we were hardly still aware that only two months ago we had lived an existence like that of the people we met on our walks in the country. If the beasts in the zoo could speak, they would tell us of similar experiences. (226)

Gál saw confinement in a restricted space as the principal factor distorting the internees' relationship to reality. For him, the ever-present barbed wire became the symbol of their imprisonment, which they internalized: 'Wer je etwas Ähnliches erlebt hat, wird die Entsetzlichkeit begreifen, die darin liegt, die Welt dauernd durch ein Gitter zu sehen' [Anyone who has ever experienced something similar will understand the horror entailed in seeing everything through bars] (46). In the brief periods when he was allowed to swim in the sea beyond the wire, Gál sensed that it was the interplay between confinement and the prospect of freedom that was responsible for the psychological distortion of the internees' perception of reality: 'In solchen Momenten wird einem plötzlich klar, wie krankhaft sich die Begriffe verschoben haben, wie entsetzlich überwertig dieser Stacheldraht in unserem Bewusstsein geworden ist' [At such moments one suddenly realizes how pathologically one's conception of the world has shifted, what a horribly excessive importance this barbed wire has assumed in our consciousness] (67).

Jacobsthal reflected on the temporal aspect of internment:

> Confinement is more than loss of freedom in the sense that the space of

> movement is narrowed [...]. Confinement means a break in the continuity of existence, an interruption of the normal flux of life, it causes a trauma; the natural relation and proportional importance of present, past and future become distorted. (223)

The element of time did indeed play a significant part in the psychological disruption suffered by the internees. They were affected by what one might call a disjunction between time and space, in the sense that whereas the space they inhabited was restricted by their confinement, the duration of that confinement seemed to extend indefinitely. The internees were not, like convicted criminals, sentenced to a defined period of detention; nor were they in the position of prisoners of war, who knew that they would be released when the war was over. The indefinite status of the detainees, which they perceived as that of free men unjustly deprived of their liberty by extra-legal means, was matched by the indefinite duration of that status. The absence of any clear limit to their detention in time stood in stark contrast to the rigid limits of their confinement in space; from that contradiction sprang much of the mental anguish of internment.

The British government reversed its policy on internment in July 1940, and the Home Office issued a White Paper listing eighteen categories of internees who would be considered for release. The publication of the White Paper gave rise to a frenzied surge of applications for release: men sought desperately to provide evidence that would qualify them as medical cases, for example, or to convince the authorities of their usefulness to the war effort. All the texts that depict internment document in some detail the frantic efforts of the internees to secure their liberty and their attempts to frame their applications so as to obtain a favourable outcome. But those attempts were futile, since there appeared to be no discernible logic or reason underlying the process of release; internees were apparently released entirely at random. Many refugees saw the logical inconsistency underlying the British policy of release: they had been interned as security risks, but were being released according to criteria relating to health, hardship, or usefulness to the war effort. Was a potential enemy agent any the less dangerous, they asked, for being an agricultural labourer? Towards the end of Leo Kahn's *Obliging Fellow*, a group of internees refuse on principle to apply for release, as the act of applying would imply the retrospective legitimation of their detention. Their resolve soon weakens, however, as the desire for freedom from the hated confines of the Isle of Man predominates. The period of internment in 1940–41 saw the refugees at their most powerless, lacking almost all agency to determine their own lives and threatened in their identity as bona fide refugees, as enemies of Nazism, and as loyal friends of Britain.

Women behind Bars

Far fewer women were interned than men, as internment was halted before Category C women, the great majority of the female refugees, could be detained. In consequence, Nazis and Nazi sympathizers represented a considerably greater proportion of the total number of women interned, which led to more situations of conflict than was the case with the male internees, among whom the Jewish and anti-Nazi refugees formed a dominant majority. The interned women escaped the dire conditions of improvised camps like Kempton Park racecourse and Warth Mill, or Prees Heath in Shropshire, where the men lived under canvas; presumably, the authorities felt that such accommodation was unsuitable for women, especially those with small children. But the consequence of this was that many women were held in prison, principally in Holloway Prison in north London, from where they were sent to Rushen, the women's camp on the Isle of Man. The differences in the internment of men and women make it possible to undertake a gender-based differentiation between them.

Among the female internees were Ruth Borchard, the second part of whose novel *We Are Strangers Here* is set in Holmdale (Holloway) Prison,[7] and Livia Laurent, who described the six weeks that she spent there in her memoir *A Tale of Internment*.[8] Laurent employed a style of light, almost whimsical humour, with an underlying strain of irony that proved to be an indirect but effective means of highlighting instances of severe injustice or gross administrative inefficiency. Although her memoir was published only a year after her release from the Isle of Man, Laurent apparently felt obliged to justify her decision to devote a book to the internment of 'a few thousand people' (7), a subject that appeared trivial when set against the momentous wartime events of 1942. Accordingly, she prefaced her text with a section entitled 'Perhaps a Justification' (7–8), in which a journalist friend persuades her to write her book by arguing that the liberty of the individual was the fundamental issue over which the war was being fought.

The 'shock of disbelief and astonishment' (11) caused by detention in a prison dominates the opening pages of Laurent's narrative (10–19). She conveys her experiences with seeming light-heartedness, in the fairy-tale image of a young girl who, expelled from her native land, comes to love and admire the country that takes her in, only to be interned there 'until further order'. She is taken first to a 'sordid prison cell' (11), where, sitting in the dark on a hard wooden bench and listening to the voices of the old lags next door, she can only stare impotently at the door that has been locked behind her. Although she resolves that she must bear her ordeal with dignity, she realizes 'that I was in the clutches of a great wheel which would rotate and rotate, taking me with it' (12), a striking image of disempowerment. From this prison, Laurent is transferred to Holloway, a fortress-like building where she is subjected to the perfunctory and demeaning procedures of reception, before being locked in a somewhat larger cell equipped with basic amenities. Next morning, she is introduced to the first routines of prison life, filling a jug of hot water to wash and breakfasting on porridge, bread, and tea from a tin plate and mug.

The realization that she is to be detained in a prison also comes with the force of a physical blow to Ruth Borchard's Anna Silver (74). The forbidding initial impression of Holmdale Prison, with its dirty cobbled yards, 'encased by greyish black walls with three long rows of hollow-eyed little windows' (75) and piled with heaps of coal, forms an appropriate backdrop to Anna's loss of her individuality and her freedom to determine her life and that of her baby. From the inside, her prison wing offers an equally bleak vista; it consists of four storeys lined on either side with narrow landings onto which open apparently endless rows of cells, with wire netting between the storeys to prevent suicide by jumping. Within this confined setting, prison life, as described by Laurent, develops its own monotonous, deadening rhythm: 'Days passed, all alike in their routine, only interrupted by such excitements as parcels, food sent in, letters and the weekly visits' (31), though visits from the world outside prove to be a strain. The food is appalling, the scope for activities extremely limited, and communication with the outside world difficult. Laurent, a cultured and well-educated woman, is reduced to taking up knitting, and almost welcomes air raids as a distraction from prison routine.

From her arrival at Holmdale, Borchard's Anna Silver faces a continuous battle over the care for her daughter Nele, since the prison is ill-equipped to cater for babies. On her first day, she has a prolonged struggle to get milk for the child's feed; when it eventually comes, it has sugar in it and Nele will not drink it. Anna faces the constant danger that Nele will be taken away from her and sent to an institution, a prospect that she finds unbearable. At one stage, when it is announced that the child cannot stay in Holmdale, the only alternative appears to be to give her to Anna's mother-in-law Ida, who lives nearby, in West Hampstead. Yet the almost Kafkaesque complexities involved in sending a telegram to Ida make Anna feel 'more helpless than ever before in her life' (97), and are only resolved by the intervention of Anna's friend, Hilde Gottschalk. Much of the later part of the novel is taken up by the difficulties Anna encounters in taking Nele with her to the Isle of Man, since a new ruling from the Home Office dictates that she must go by herself, even though she has repeatedly been promised that she will be reunited with her child. This heartless and senseless ruling leaves Anna feeling 'helpless, powerless' and despairing of having brought a child into such a world (139). But her determination not to give way to the situation ultimately enables her to overcome all these obstacles.

The resourcefulness and determination displayed by the female detainees is a principal theme in both texts. Far from lapsing into tearful weakness and submissiveness, in line with the stereotyped image of females in distress, they develop an admirable sense of solidarity and strength through comradeship. Although more ready than the male detainees to express emotion, even through tears, the women develop their own way of meeting the challenges of imprisonment. On her first morning in Holloway, Laurent discovers that those in the neighbouring cells are not dangerous criminals or spies, but friendly and sympathetic women who invite her to breakfast with them and do their best to make her feel at home. Whether creating a wholesome meal from the unpromising ingredients provided for them, or establishing their own routines for dealing with the nightly air raids, the women learn to cope with prison life in a defiant spirit of independence. As Laurent's new friend Elsa puts it: 'It's amazing what women can stand. A man under the same circumstances would go crazy. [...] Women have deeper resources' (26). Laurent herself was greatly impressed by her fellow detainees: 'I was only conscious of my profound astonishment at finding such extraordinary comradeship among so many women of different types, classes and countries.' She concludes that this solidarity is not merely a response to prison conditions, but an indication of the women's true qualities, which should not be obscured by male prejudices against their allegedly 'lesser' strength of character: 'Was it something deeper, a sense for the preservation of the best in one which evened out inequalities, jealousies and many of the lesser feminine characteristics?' (28).

Borchard's depiction of the detainees is more mixed:

> The landings upon landings were thronged with women pressing in both directions. The buildings vibrated with noise. It was a particular high drone, kept at the same level incessantly, which somehow pierced the nerves. The noise of a huge, excited female crowd, unrelieved by any deeper male tones. Anna always remembered it as the very note of women's internment. (102)

Anna Silver, a serious-minded graduate of a respected German university, plainly finds her Viennese fellow prisoners, who are obsessed with film stars, gossip, and make-up, frivolous and lacking in strength of character; it is detainees like these who allow themselves to be browbeaten into a servile display of submission by the prison governor's assistant (118–19). Yet when Anna joins forces with the energetic Frau Dr. Kalmus to establish some order amidst the manifold inefficiencies of the British administration, they display a strength of purpose and an organizational ability that belie the traditional view of women as passive objects of masculine administrative systems. In setting up an enquiry office that helps to resolve the many problems of the distressed detainees, the two women assert their status as superior to that of common criminals and rise above their detention, at least in spirit. This enables them to overcome the impact of British prejudice and ignorance, as demonstrated by a warden who declares, after a confrontation between refugees and interned British fascists: 'To us, you are all suspects, or else you wouldn't be here' (123). Laurent also regains some of her self-confidence and self-esteem when she observes the derisive humour with which the criminal element treats the expensively dressed, upper-class British fascists at Sunday church services.[9]

The British, represented in these texts by prison administrators and wardens, are cast in a poor light. The senior staff are depicted as aloof and indifferent to the plight of the detained refugees; something of their quality is conveyed when Borchard describes two of the governor's assistants as 'abbess-like' and 'mannish' respectively (118). Anna's initial view of the wardens in Holmdale is that of a monolithic group, an impression reinforced by the coldly distanced order, 'Come along', with which they customarily address the detainees. This presumably reflects their attitude to their usual charges, convicted criminals, whom they have learned to treat as a mass, not as differentiated individuals. Occasionally, an individual warden emerges from the collective, like the kindly officer who makes an extra effort to have Anna's telegram sent to Ida (86–88), but others are callously indifferent to Anna and her child, hardened, perhaps necessarily, by their profession.

The inefficiency and indifference of the authorities reaches a low point when Laurent leaves Holloway for the Isle of Man, as described in her chapter 'I Go on a Journey' (49–57). She begins by listing some of the skills necessary to organize a mass transport, only to highlight their total absence in this instance. The search of the women's belongings that precedes their departure has already reduced their careful packing to chaos, 'the aim being', as Laurent puts it ironically, 'to create disorder in the shortest possible time, which was accomplished with a rare degree of efficiency' (44). The journey begins with the customary hours of waiting outside Euston Station, before it is announced that their train is about to depart and a mad rush of women and children ensues. On arrival in Liverpool, one hundred and fifty women with several exhausted children are deposited at a seamen's home where nobody has thought to provide them with food or bedding. When the air-raid alarm sounds, they are taken down to the basement to sleep in washrooms on stone floors:

> When morning came I knew that after that night, there really was nothing in the world for me to be frightened of. There might be more dramatic events before me, I might get hurt or killed, but for sheer discomfort, sordidness and hopelessness that night could not be surpassed by anything. (53)

For Laurent, Rushen Camp on the Isle of Man, the women's camp where she spent almost a year, comes as an anticlimax after Holloway. (Ruth Borchard's novel ends with Anna Silver's arrival on the Isle of Man.) Laurent provides an instructive picture of the camp, which was divided into the larger village of Port Erin, where some women were accommodated in large hotels, and the smaller village of Port St Mary, where they were billeted in private boarding houses (the exception being the Ballaqueeny Hotel, the butt of Laurent's special disfavour). Unlike the men, the women lived in these boarding houses with their landladies, which enabled Laurent to find a sympathetic landlady but exposed other detainees to exploitation and capricious treatment. Laurent singles out the commandant, Dame Joanna Cruickshank, for criticism, in particular for stopping the functioning system that the internees had developed for paying their bills. Addressing the internees, Dame Joanna announces, with scant regard for logic, that 'there were some Internees who had actually reverted to dishonesty in order to obtain some of their own money' (87). Laurent observes with bitterness the way in which internment causes the women, who are entirely blameless of any financial impropriety, to accept the accusation; this internalization of their inferior, semi-criminal status is a clear case of the psychological impact of detention, which Laurent calls 'the quiet degradation of the human soul' (89).

The mental and emotional effects of life in what Laurent terms 'the ladies' paradise' (58) form a significant part of her description of life in Rushen Camp. Her own feelings about internment in Rushen swing wildly from one extreme to the other: at one stage she refers to it as 'a time of comparative contentment and inner freedom' (61), but when writing her weekly letters — restricted to twenty-four lines in length — she realizes that they were all 'variations of the one theme: "Get me out of here, do all you can, I can't stand it much longer"' (77). She greatly misses the comradeship and solidarity of Holloway, which has dissolved into petty feuds and enmities on the Isle of Man. She contrasts the uncertain and indefinite nature of her stay there with the certainties and apparent solidity of prison life: 'At least you knew where you were. If one is a prisoner, one should be in a prison. It's only fair. This half and half business doesn't impress me at all. It's so aimless' (63). As in the texts by male detainees, it is the barbed wire that becomes the all-encompassing symbol of her incarceration: 'I dream barbed wire, I think barbed wire, I see barbed wire. Soon my brain will snap, and then I'll probably eat barbed wire', she tells an unnamed internee whom she meets while taking a solitary walk on her twenty-sixth birthday (74).

The unnamed woman finds the view out to freedom across the barbed wire particularly disturbing: 'It's worse than a prison. There you don't see what you are missing. The walls shut you in, the world is far away; here it is all in front of you, you see it, and can't have it' (73). Here again, the vista across the barbed wire, which sets limits on the internees' liberty but at the same time allows their gaze to wander freely beyond, reflects the uncertainty of the women's status and the indefinite nature of their detention. One can observe in a poem inserted into Laurent's text the familiar disjunction between the physical restriction of her liberty in space and the potentially unlimited duration of her detention in time:

> A strange gift was given me,
> A slice of time apart of time
> Removed from the stream of event,
> To do with as I think it fit
> In purpose and intent. (76)

Laurent is detained 'until further order' (11), until she is released from what she sees as the enforced state of limbo in which she has been held. Her release, which is completely unexpected, demonstrates again her lack of agency, her disempowerment; by writing *A Tale of Internment* with ironic distance and detached humour, she was arguably able to reassert a measure of retrospective control over the events of that period in her life.

Narratives of Internment

The texts written by former internees after the end of their internment differ significantly from earlier diaries like Gál's and Jacobsthal's that were written during the authors' detention (though only published long afterwards). The texts written after internment are mostly considerably less bitter and angry in tone; they also engage more fully with the British, often because they extend beyond the period of internment to take in the events of 1940–41, the Battle of Britain and the bombing of British cities by the Luftwaffe. It is usually argued that texts as critical of the British as Gál's or Jacobsthal's could not have been published during the war, or even in the years after it, given the quasi-mythical status that the year 1940 had acquired in the public consciousness. Robert Neumann and Fred Uhlman, whose memoirs will be discussed in Chapter 5, both published, in later decades, accounts of their internment that were markedly less critical of the British than their diary accounts written at the time. However, Livia Laurent's *A Tale of Internment* and a section of Ruth Borchard's *We Are Strangers Here*, both highly critical of the internment of refugee women, were in fact published during the war.[10] It may be that an erstwhile detainee like Gál did not wish to publish a text as personal as his internment diary during his lifetime, or that he was unwilling to re-engage with so painful a period from the past.

The four texts to be considered next, all written within a few years of their authors' release from internment, are distinguished by their strong narrative frameworks, unlike the more unmediated accounts of internment to be found in the diaries. Alfred Lomnitz's *'Never Mind, Mr. Lom!'; or, The Uses of Adversity* appeared in 1941.[11] Lomnitz, an artist born near Kassel in Germany, had come to Britain in 1933 and was aged forty-eight when he was interned in June 1940 and spent three months in Huyton. The external events of his arrest, detention, and release form the framework for the deeper narrative revealing the inner journey that his autobiographical counterpart, Lom, undergoes during his internment.

The words 'Never Mind, Mr. Lom!', first uttered 'with fatuous sympathy' by his loyal charwoman when he is arrested (1), take on a deeper significance for him as he realizes that he must make use of adversity by accepting and transcending it, not with submissive fatalism but in the spirit of the Taoist teachings of Laozi (Lao-Tze), who advocated flexibility, not anger and bitterness, in face of adversity and whose lines form the book's motto: 'Be humble, and you will remain entire. | Be bent, and you will remain straight.' Lom's ability to cope with internment emotionally and psychologically is reinforced by his thoroughly positive view of Britain and the British. The process of integration in Britain was easier for assimilated German Jews like Lom, who had already been integrated well into German society: he recalls his service in the German army in World War I with pride, never mentions his Jewish origins, and sends his son to a British boarding school, where he will be conditioned to the social culture of the British upper classes.

Lom's arrest on a fine summer's day comes as a brutal shock: two impatient detectives hustle him into a taxi and convey him to a grubby, oppressive cell in a police station, where the mood among the detainees combines despair with anger at the injustice done to them. But even here a note of humanity is interposed, as a kindly warden hands a lighted cigarette into the cell, an example of 'this human touch, which Lom had admired all the time since his arrival on this island' (4). In contrast to the unquestioning obedience to orders in Germany, this open breach of regulations exemplifies the British tendency to place the dictates of humanity above those of authority; refugees like Lom repeatedly praise the flexibility and ability to improvise that they perceive as characteristic of the British, in contrast to the soulless, mechanical efficiency of the Germans. Conditions do not improve when Lom is transferred to an unnamed racecourse, where only rudimentary provision has been made for the internees; they are kept under armed guard, in an atmosphere of tension, confusion, and outraged indignation that he describes as 'intolerable' (10). Lom struggles to reconcile his internment with his experience of living in Britain for seven years: 'He had formed the greatest admiration for the culture and style of living of the people of this friendly island' (24).

The low point in Lom's internment occurs when he is transferred to Huyton, where the detainees' morale is shattered by the misconceived and inhumane policy

Fig. 2.2. Alfred Lomnitz (Lom), *Girl behind Barbed Wire*.
Courtesy of Julie Seldon and the Ben Uri Gallery.

of deporting 'enemy aliens' overseas. Aware of the sinking of the *Arandora Star*, with heavy loss of life among the internees aboard (146 Germans and Austrians and 453 Italians), they await the selection of men for an impending transport — unknown to them, the Australia-bound *Dunera* — in fear and impotent rage. The inadequacy of the food, accommodation, and postal system at Huyton, along with rainy weather that turns the ground into mud, forms the dismal backdrop to the 'new week of torment' (62) as the internees wait desperately to see the lists of those to be deported. The criteria by which the British authorities have selected men to fill the quota of 1,500 to be deported from Huyton are crude and arbitrary; the men selected spend their last hours on British soil anxious and depressed, knowing only that they must leave the following day for an unknown destination, with little certainty of seeing their families and friends again soon. The spectacle of men packing their scanty possessions for a journey into the distant unknown, leaving behind such security as they have been able to create for themselves in Britain, is pitiful, and an indictment of British policy.

With the arrival of a new commandant, however, morale in Huyton improves sharply. The camp authorities have already started to organize a programme of activities, such as classes and lectures; an orchestra and a Viennese cabaret spring up, and Lom begins to paint again. The new commandant immediately sets about remedying the kitchen and postal arrangements, to the delight of the internees, but his principal innovation lies in his attitude to his charges: while he will countenance no contravention of regulations, he declares that his sole aim is to ensure that every innocent man is released and that nobody will be detained in the camp for longer than is necessary (99). Lom, impressed by the commandant's humanity, differentiates between him and his German counterparts:

> Strip off his uniform, and examine him as a man. You'll find that our Commander has a number of indescribable and very real qualities anchored firmly within himself. They shine through all the military pomp. He speaks in a friendly way — friendly, not ingratiating or supercilious or over-hearty. He's fundamentally a natural person who instinctively treats everyone as his equal.

Lom relates these qualities to a broader democratic mentality that he perceives as ingrained in the British character:

> People call them — Democracy. Myself, I'd rather call the whole mental outlook 'democratic-minded'. You see, democracy is so much more than a mere system of government. And so our Commander, with the best of England in him, is really and truly democratic-minded. He can't help it. It's simply there, it's part of him. (101)

In Germany, by contrast, the parliamentary democracy of the Weimar Republic had failed, precisely on account of the lack of such a broadly based democratic consensus (102).

As news of the Battle of Britain filters through to Huyton, the internees experience an intense feeling of solidarity with the British people in their stand against Hitler. They stage a show called *Round the World in Song*, whose rousing internationalism convinces Lom that a new spirit of anti-fascist resistance has spread across Britain, embracing even the interned 'enemy aliens'. Although cut off from the outside world, the internees are aware that the momentous events taking place in the skies over Britain will have a transformative effect on society outside the barbed wire: 'There was *something going on*, something astonishing and uplifting, something they had long been waiting for. Jealously, Lom and Co. felt excluded from an important event. They were only too anxious to see it and be part of it' (139). They seize on the use of Underground stations by the people of London as air-raid shelters, forbidden at first by the authorities but swiftly approved, as an inspiring example of popular democracy in action:

> The people had decided what was the best thing to do, and the government had legalised it. Never was there a clearer case of the will of the people finding direct and prompt expression in administrative form. The English reader must please realise how important this appears to a foreign mind. Lom and his friends agreed that this was the first *aggressive* action taken by the British people: not against their own Government, but simply for the cause of freedom. (140)

When Lom is released, he returns to a society that is described in the final chapter of the book, 'Mr. Lom Comes Home', as imbued with a new, energizing spirit of comradeship and solidarity in face of the Nazi onslaught. On his journey back to Oxford, he meets with extraordinary helpfulness and friendliness from ordinary British people. At Rugby station, where he is stranded by a combination of air raids and the Sunday timetable, the staff go to exceptional lengths to assist him, culminating in a porter's kindness in finding Lom overnight accommodation in a first-class carriage in a waiting train:

> Lom didn't know what to say. He was a man from Huyton, a foreigner. He'd never felt such a foreigner as at this moment. And yet he was being treated in this trustful, unselfish, human way. It was unbelievable. Could that have happened in Germany? No; a uniform, even a railwayman's uniform, meant officialdom there. (159)

Lom returns to the cottage that he has rented in the Oxfordshire countryside. When he visits the village pub, Lom is greatly reassured by the warm welcome that he receives from the local inhabitants, who now accept him fully into their community: 'He was — and there is no higher testimonial in England — he was ALL RIGHT' (181). Travelling to London, where he finds his flat destroyed by a bomb, Lom is struck by the resilience of the population during air raids, sensing the new and unexpected potential displayed by the British during the Blitz.

These qualities, the flexibility and energy newly unleashed by the war but operating within the framework of a long-established system of values, convince Lom that wartime England 'was even more delightful and astonishing than peacetime England' (181). To remain close to the living essence of the country, he decides to stay in Oxfordshire and commute to work in London. Lomnitz's depiction of Britain in 1940 may be dismissed as uncritically admiring, even as a form of wartime propaganda, but in its affection for the British people at war and in Lom's pride at being accepted by them, it reflects a perception of British society that was deeply held among the refugees from Nazism and that persists to this day.

Obliging Fellow by Leo Kahn, a lawyer from Germany, born in 1894 and a refugee in Britain since 1937, is unusual in that it is not autobiographical but instead charts the fortunes of the fictional Leo Raphaelsohn, a wily, unscrupulous commercial traveller, who contrives to work himself into positions of importance in internment, ending up as camp supervisor — the senior internee — in Onsay (Onchan) Camp on the Isle of Man. Raphaelsohn's internment follows the same path as his creator's: from a London police station he is transferred to a barracks, formerly a riding school, and thence to Mudfield Park racecourse (Kempton Park), to Blake Mills (Warth Mill), and finally to Onsay. Kahn's use of a thoroughly unattractive protagonist for satirical purposes is unusual, though by no means unjustified, given the essential absurdity of the entire process of internment. Writing after the end of the war, Kahn would have felt free to adopt a sharply satirical attitude to internment, emphasizing the human deficiencies of both the detainees and their British captors, and subjecting them to ridicule in a darkly humorous style.

Kahn presents Raphaelsohn with a sceptical, knowing humour that reveals the petty, sordid reality behind his picaresque adventures in internment. By the end of the novel, Raphaelsohn is morally compromised by his obsessive desire for office: to that end, he has been instrumental in the betrayal and deportation to Australia of his comrades; he has consolidated his position by having his predecessor as camp supervisor deported to Canada; and, finally, he fakes a medical condition to engineer his release. Negative qualities also predominate among Raphaelsohn's fellow internees; they appear as gullible, naive, self-absorbed, volatile, and easily swayed, determining to take courses of action, like a hunger strike in protest against conditions in Blake Mills, which they are too cowardly to carry through. Although the tone of the novel seems light-hearted, it nevertheless represents a stinging indictment of internment, both in its injustice and in the conditions it inflicts on the internees: the description of the aptly named Mudfield Park demonstrates this, while Blake Mills fully lives up to the dark, satanic connotations of its name.

The British are also presented with critical humour from the start of the novel. The detectives from Scotland Yard who come to arrest Raphaelsohn display more interest in his landlady's attractive young daughter than in him and his fawning attempts to ingratiate himself with them. Raphaelsohn's behaviour reflects the widespread tendency among the internees to treat the British as superior beings and to demean themselves by trying to curry favour with their captors. At Mudfield Park, those who do not speak English well enough to understand a sergeant major's bellowed warning that any internee approaching the barbed wire will be shot, chorus 'Thank you, sir' in response (26). To imitate the English is the greatest ambition of many internees, though seldom fulfilled: Raphaelsohn, seeking to enhance his standing among his fellow detainees, claims to be familiar with British institutions like Ascot and to have mastered the English language, which in reality he speaks incorrectly and with an atrocious accent (13).

The attitude of the British officers towards the internees is characterized by incomprehension and indifference. When the internees arrive at Mudfield Park, they are treated as dangerous Nazis, enemies of Britain, whereas in reality their eagerness to prove their loyalty to Britain verges on servility. When Raphaelsohn addresses some friendly words to one of the soldiers escorting them into the racecourse, the reply is a bayonet pointed at his stomach. The inability of the British to distinguish between anti-Nazi refugees and pro-Nazi Germans extends to the commandant, Major Peacock, who, baffled by the otherness of foreigners, takes refuge in simplistic, outdated national stereotypes: 'A Hun is a Hun. Don't trust them. No use bullying them, of course, but teach them to know their place' (41). Peacock adopts a tone of lofty indifference to his charges, commencing his address to the newly arrived detainees with the words: 'I do not know for what reasons you have been brought here and, indeed, I do not care.' He narrowly avoids informing them that the British flag, under whose protection they supposedly find themselves, 'stands for humanity and liberty', switching hastily to the hardly less misconceived phrase 'humanity and justice' (26–27).

The discussions between Peacock and his staff, Lieutenant Peck and Lieutenant Campayne, reveal their true opinion of their charges; they speak of them with patronizing contempt, and do not hesitate to conceal the truth from them when expedient. At Mudfield Park, Peacock knows that his orders do not allow any of the thousands of letters written by the internees to be sent for three weeks, but cynically instructs his staff not to tell them, as writing letters will keep them occupied. Peck, possessed of a droll sense of humour and a bent for gadgets, suggests fixing a pneumatic tube directly from the camp letter box to a fire (41). Campayne, a serious young man with humane, progressive views, is more concerned about the internees' well-being, realizing that they are opposed to the Nazis and pose no danger to Britain. The absurdity of British assessments of such dangers is illustrated later by the reports in the press on the Isle of Man about the official opening of the Popular University at Onsay.[12] One headline reads 'Interned Aliens Inventing Secret Weapon Against Former Fatherland', a stupid and wholly implausible misunderstanding of a speech made at the opening ceremony, while the other appeals crudely to nationalistic prejudice: 'German Prisoners Being Coddled While Britain Bleeds' (135).

The British authorities appear at their worst when compiling the lists of men to be deported to Australia. Initially, they wish to deport 'undesirables'; Raphaelsohn, correctly guessing the political bias behind this objective, puts forward the name of his friend Kolka, a left-wing radical. When the number of 'undesirables' turns out to be too small, Raphaelsohn becomes complicit in filling the quota by the addition of names more or less at random. He and his predecessor as camp supervisor act as informers who denounce and betray their unknowing comrades. But responsibility for the dishonesty and deception that accompany the deportations ultimately rests with the British, whose inefficiency and negligence lead them to delegate the morally reprehensible task of selecting men for the *Dunera* to the senior internees.

The procedures surrounding Raphaelsohn's release are recounted with similar dark humour. The White Paper with its categories of men to be considered for release is shown to be a mere expedient designed to conceal the truth, which is that the interned 'enemy aliens' should never have been detained in the first place.

As Lieutenant Peck admits, its main purpose is to save the face of the British authorities, not to serve the interests of justice: 'They couldn't release the lot of you at once, after all the fuss they made over your internment. It would look too silly' (164). Four of Raphaelsohn's friends refuse on principle to apply for release on the basis of the White Paper, as that would imply that their internment was somehow justified: 'We demand to be released simply because there never was a valid reason for depriving us of our liberty' (166).

Raphaelsohn is among the first to be released. He departs, convinced that his conscientiousness as camp supervisor has won him the respect of the British officers:

> Raphaelsohn thought happily, as he closed the door behind him: the Englishmen in the camp, at any rate, will retain a good impression of me. I am not just a b...y foreign Jew to them any longer. I've made them respect me. (170)

Peck, however, refers to him as a 'funny little blighter' and a 'bit smarmy' (171), while Campayne regrets having put him in charge of the camp university. The British fail to understand Raphaelsohn, as he fails to understand how they see him. Campayne believes that Raphaelsohn 'means well', whereas in reality he has used his time in internment to advance his own interests deviously and without scruple. In the novel's final sentence, Lieutenant Poffert, who has to be reminded who Raphaelsohn is, dismisses him with airy indifference: 'Oh him. He's all right. He never caused any trouble. He'll make his way' (171). The cunning and manipulative Raphaelsohn, who has every intention of 'making his way' by taking advantage of the commercial possibilities offered by the war, is transformed by his ill-informed hosts into the 'Obliging Fellow' of the novel's title.

Unlike such narratives of individual protagonists, Eugen Spier's internment memoir, *The Protecting Power*,[13] places its author's experiences firmly in the context of a higher destiny that transcends the fate of any single detainee. Spier was a deeply religious man; the 'protecting power' of his title was the God in whom he trusted with absolute and unswerving faith. As the narrative of Spier's memoir is shaped by his personal credo, it cannot be taken as a straightforward, historical record of events; but it demonstrates the narrative strategies employed by refugee writers to present the injustice of internment within the context of the wider justness of the Allied cause. Spier had lived in Britain for many years, but as a Jew and known anti-Nazi could not return to Germany after 1933. He was among the more unfortunate detainees in that he was arrested as early as 1 September 1939. He was held at Olympia Exhibition Centre, at Clacton in Essex, Seaton in Devon, and Lingfield in Surrey before being deported to Canada in July 1940; he spent over a year there before being returned to Britain, where he was held on the Isle of Man and released in November 1941. Spier spent over two years in internment, an unusually long period; in the early part of his detention he was constantly surrounded by Germans, prisoners of war and other Nazis, who delighted in taunting the Jews detained by the British and gloated over their fate in the event of a German victory.

Spier's memoir, which is based on his diary written at the time of the events described, contains much information about conditions in internment. However, as he states in his preface, since these events 'provide but the external background, they become only of secondary importance, compared with the everlasting significance of which the spiritual experiences in the following chapters give an account' (5). The primary object of the memoir is to chart the course of a moral and spiritual conflict, the conflict of values between the totalitarian barbarity of Nazi Germany and the forces of liberty and democracy, between inhumanity and humanity. That conflict is fought out by military means in the arena of war, but also by spiritual means among such groups as the internees. In his introduction, Spier declares that, during his time in the internment camps, he

> witnessed and experienced, as never before, the great and miraculous manifestations of the Spirit, by which my inner happiness was upheld and enhanced, and which endowed me with a power to bear the heavy strain of adverse circumstances which so often appeared desperate.

For Spier, moral and spiritual considerations play a determining role in the war; by allying themselves to the Allied cause, men of faith like himself, however remote from the military arena, place themselves on the side of humanity, at a time when 'the great religious values of mankind' are under threat from Nazi Germany (7).

At first, Spier is dismayed by the repeated failure of the British government to behave in accordance with the dictates of humanity and justice, citing the arrest, without judicial warrant, of avowed anti-Nazis like himself. He attributes this to a fundamental flaw in the Chamberlain government's conduct of the war as if it were a traditional war between nations, not a war of moral values and principles:

> The old conception of friend and foe based on a narrow patriotism and determined by one's nationality at birth was no longer valid in the ensuing struggle which was declared by the conscience of mankind against the followers of the totalitarian Powers inside and outside Germany. (16)

The detention of Jewish refugees appears to fly in the face of the very principles for which Britain claims to be fighting; tormented by the thought that Britain might be betraying its heritage of liberty and democracy, Spier only regains his inner peace by reading from his prayer book. This forms a pattern: at moments of despair, he recites from the Bible, mostly from the Psalms, which are rich both in lamentations and in thanksgivings to God. Even at his lowest point, when he is being deported to Canada, painfully aware of the distance separating him from his wife and son and amidst the appalling conditions prevailing on the *Duchess of York*, Spier finds comfort in a quotation from the Book of Jeremiah (134).

Spier perceives the events of May 1940 as stark evidence of Britain's parlous situation, both in military and in spiritual terms. The jingoistic hysteria leading to the mass internment of anti-Nazi refugees causes him to exclaim in bewildered despair: 'This, then, was to be the human and democratic approach to defeat Nazi ideology and to promote a peace based on freedom and justice' (100). The conduct of the war up to that point, still influenced by Chamberlain's policy of appeasement, has been both morally and militarily misguided: 'To act as the strong man against the helpless and the weak and to practise a soft attitude towards the strong was an indisputable and open admission of one's own fear, helplessness and weakness.'

The moral deficiencies revealed by the internment of thousands of defenceless and blameless refugees are, for Spier, as serious a setback to the British cause as any military defeat:

> I felt that the adoption of these methods by the British Government was a shocking degradation of the Democracy which the country was so eagerly purported to uphold. This partial collapse of the democratic spirit appeared to me to be a far greater misfortune than the collapse of an army. (101)

But at this moment of supreme national crisis, the one man who can rally the moral forces of the world against Nazism is at hand, in the person of Winston Churchill: 'He could bring about the much needed democratic solidarity which does not accept geographical, national, racial, or religious boundaries', thereby transforming the war into a moral crusade against tyranny (90–91).

Greatly as Spier is impressed by news of the Battle of Britain, the decisive factor that restores his confidence in Britain is the triumph of moral values that he discerns in the debate on internment that took place in the House of Commons on 22 August 1940:

> At such a fateful hour men of Great Britain had the moral courage to stand up, unmoved by the military triumphs of the Nazis, to demand a rectification of our deplorable situation and insist that they should put right what was so obviously wrong in the actions taken against those of us who were the arch enemies and first victims of Nazism. I cautioned my listeners not to dismiss this event in the House of Commons as a small and only rhetorical matter, but to believe me that it was indeed an event of the deepest significance. The ears of the whole world would be centred upon these speeches, which put human considerations above political expediencies and as such they were representative of a vital effort to advance the faith of mankind in the true and constructive values of democracy. (175)

Spier's reading from the record of the debate has a profound effect on his fellow inmates: 'We all felt that the power of the spirit had reasserted itself and had become manifest on our behalf' (199). From this juncture onwards, the British cause appears as morally, indeed divinely sanctioned:

> This rallying of the moral powers of the world with their invincible strength would surely reverse the triumphs of the Nazis as surely as the day would follow the night, however long the night might yet last. I was overjoyed by the thought that once again we would experience in our days, that the totalitarian's device to ignore and to reject the eternal laws of God, which are the foundation of our religion, were as futile as 'if the stars were to combine to abolish gravitation'. (200)

During his return across the Atlantic to Britain, Spier becomes convinced of the invincibility of the Royal Navy, less because of the might of the assembled warships than because of his belief that, by devoting scarce shipping resources to repairing the injustice inflicted on the internees, Britain is following the dictates of the supreme power:

> Who then was this commanding and protecting power at work? It was the

still but persistent inner voice of the conscience of mankind, it was the spirit
of God in the hearts of men, which commanded that these things should be
done. (240)

The book's final pages read like the working out of a divine purpose. Spier is
reunited with his wife in what appear to him as the agreeable surroundings of the
family camp at Port Erin on the Isle of Man, then is released, a proudly free man,
into civilian society, where he joins his fellow internees in contributing to the war
effort. He observes a spiritual transformation in British society:

> Everywhere I discovered a new and happy and lofty comradeship and
> brotherhood in the united effort to withstand the Nazi onslaught and to
> defeat the forces of barbarism and enslavement in order to gain victory for the
> establishment of a world in which men and women may live a life of freedom
> on a higher standard of happiness.

His experiences over the preceding two years have led him to conclude that

> it is indeed practically possible for us to bring about such a change in our
> attitude towards God and towards our fellow-men so as to develop thereby
> a reciprocal respect for the dignity and the life of every individual human
> person. (252)

Once the conduct of the war is determined by the divine principles of justice and
humanity, it cannot but result in the victory of the forces of good. *The Protecting
Power* closes with an affirmation of faith in God and his designs for humankind:
'Whoso is wise let him observe these things and consider the mercies of the Lord'
(252; Psalm 107).

Among the most accomplished literary depictions of internment is Richard
Friedenthal's *Die Welt in der Nußschale* [The World in a Nutshell].[14] Friedenthal,
born in 1896, had made a career as a writer and in publishing before emigrating to
Britain in 1938. *Die Welt in der Nußschale* follows the internment itinerary of Konrad
Gärtner, a civil engineer from Germany, aged fifty, who is arrested on 3 June 1940,
taken to a police station and thence to Kempton Park racecourse, and then spends
four weeks in thoroughly uncomfortable conditions at Prees Heath in Shropshire,
before being transferred to Huddlestone (Hutchinson) Camp on the Isle of Man.
The book focuses predominantly on the internees: on the group of six men that
forms around Gärtner and on characters based on the artists, intellectuals, and other
prominent figures that the author encountered, among them Lebrecht 'Baby' Bitter
(Kurt Schwitters) and Jack Wunder (the flamboyant artist and art gallery owner Jack
Bilbo, originally Hugo Baruch). The British remain somewhat in the background.

A central theme in the novel is the solidarity that develops between the six
apparently ill-assorted men who form a group around Gärtner. In the opening
lines of his preface, Friedenthal speaks of these people as a 'Schicksalsgemeinschaft',
a randomly assembled group brought together by a shared fate; they overcome
the adversity of internment and form a tightly cohesive unit of mutual support
(5). Friedenthal argues that the experience of detention behind barbed wire has
become so common in the modern era that the 'world in a nutshell' on the Isle
of Man is an accurate reflection in miniature of the larger world beyond (6). But

FIG. 2.3. Hugo Dachinger, *Portrait of a Man*, painted in internment on the Isle of Man. Shortly after the first hardback edition of this book was published, Dame Margaret Hodge, the long-serving Member of Parliament for Barking, saw the painting and immediately identified the previously unknown subject as her grandfather, Wilhelm Hollitscher. Wilhelm's daughter Lisbeth had found her way instead to Egypt and there married a fellow Jewish emigré, Hans Oppenheimer: Dame Margaret was born stateless in Cairo in 1944, and the family did not reach England until 1948. Photograph courtesy of Anne Dachinger and the Ben Uri Gallery.

the book's title has another meaning: it refers to the nutshell shape of the Isle of Man, which Friedenthal repeatedly calls 'die Menscheninsel' [the human island], an unexpected but heartfelt compliment to the relative humanity of the detainees' treatment; reflecting on their internment as it nears its end, Gärtner employs the lapidary phrase: 'Es gibt andere Lager und anderen Stacheldraht' [There are other kinds of camps and barbed wire] (407). Although the policy of internment is seen as wasteful, misguided, and unnecessarily cruel, the internees' final judgement on their time on the 'Menscheninsel' is mild, even conciliatory.

The underlying humanity of the better part of the British is demonstrated in the opening pages, when Gärtner's kindly landlady discusses his arrest with another tenant, an embittered, shrewish governess (9–10). Whereas the latter gives full vent to her prejudices against foreigners and would gladly incarcerate them all, the landlady is disgusted by the arbitrary arrest of a decent, innocent man, describing his transfer to prison in a Black Maria as a disgrace. Before Gärtner is taken away, she insists on serving him a hearty breakfast of bacon and eggs. The British authorities are portrayed less as cruel or heartless than as disorganized and incompetent. The incompetence is in evidence from the start, when the police arrest an indignant American whose name happens to resemble one on their list (22). It reaches its low point in the lack of organization at Prees Heath, where the detainees have to live under canvas, with only the most rudimentary facilities and lacking certain basic necessities. A sharp contrast emerges between the utter chaos created by the British and the ingenuity and resourcefulness of the internees, who bring some order into the situation.

The British are depicted as astonishingly ignorant about the refugees in their midst, labouring under misconceptions that would be laughable in a less serious situation. Friedenthal gives voice to this through the comments of anonymous British soldiers in the camps. Two of the Guards officers overseeing the reception of the internees at Kempton Park speak with disdain of the crowd of foreigners, with their loud voices and unwillingness to form an orderly queue, assuming them to be the dregs of society (38–41). They cannot understand that a man with a Czech birthplace should be amongst them, for surely, as one asks, the Czechs are allies. When a detainee makes desperate attempts to keep his passport, the officer cannot comprehend its importance to him: 'Grotesk. Ich dachte, er wollte seine Goldstücke grapschen, aber der Paß, was hat er sich so mit dem Paß? Ich habe mein Lebtag keinen Paß gebraucht. Komische Vögel' [Grotesque. I thought he wanted to grab his gold coins, but a passport, what's so special about a passport? I've never needed a passport in my life. Odd birds] (41). Two of the soldiers carrying out a count of the internees at Prees Heath — arriving at totals that never match — can see only that the men have been arrested and must therefore be dangerous criminals whom one would not wish to encounter in the dark. One soldier is convinced that Gärtner's friend Krohnert is a hard-boiled career criminal, a pickpocket at the very least, when in fact he is a highly respectable senior judge with the rank of Senatspräsident (79–80).

The most serious fault of the British is their failure to distinguish between Nazis and anti-Nazis; for most of them, a German is a German. The young lieutenant who strikes up a conversation with Gärtner on the Isle of Man cannot understand that his polite attempts to make conversation, about the similarity between the swastika and the emblem of the Isle of Man, the greatness of Adolf Hitler, and the efficient organization of the 1936 Olympic Games in Berlin, evoke a less than enthusiastic response. In this dialogue of mutual misunderstanding, Gärtner despairs of overcoming the officer's boundless ignorance (248–50). When a detainee at Kempton Park, mentally unhinged by his experiences in a Nazi concentration camp, rushes at the barbed wire, a British sergeant upbraids him for trying to escape, since 'Hitler ist doch bald hier!' [Hitler will soon be here!] (46), and then he will be freed by his countrymen.

Particularly egregious in this respect is the commandant of Prees Heath, Major Pointer, an officer of the reserve, who is presumably representative of the low-quality staff initially placed in charge of the internment camps at a time when able officers could not be spared. Pointer is ill-equipped for the position allotted to him: he sits perspiring in his office, overwhelmed by the paperwork piled high on his disordered desk. His intellectual limitations become clear at a meeting with the three elected representatives of the detainees, as a series of exchanges demonstrate (92–95). Pointer cannot see why the internees should need papers, as at the end of the war they will surely go straight back to Germany; he cannot distinguish between them and their compatriots who are currently dropping bombs on London; and he reproaches the Jewish internees sternly for their support of Hitler, assuming that they have Nazi sympathies from the mere fact of their arrest. He dismisses their horrified remonstrations with the words: 'Ich muß schon sagen, das übersteigt mein Vorstellungsvermögen' [I must say, that is beyond the limits of my comprehension] (95). Pointer's narrow insularity and limited intelligence stand in inverse proportion to his vanity: when the internees leave the camp, he insists on marching them in columns through the streets of Shrewsbury, with himself at the head, ensuring only that they arrive late for the train to Blackpool for the sea crossing to the Isle of Man.

Pointer's counterpart at Huddlestone Camp, Major Hicks, is depicted more affectionately, for all his foibles and limitations. Hicks has seen service as an officer in a wide variety of British colonial territories; he has a shrunken head from Sarawak on his desk, refers to the camp as a kraal, and dreams of his days riding his favourite Arab mare. His previous service hardly equips him to cater for the requirements of a group of educated and cultured European internees. Ignoring the high level of artistic and intellectual culture in the camp, he decrees that the camp must form a football team and arranges a match against the younger and fitter team from Peel Camp, which predictably ends in a humiliating defeat for Huddlestone. But Hicks has learnt the advantages of respecting the religious customs and sensibilities of the tribes under his administrative control; he ensures that the devout Jews in the camp have kosher food and are able to practise their religion as they wish. More important in the daily life of the internees than Hicks is the senior NCO, Sergeant Monihan,[15] formerly of the elite Coldstream Guards, subsequently head porter at a complex of flats in a select district of London. Monihan understands the internees;

he knows that they are not enemies of the British, considers it stupid to assume that they will try to escape, and develops a friendly respect for them. In the epilogue, set during the Blitz, the former internees stage a reunion, where they speak almost nostalgically of Huddlestone Camp. But the building where they meet is bombed; they manage to escape, emerging into a wartime world lit up by fires and explosions, yet infused with a fresh spirit of solidarity and defiance of the Nazi threat.

To be deprived of their basic civil rights and incarcerated without trial or appeal was a severe blow to the internees. They were acutely conscious of the injustice of the process, and of the utter senselessness of interning Jewish refugees as potential Nazi sympathizers. The psychological and emotional consequences of internment weighed more heavily on many detainees than did the material privations, at least once insalubrious transit camps like Warth Mill and Prees Heath were in the past. The loss of their freedom, symbolized in written accounts of internment by the ubiquitous barbed wire, proved hard to bear; it was only made worse by the uncertain duration of detention and by the apparently random and opaque process of release. But arguably the greatest burden was the consciousness of their powerlessness, the loss of their ability to determine the course of their own lives while interned. It was never easy for this group of Jewish refugees from Nazism to establish a clear collective identity in face of the ignorance, prejudice, and indifference of the British. In internment, where they had the identity of 'enemy aliens' suspected of Nazi sympathies imposed on them, that denial of their true identity and that loss of agency were deeply unsettling experiences, however much they were to make light of them in accounts written in later years.

Notes to Chapter 2

1. François Lafitte, *The Internment of Aliens* (Harmondsworth: Penguin, 1940); Leni Gillman and Peter Gillman, *'Collar the Lot!': How Britain Interned and Expelled Its Wartime Refugees* (London: Quartet Books, 1980); Ronald Stent, *A Bespattered Page? The Internment of His Majesty's 'Most Loyal Enemy Aliens'* (London: Deutsch, 1980); *The Internment of Aliens in Twentieth Century Britain*, ed. by David Cesarani and Tony Kushner (London: Cass, 1993); *'Totally Un-English'?: Britain's Internment of 'Enemy Aliens' in Two World Wars*, ed. by Richard Dove, Yearbook of the Research Centre for German and Austrian Exile Studies, 7 (Amsterdam: Rodopi, 2005); Rachel Pistol, *Internment during the Second World War: A Comparative Study of Great Britain and the USA* (London: Bloomsbury, 2017).
2. Some 600 people were allocated to Category A, 6,800 to Category B, and 64,200 to Category C, of whom 55,400 were classed as refugees from Nazi oppression.
3. Paul Bondy, 'Internment Notes', in *Civilian Internment in Britain during WW2: Huyton Camp: Eye-Witness Accounts*, ed. by Jennifer Taylor ([London]: Anglo-German Family History Society Publications, 2012), pp. 15–37.
4. Paul Jacobsthal, 'The Long Vac', in *Refugee Scholars: Conversations with Tess Simpson*, ed. by R. M. Cooper (Leeds: Moorland Books, 1992), pp. 198–228. The period of Jacobsthal's detention, from 5 July to 30 September 1940, coincided approximately with Oxford University's long vacation.
5. Hans Gál, *Musik hinter Stacheldraht: Tagebuchblätter aus dem Sommer 1940*, ed. by Eva Fox-Gál (Berne: Lang, 2003).
6. Leo Kahn, *Obliging Fellow* (London: Nicholson & Watson, 1946).
7. See Chapter 1 for a discussion of the first part of the novel.
8. Livia Laurent, *A Tale of Internment* (London: Allen & Unwin, 1942). Livia Laurent was the

pseudonym of Eva Meyerhof, born in 1914, who left Frankfurt am Main for Britain with her mother in 1933.
9. The fascists were known as '18Bs' as they had been detained under Regulation 18B of the Defence (General) Regulations 1939.
10. A section of Chapter 4 of Borchard's novel appeared in a prose anthology in 1944.
11. Alfred Lomnitz, *'Never Mind, Mr. Lom!'; or, The Uses of Adversity* (London: Macmillan, 1941).
12. Kahn depicts the idea of a camp university as a device that Raphaelsohn exploits to claim a position of importance. The lecturers, far from being intellectually distinguished, are presented comically, as vain, inept, or simply senile.
13. Eugen Spier, *The Protecting Power* (London: Skeffington, 1951).
14. Richard Friedenthal, *Die Welt in der Nußschale* (Munich: Piper, 1956).
15. Monihan is probably based on Quartermaster Sergeant Potterton, who appears in Fred Uhlman's autobiography, *The Making of an Englishman*, discussed in Chapter 5.

CHAPTER 3

Memories of Wartime Service and Combat

The wartime years marked a crucial stage in the development of the relationship between the Jewish refugees from Nazism and the British, certainly once the period of internment was over and the refugees were permitted, as the war progressed, to volunteer for almost all branches of the British forces. Their eagerness to join the anti-Nazi cause has been thoroughly documented, from the early post-war years to the present century.[1] It has been calculated that some ten thousand refugees served with the British forces. The war afforded the refugees the opportunity to fight against the hated Nazis while identifying themselves with the country that had, since the events of 1940–41, come to symbolize principled resistance to Nazi might and arrogance. This mood of solidarity with the British extended to civilian refugees on the home front, working for the war effort in factories and offices or partaking in civil defence. The period of the war arguably represented a decisive shift in refugee attitudes to Britain, preparing the way for the relatively smooth settlement of the bulk of the refugees in the post-war decades. The admiration and affection for the British that was and remains so pronounced among broad sections of the refugee community largely has its roots here.

As it is not easy to find accessible texts by refugee authors about wartime service written contemporaneously with the events described, all bar one of the texts discussed in this chapter were written — though they sometimes draw on diaries from the time — well after the war. Consequently, the intention here is not to treat these texts as if they replicated faithfully the details of wartime service — though often enough they do. Rather, the focus of the analysis lies on the impact of the war on refugee perceptions of and attitudes to the British, and in particular on the very marked change in the self-image of refugees who, initially seen as transient and not always welcome immigrants and then interned as 'enemy aliens', came to wear a British uniform with a renewed sense of pride. That did not, however, always prefigure their happy integration into British society after the war; two of the authors discussed here, Walter Eberstadt and Mark Lynton, left for the United States soon after the war's end. Lynton's memoirs, which indulge in a considerable amount of satirical exaggeration and distortion and are not always wholly trustworthy in their account of events, are nevertheless valuable for their vivid presentation of a young refugee soldier's attitudes and state of mind in relation to the British around him.

A Contemporary Account

One of the earliest accounts of combat by a Jewish refugee from Nazism serving with the British forces in World War II was Louis Hagen's *Arnhem Lift*, which tells the story of the author's experiences during the Battle of Arnhem in September 1944.[2] The feats of arms performed by the British 1st Airborne Division at Arnhem, most notably the defence of the bridge over the Lower Rhine by a small force of paratroopers under Lieutenant Colonel John Frost, passed almost immediately into legend; in the characteristically British mythology of heroism in defeat, Arnhem came to rank next to Dunkirk, and is probably the best-known land battle involving British forces in the entire war after the Normandy landings and the Battle of El Alamein. Hagen's book was published in January 1945, barely three months after Operation Market Garden, and rapidly became a best-seller. It would have been a considerable source of pride to the refugee community that one of their number had taken part in such a celebrated action;[3] Hagen was decorated with the Military Medal — which he does not mention in *Arnhem Lift* — and his name and his book became widely associated with Arnhem.

Hagen was born in Potsdam in 1916 and fled to Britain in 1936, after enduring a spell in a concentration camp while still a teenager. After service in the Pioneer Corps, he was accepted into the 1st Airborne, changed his name to Lewis Haig, and was trained as a glider pilot. It was in that capacity that he flew to Arnhem, where he took part in the desperate defence of the pocket at Oosterbeek, west of Arnhem, by lightly armed and heavily outnumbered British troops. His account of the action is divided into eight sections, each covering, in diary form, one of the eight days from the glider lift on Monday, 17 September to Monday, 24 September 1944, when the British paratroopers made their escape from the Arnhem area — in Hagen's case by swimming across the Rhine — and were then transported back to Britain. Of the ten thousand men of the 1st Airborne who went into action at Arnhem, only some two thousand returned. Hagen wrote what is believed to be the first book about the battle.

Arnhem Lift gains much of its impact from its simplicity and directness, giving it the immediacy and authenticity of a day-by-day report on a military action, an authenticity underlined by the book's subtitle, *Diary of a Glider Pilot*. Although Hagen had never written anything before, he completed *Arnhem Lift* with remarkable speed. His publisher describes the process of its composition in a 'Prefatory Note':

> When the author of this book arrived home on leave after fighting right through the Arnhem action, everybody wanted to hear his story. After telling it several times, he began to find the repetition irksome. So he spent the rest of his leave writing it all down, while the events were still vivid in his mind. Any more friends who asked him for the story would get a type-written document! That is his explanation of how it came to be written. (9)

While this may oversimplify its genesis, the book's slice-of-life realism takes the reader straight to the heart of the battle experience. In a manner familiar from novels about World War I like Erich Maria Remarque's *All Quiet on the Western Front*, *Arnhem Lift* is written from below, from the perspective of the fighting man

FIG. 3.1. Lt. Rudolf Falck, friend of Walter Eberstadt and fellow refugee, killed at Arnhem, September 1944. Courtesy of Christa Laird.

at the front. It records the apparently spontaneous reactions of an ordinary soldier to the daily events of war, its vividness enhanced by its protagonist's unawareness of high strategy: 'This is the story of one man's battle. It doesn't purport to describe the action as a whole. It gives instead a series of ultra-vivid images and experiences. Like real life, it is inconsequent and surprising' (10).

The book begins *in medias res*, catapulting the reader into the prelude to the action, the departure of the gliders for Arnhem:

> We knew it was coming off this time as the first glider lift had left on Sunday morning. We were waiting in the mess for the tug pilots to return and give us the Gen. All seemed well. They had found the L.Z. — Landing Zone — quite easily, with no flak to complain about. (11)

The narrator presents himself as an anonymous representative of a clearly defined collective, the crews of the Glider Pilot Regiment who transport the men and equipment to Arnhem. He is at pains to explain the terminology used by the pilots, such as 'L.Z.' for 'Landing Zone', to civilian readers outside that collective. He also employs the idiom of the military, in such terms as 'Gen' (information), thus identifying himself as an insider among the fighting men of the 1st Airborne. In the opening pages, Hagen makes frequent use of British slang and colloquialisms. His comrades are 'blokes' (16); the pilot who tows their glider across the Channel gives them a 'wizard ride', and Hagen 'made a mental note to buy him a pint when we got back' (12); he castigates a man who delays the unloading of the glider as 'a bloody fool of a parachutist' (13), then unexpectedly spots 'a chap' who had borrowed 'a couple of quid' (15) from him without repaying it. Hagen as narrator refers to his comrades as an insider who knows them so well that he does not need to introduce them: he acts as second pilot to 'Mac' (Sergeant Mac Wheldon), while other men are known simply by their first names, their nicknames ('Smithy' or 'Fearless Frank'), or, in the case of senior officers, their rank.

This is all designed to demonstrate that Hagen is no more than an ordinary member of his unit, typical of the men who fought at Arnhem, thus adding credence to the note placed immediately after the title of his book: 'Anyone who went to Arnhem could have told this kind of story.' But Hagen, a Jew from Germany who had been in Britain for only eight years, was anything but a typical British soldier. This makes *Arnhem Lift* exceptional, even unique, among autobiographical texts written by refugees: by writing from the perspective of a British soldier, Hagen rejects the perspective of the refugee from Nazism, preferring to depict the British around him as if he were one of them. As a narrator, he remains anonymous: we learn almost nothing about him and his German-Jewish past, while his perfect command of English adds to the impression that the narrator is British. Only a few small details, relating to his knowledge of German, betray his background. He can understand what enemy troops within earshot are saying, and proves useful in the interrogation of German prisoners. With difficulty, too, he convinces his hungry comrades to eat Dutch preserves, 'Continental concoctions' (40) in their view, which he, being 'Continental' himself, knows to be eminently edible. Otherwise, Hagen appears to be accepted without reservation by his fellow soldiers and to have been absorbed totally into the unit with which he fights. There is no national, cultural, or linguistic distance between him and his comrades; his narrative perspective could be theirs.

The superiority of that British fighting collective over its German counterpart forms one of the principal themes of the book. Hagen's opinion of the German troops whom he encountered in the wood between the landing zone and Oosterbeek was that they were 'a badly disciplined and poor crowd' (21). The Germans' low morale and reluctance to fight is evident in the failure of an SS panzer division to wipe out the vastly inferior British force confronting it in Oosterbeek; instead, Hagen and his comrades repeatedly repel attacks by German armour, with only a hand-held anti-tank weapon at their disposal. Except for a small number of fanatical SS officers, the German soldiers have lost their spirit: 'There was nothing left of the old arrogance and cockiness' (57). By contrast, the British troops, largely civilians in uniform, maintain their discipline and order under extreme pressure, fighting with selfless solidarity as part of a unit that believes in its collective cause. Their quiet, understated heroism, reflecting their inner confidence in their superiority, infuses the book with the spirit of optimism that turns defeat into a stage on the path to ultimate victory. The only sour note regarding it came from Hagen's commanding officer, Lieutenant Colonel Iain Murray, who was infuriated by the criticism of the pilots' training regime in the manuscript: 'No Britisher would ever have let his comrades down by writing stuff like this. It lets down the whole regiment!'.[4] But this crass expression of xenophobic prejudice was drowned out by the acclaim with which *Arnhem Lift* was greeted on its publication and which has accompanied its depiction of a British unit in action ever since.

Refugee Officers, British Citizens

The following two sections examine the experiences of two pairs of refugee combatants whose lives took very different directions after the war. To understand the impact of their wartime experiences, it is necessary to consider the trajectories of their lives and to highlight the factors that led them to negotiate their wartime and post-war identities and allegiances as they did. Like the great majority of the refugees who fought in the British forces, those mentioned in this chapter first joined the Auxiliary Military Pioneer Corps; the sole exception was Charles Hannam, who joined up late in the war, so late that he never saw action in battle. Refugees were at first only permitted to join the Pioneer Corps (as it was renamed in November 1940), a non-combatant formation used for light engineering, labour, and construction work. Six companies of pioneers, almost two thousand men in all, were raised at Kitchener Camp, near Sandwich in Kent, which housed so-called 'transmigrants', refugees admitted to Britain, often from Nazi concentration camps, on the understanding (mostly fictional) that they would re-emigrate elsewhere. By 1943, refugees were allowed into almost all branches of the British forces. The younger male refugees, eager to play their part in fighting the Nazis, often became frustrated at being excluded from active service. Those who served in the

Pioneer Corps either joined up after being interned, in some cases securing their release from internment by 'volunteering', or had already joined the Pioneer Corps before internment commenced. Refugees who joined fighting formations from the Pioneer Corps were instructed to change their names in case they were captured by the Germans; they were not, however, able to apply for British nationality until after the war.

The brothers Peter and Geoffrey Perry were born in Berlin, as Joachim and Horst Pinschewer, in January 1920 and April 1922 respectively. They grew up in a prosperous, middle-class German-Jewish family: their father had served in World War I, and was thoroughly assimilated and deeply devoted to Germany, though not to the extent of abandoning Jewish observance. Peter Perry in particular preserved his Jewish faith and its practices throughout his life. The Perry brothers demonstrated the ability of assimilated German Jews to continue the process of integration, interrupted by Hitler in Germany, after their emigration to Britain: they resumed the upward social and occupational mobility characteristic of German Jewry before 1933; they became deeply loyal to their adopted homeland and acculturated to its values and customs; and they remained proud of their Jewish heritage, including its German-Jewish components. Their ready integration into British society gained an early impetus from the remarkably friendly reception accorded to their parents, who arrived in Britain exhausted and penniless in November 1938, to find that a benefactor had provided them with accommodation in a village near Wimborne in Dorset, where they were greeted by baskets of fruit left by neighbours on their doorstep (GP, 12; quotations from Geoffrey's and Peter's accounts will be denoted by 'GP' and 'PP' respectively).[5]

Peter Perry left Germany in late 1935, his brother following a few months later. The brothers were fortunate in being able to continue their education at Buxton College in Derbyshire, an establishment that provided an environment unusually conducive to their smooth integration into British society. The atmosphere in the school, where the brothers found security and understanding, was a revelation after their treatment as Jewish pupils at their Berlin Gymnasium (roughly akin to a grammar school). The headmaster, A. D. C. (Dennis) Mason, became something of a role model for Peter and 'had a profound influence on us becoming Britons' (GP, 9), while Geoffrey was 'semi-adopted' by a young chemistry teacher, George Harding (GP, 8). Mason inspired the brothers with a love of fair play and classical music, and they soon acquired a taste for British products and customs, ranging from grilled kippers to Anglican hymns; when Peter requested a Jewish religious service, Mason also agreed. From cold showers in the morning to Armistice Day ceremonies, the brothers were initiated into the routines of British school life.

Buxton College also inculcated British values into them, thereby supplying the foundation for their construction of a new identity — part British, part German-Jewish — and a new allegiance to their adopted homeland. Peter Perry established an instinctive rapport with British life on arrival in London: 'Life in Germany seemed menacing and mediaeval by comparison. London's image, on the other hand, struck an immediate chord in my mind with the kind of society in which I hoped to live' (PP, 21). Buxton College appeared as a microcosm of British life: 'I found myself instinctively attracted to the habit of deliberate under-statement, to the self-deprecating sense of humour and the aversion against interfering in other people's private affairs, which seemed to mark my new environment' (PP, 22). He soon felt accepted into the school community, in consequence of which his English improved rapidly, and he willingly internalized the values of the school:

> The feature that impressed me with particular reference to my German experience was the co-existence of a highly competitive spirit on one hand, and the general feeling of tolerance on the other. The opponent's efforts, we were told, deserved to be respected. The cultivation of a feeling for fair play, combined with hard effort, was the philosophy underlying the school's educational aim.

The school's debating society was conducted on lines diametrically opposed to those Peter had observed in Germany: 'Expressing one's views with moderation and courtesy, and listening to opposing views with tolerance and an open mind were extra-curricular lessons which proved of inestimable value to me in later life' (PP, 25).

The family's straitened financial circumstances meant that neither brother was able to study at university. However, the first jobs that they took between leaving Buxton College and the outbreak of war became indicators of their post-war careers, demonstrating both their considerable abilities and the drive and dynamism that enabled them to fulfil their ambitions. After a dead-end starter job, Peter undertook a course of study at Willesden Technical College in north-west London, acquiring an interest in vocational training, the field in which he was to build a career of national importance. Geoffrey overcame the obstacles of his youth and foreign birth to secure highly desirable positions as a photographer, first at the London office of the *New York Times*, then as a staff photographer for a British national newspaper, the *Daily Mirror*. This set him on course for a successful career in publishing, including the foundation of his own company, Perry Press Productions, and positions with such major firms as the Thomson publishing empire. Both brothers came to admire and respect Britain, adapting easily to its customs, values, and attitudes. But the outbreak of war marked a change for the worse in their situation: Geoffrey lost his job, while Peter attempted in vain to join up. On 19 July 1940, the police arrived at the family's flat on Haverstock Hill in Hampstead to arrest them and their father. The latter was exempted on health grounds, and Peter's application to join the Pioneer Corps, though not yet accepted due to bureaucratic tardiness, saved him from detention; but Geoffrey, who was too young to apply to join the Pioneer Corps, was for that reason arrested and interned for four months.

In November 1941, Geoffrey enlisted in the Pioneer Corps and was sent to Ilfracombe, Devon, where his command of English secured him promotion to lance corporal; the army's attempt to make NCOs of older men who had served in the German and Austrian armies in World War I had turned into something of a farce, on account of their hilarious lapses in English (GP, 50). With 248 Company of the Pioneer Corps, Geoffrey was then posted to Catterick, Yorkshire, where he spent more than two uneventful years, engaged in maintenance duties and such tasks as constructing Nissen huts. During this tedious time, he did, however, take over editorship of the noticeboard bulletin that served his company, turning it into a proper company newspaper; and he first met his future wife, the daughter of one of his older comrades, whom he was to meet again ten years later. In summer 1943, his exceptional abilities were recognized when he became one of the first 'aliens' to be commissioned, passing a series of testing interviews and emerging as a second lieutenant.

Peter Perry's career in the Pioneer Corps was more eventful. He enlisted at the recruitment centre in Euston on 20 July 1940 and was first stationed with 137 Company of the Pioneer Corps at Westward Ho!, North Devon, before being posted to his unit's first assignment at the Fleet Air Arm station at Yeovilton, Somerset. The NCOs from the regular army who were tasked with their training found it hard to instil discipline into the 'rag-bag' of 'aliens', and their expletive-ridden language reached 'heroic heights' in the effort to do so:

> This outward show of uncouthness, however, hid an inarticulate fellow-feeling on the part of many of them for the men under their command. They clearly realised that those, especially of middle age, who had lost their homes, and often their families, faced serious emotional problems, and this realisation led to many acts of kindness. (PP, 41)

The unexpectedly positive gloss that Peter retrospectively put on his basic training owed much to his experiences between October 1940 and January 1941, when his company was drafted into the Docklands area of London, hard-hit by air raids, to help with the work of rescue and demolition. His diary entries from that time, which included the firebombing of the City of London on 29–30 December 1940, showed his admiration for the courage, unbreakable morale, and self-discipline of those who took shelter nightly in the local Underground stations. Peter's company was subsequently posted to a variety of locations across the country, which he experienced as

> a welcome introduction to the variety and beauty of the land I was helping to defend. In particular, I valued the chance to meet a wide and representative cross section of people, and to admire the innate courtesy and open-mindedness which I tended to find. (PP, 47)

The brothers' path to active service began with their selection for training as officers. Geoffrey, who had been commissioned in October 1943, was sent by his new unit for training as a transport officer in preparation for the invasion of France. After landing with his unit in Normandy on 20 July 1944, he 'witnessed the terrible slaughter of Germans who were bottled up in the Falaise gap' during the Allied breakout from the Normandy beachheads (GP, 37). He was then posted to Second Army's order of battle unit, which was responsible for interrogating German prisoners of war, and was subsequently assigned to one of the Information Control Units that formed part of the Psychological Warfare Division. In April 1945, with his commanding officer, Lieutenant Colonel Lieven, and Major Finlay, both of whom had experience in the media, Geoffrey was posted to T (for 'Target')

Force, tasked with the taking over of Radio Hamburg and the city's newspaper offices.

Peter was recommended for an interview for appointment to a commission in summer 1942. He left a detailed account of the arduous training that he underwent, first at a three-day War Office Selection Board, then at the Officer Cadet Training Unit (OCTU) at the Royal Military College, Aldershot, and before that at a 'Pre-OCTU' at Wrotham, Kent (PP, 51). At his passing-out parade, on 24 August 1944, 'one of those occasions which will remain in my mind all my life', he felt 'a sense of achievement and satisfaction' as well as great pride, a pride that his parents shared on seeing their son in the uniform of a British officer (PP, 57). Peter was commissioned into the Royal Fusiliers as an infantry platoon commander. He disembarked with his unit at Ostend in January 1945 and took part in the clearing of mines on the edge of the Reichswald, on the German-Dutch frontier, in preparation for the Allied crossing of the Rhine.

For both brothers, the high point of their service in the British army came during the early existence of the British Zone of Occupation in Germany. This confirmed their new sense of identity as British officers, especially in relation to the vanquished Germans. However, in their dealings with Germans, they displayed none of the attitudes of the colonial administrator that were often ascribed to the British military authorities. The brothers certainly felt morally superior to the Germans, contaminated as they were by their complicity or acquiescence in the crimes of the Nazis. But they both determined to conduct themselves in their relations with Germans according to the values and standards inculcated into them in Britain from their time at Buxton College onwards; it was in the name of what they perceived as British values that they carried out their duties, performing services of great value to those for whom they were now responsible.

Geoffrey made his principal contribution to post-war Germany in the areas of broadcasting and the press. When Hamburg surrendered to the British on 3 May 1945, he played a key part in the takeover of Radio Hamburg, so that within thirty-six hours it was broadcasting for the British military administration; he acted as station announcer for the first two days. He used the same microphone that William Joyce, the notorious traitor 'Lord Haw-Haw', had used for his final, drunken broadcast for the Nazis — ironically, in view of the fact that Geoffrey captured Joyce outside Flensburg shortly afterwards. His greater achievement was his part in the creation of a free press that preserved a measure of balance and impartiality in its reporting after the years of Nazi propaganda and distortion of the truth. He was involved in the production of the *Hamburger Nachrichten-Blatt*, which was published as early as 9 May 1945, and then in that of the larger *Neue Hamburger Presse*, whose circulation reached over a million in June 1945 and met the hunger of its German readers for reliable, objective news.

Later, promoted to major, Geoffrey was involved in setting up *Die Welt* (prior to its sale to Axel Springer) and the press agency DPD. The newspapers published under his unit's control were produced to strict standards of impartiality, restricting themselves to 'straight reporting' and eschewing political opinions. When political life resumed in Germany, Geoffrey insisted on equality of treatment for the newly established political parties; with scrupulous fairness, he measured the column inches received by each party — Social Democrats, Christian Democrats, and Communists — to ensure that their activities were treated equally. This insistence on fairness, impartiality, and political evenhandedness was a small but significant contribution to the creation of a new democracy in West Germany. Geoffrey's willingness to contribute to the building of a better Germany was only made possible by his decision not to hate all Germans indiscriminately. As a Jew who had suffered persecution at the hands of the Germans, it would have been natural for him to hate them:

> But so many of the relationships I had with Germans later, when we started the newspapers and after the war, were good ones. They were not founded on hatred, or hate ameliorated by getting to know the individual later. [...] I may hate specific Germans, but not the whole German people. (GP, 48)

This attitude of rational humanity that saw the good or bad in individuals, rather than condemning an entire nation en masse, owed much to Geoffrey's education and social formation in Britain.

This was also the case with Peter, whose duties with the British Military Government raised the question of his relations with Germans more insistently. After a spell at the headquarters of 21st Army Group at Bad Oeynhausen, he was transferred in September 1945 to Berlin, where, as Food and Transport Officer for the Charlottenburg district — where his family had lived prior to emigration — he became responsible for the supply and distribution of food to the local population, then numbering over two hundred thousand people. Aged only twenty-five, with the rank of captain, he was faced with the tasks of making the rationing system function, combating the ubiquitous black market, and ensuring that the population did not starve; conditions throughout the British Zone of Occupation were dire, but food shortages were most pressing in West Berlin, an enclave within the Soviet Zone to which the Russians were able to restrict supplies when it suited their political purposes. Peter worked devotedly to alleviate the suffering of the inhabitants of Charlottenburg. It was then that he met his future wife, still a young girl.

Peter adopted an attitude to Germans very similar to that of his brother:

> I quickly came to the conclusion that I would not — indeed, could not — act as an avenger. I felt too much sympathy for the magnitude of the suffering that surrounded me on all sides. Revenge for its own sake was demeaning and self-defeating. My priorities, I felt, were the eradication of all traces of Nazism wherever I might find it; and the seeking out of the victims of Nazi persecution and the alleviation of their mental and physical agony. Within these guidelines I saw my duty in the fair and equitable distribution of the food supplies and transport services for the 206,000 inhabitants of Charlottenburg, who were relying on the integrity of the administration which I now represented. (PP, 89)

Peter saw himself as the representative of the British administration whose 'fair and equitable' behaviour towards the Germans demonstrated its moral integrity. He explicitly related his own humane and unselfish work to the British values that he had adopted, as when he assisted in Operation Stork, the evacuation of children from Berlin, even though he could not help being reminded of other transports organized by the Germans: 'Yet I endorsed the important and humane gesture of "Operation Stork" and was happy to be an active participant. Anything else would have seemed a negation of all the values in which I believed and for which I had fought' (PP, 108). Reflecting on his work in Berlin, he recognized that its effectiveness was underpinned by his consciousness of the overall humanity and integrity of British policy in occupied Germany: 'My appointment enabled me to intervene effectively and positively in the events facing me; and I was convinced of the justice and fairness of British policy in Berlin. I carried it out with conviction' (PP, 135).

When the brothers were demobilized in late 1946, they still did not hold British nationality; their status as 'aliens' required them to register with the police. Accordingly, both brothers presented themselves at West Hampstead Police Station, resplendent in the full uniform of British officers and wearing their campaign ribbons, to the embarrassment of the bewildered desk sergeant who had to register them (PP, 144; GP 71–72). The brothers were naturalized shortly afterwards. The delay in their naturalization did not cause them to take lasting offence at the behaviour of the British authorities; on the contrary, Peter recorded his gratitude at the War Office's recognition of the services that he had rendered to Britain:

> For most of the home-coming servicemen and women these thanks and privileges represented nothing more than polite formalities. For former refugees, who had been able to demonstrate their devotion to Britain, it was tangible proof of acceptance by their adopted country. (PP, 144)

This attitude underlay the long, happy, and successful lives that both men subsequently enjoyed in Britain. Although they retained elements of their native identity — both married wives of German-Jewish origin — they came to consider themselves as primarily British, and were proud to do so. Looking back at his life and that of his family, Geoffrey Perry concluded: 'Three new generations of this new branch of our family have taken root and flourished in England. And I hope there will be Perrys in England for many generations to come' (GP, 129).

Refugee Officers, American Citizens

The lives of the authors of two of the most interesting memoirs by German-Jewish refugees who fought in the British army in World War II, Walter Eberstadt and Mark Lynton, followed paths very similar to those of the Perry brothers until the war ended and their paths diverged sharply. On the surface, it appears that Eberstadt and Lynton enjoyed a more privileged situation than the Perrys and might have been expected to adjust easily and contentedly to British society. That, however, was not the case, as both men left for the United States after the war. Walter Eberstadt's memoirs, *Whence We Came, Where We Went*, are subtitled on their jacket cover as *A Family History*; they are imbued with pride in his family's achievements and connections.[6] His father's family had long played a leading role in the Jewish community in Worms, before moving to Frankfurt am Main in 1867, where they became bankers and where his mother's family, the Flersheims, were established. Eberstadt was born in Frankfurt in 1921 and moved to Hamburg in 1924 when his father took up a position there. The early sections of his book are replete with the names of important bankers, both German and British, sometimes ennobled and representing the aristocracy of the British merchant-banking elite. Eberstadt's penchant for and pride in connections with a high social cachet became particularly evident during his time at Christ Church, Oxford, where his many upper-class friends included Angus Ogilvy, who married Princess Alexandra, the Queen's cousin. Eberstadt, a dynamic and ambitious man, had a sense of entitlement to access to the highest strata of society. Sensing that, as a German Jew, he would never be fully accepted as an equal in such circles in Britain, he opted for the United States, where immigrant status was unexceptional and merit more amply rewarded.

Mark Lynton was born as Max-Otto Loewenstein in Stuttgart in 1920 and moved with his family to Berlin in 1922. Like Eberstadt's father, Lynton's was the model of a patriotic, affluent, assimilated, middle-class German Jew. On both sides, Lynton's family was well established in the Stuttgart area, boasting numerous lawyers and bankers among its number. He retained his attachment to the country of his origin, which continued to shape his identity in later life: 'Overall, my German roots go deep and remain so' ('Foreword', unnumbered page).[7] Lynton's memoirs, *Accidental Journey: A Cambridge Internee's Memoir of World War II*, cannot be considered as a broadly accurate autobiography in factual terms, since the author presents a consciously stylized, satirizing picture of the British institutions and people that he encountered on a picaresque trajectory across various aspects of British society. Seen through the eyes of an outsider, a young refugee cast in the role of the innocent abroad, British institutions come across as inefficient, incompetent, enmeshed in arcane, archaic traditions, and vitiated by class and social distinctions so indirectly encoded that they almost defy detection by the uninitiated observer.

That technique of satirical exaggeration is applied to the depiction of the Briggs family, who took Lynton in after he came to Britain in 1936 to study at a prestigious public school, Cheltenham College, and to the village where they lived:

> If Stanford-on-Soar did not exist, Trollope would have invented it. Five miles from Loughborough, a county seat of dim distinction, Stanford was a tiny village in the very heart of England's county shires, where foxes, dogs, and horses not merely outnumber humans, but regularly outsmart them. (7)

The Reverend John Briggs, the father of a school friend of Lynton's, is presented as a comic original, but one whose essential decency and tolerance inspire deep affection:

> The Reverend Briggs, looking just like Punch with a dog collar, owned a halo of white hair, a high-pitched, rather querulous voice, button-bright eyes, a perpetual pipe perpetually being relit, and was a bustling, opinionated, stubborn, nosy, thoroughly decent, and deeply kind little man. (8)

Cheltenham College, which Lynton describes as 'an English public school of indifferent academic reputation, sterling social standing, and towering military distinction' and as an 'academic wasteland', nevertheless 'taught me a good deal about relationships, team spirit, and camaraderie, concepts [...] which, as I was to find out, have their uses' (5). If Cheltenham was in thrall to obscure imperial military traditions, Cambridge, where Lynton went in 1938 supposedly to study law, seemingly existed in a realm remote from the realities of 1939:

> Within a thousand-year-old institution, news of an occasional war hardly gets around, and where it had, it was treated with faintly irritated indifference. Since there was no likelihood of a Cromwellian confiscation of college plate to finance such an enterprise, Cambridge did not seem to feel any cause for concern. (12)

Lynton spent a 'lotus-eating' time at St John's College (5), drinking and playing sports; even after the outbreak of war, 'enemy aliens' like Lynton were initially treated with 'benign neglect, bordering on outright idiocy, generally acclaimed as the British way of "muddling through"' (13) — a combination of inefficiency with humanity that was to surprise him throughout.

Walter Eberstadt came to Britain in 1935 with his parents and sister, attended another leading public school, Tonbridge, and went on to study at Oxford. But he found it hard to accept the fall in status suffered by his parents as refugees in Britain, where they lived in reduced, slightly shabby circumstances and were instantly recognizable as foreigners, tolerated by the British but never fully accepted. Alongside the affection and admiration that he felt for the British, Eberstadt harboured a sense of grievance at their treatment of him and his family as outsiders. He was dissatisfied with their accommodation, though they lived in good areas of London, at first in Marylebone, then in Holland Park. Although he admits that Tonbridge had a profound formative effect on him, not least in his conversion to Anglican Christianity, he found the school's routines peculiar and the social composition of its intake unattractively middle class. Even at Christ Church, where he was admitted thanks to a family connection with Professor Frederick Lindemann, Churchill's wartime scientific adviser, and where he mixed freely with socially impeccable Etonians and Wykehamists, Eberstadt continued to cast himself as the outsider: 'Everyone seemed friendly but I can't believe I was accepted fully — and why on earth should I have been — by the *jeunesse dorée* whose families had been at the House [Christ Church] for generations' (155).

That sense of grievance was greatly exacerbated by the shock of his internment in June 1940, an injustice that he never forgave the British. Eberstadt is critical, at least implicitly, of his own youthful desire to recreate himself as an Englishman, partly because it represented a betrayal of his true identity, and partly because it was doomed to failure, as his internment all too brutally revealed:

> I came to worship England and the English, and for a while considered myself to have become one of them. In 1940, internment came as a rude reminder that I was after all an alien, an enemy alien at that. Never mind that the English let us join the army, which got us out from behind barbed wire. Since the morning the police came to arrest me at my parents' home, England has not been the same for me. (xii–xiii)

But Eberstadt's identity had been in large measure formed in Britain, and his affection for the country caused him to reach a more conciliatory conclusion only two pages later:

> With the Nuremberg Laws of 1935 my parents saw the writing on the wall. They sent me to school in England, my sister followed a few months later. My English school, Oxford, and six years in the British army left more than an Anglicized veneer. To this day I feel at home in Britain, though my onetime almost passionate love for the British has long since given way to a deep affection and respect for the United States.[8] (xiv)

Though Eberstadt spent only some three months in internment, at Kempton Park and Huyton, he felt himself to have been severely affected by the experience, citing it as a major factor in his decision to leave Britain for the United States. His time in the Pioneer Corps did little to endear Britain to him. He was sent to Ilfracombe, then was stationed at Lydbrook in the Forest of Dean with 220 Company, carrying out forestry and sawmill work. He was commissioned as an officer in July 1942 and was posted to 87 Company, stationed first outside Swansea, then for a pleasant year at Long Marston in Warwickshire. He was eventually posted to a fighting unit, the Oxfordshire and Buckinghamshire Light Infantry, in October 1943.

For Lynton, internment represented a rich source of material for satirical humour, starting with the tribunal before which he was summoned to appear as an 'enemy alien'. 'This geriatric gaggle set to in the finest Colonel Blimp tradition', certifying him as a 'friendly alien' (14) on the strength of his sporting record at Cheltenham and the military credentials of his referee (whom he had never met). Lynton was arrested on Whit Sunday 1940 and spent seven months in internment, five of them in Canada, where he was transported in disgraceful conditions aboard the *SS Ettrick*. The inefficiency and bizarre lack of logic that, in Lynton's view, governed the policy of internment and its implementation did not, however, prevent him from seizing the first opportunity to return to Britain instead of staying comfortably in Canada:

> I never seriously considered that choice, since I had a lemming-like urge to return to England without, just like any good lemming, being able to explain why. Clearly the war was not going to make significant progress by my being involved in it, but I was quite convinced that I ought to go 'home'. (51–52)

Lynton spent two essentially unproductive years in 251 Company of the Pioneer Corps, before being commissioned into the 3rd Royal Tank Regiment in April 1944. Like the Perry brothers, he passed through the War Office Selection Board, the Pre-OCTU, and, in his case, the Royal Military Academy Sandhurst, an august institution where the training was fierce in its intensity and the rituals, like his passing-out parade, impressively anachronistic.

Both Eberstadt and Lynton had distinguished war records, both being promoted to the rank of major, but in neither case did this cement their identification with Britain or consolidate their sense of British identity. Both men took part in the bitter fighting in Normandy, of which Eberstadt, in command of an infantry platoon, has left a vivid picture, taken from the diaries he kept at the time. Posted to the Worcestershire Regiment, he was involved in actions at Mouen, Caumont, and the hotly contested Hill 112, before being wounded in August 1944 while leading a charge across open country during an attack on Mont Pinçon. He was justly proud of his record in the front line. He had formed a close bond with the men under his command, and he respected his senior officers. He was treated as a wounded hero on his return to Britain, where he was posted to Colchester to train new recruits, and made a 'boon companion' of a fellow officer, Tony Paget, from a suitably long-established English upper-class family (217).[9]

Despite all this, Eberstadt had considerable difficulty in assuming the role and identity of a British officer. When he was first commissioned, he felt that his application had been successful 'for all the wrong reasons'; the English veneer that he had acquired at Tonbridge did not qualify him to command 'aliens' in the Pioneer Corps, but 'it might make me a conventionally more agreeable member of an English officers' mess' (170). He describes himself at this stage as excessively eager to appear immaculately British: he bought his dress uniform from the select establishment of Bernard Weatherill in Mayfair and celebrated his twenty-first birthday with an initialled silver cigarette case, 'very appropriate and very English' (171). He was reluctant to anglicize his name, a key indicator of adaptation to Britain:

> I had changed my name from Eberstadt to Everitt. I did not have my heart in the name change, but with the stigma attached to anything German I quite liked it at a time when I still wanted to be very, very British. (219)

He later reverted to his original name in reaction against what he felt to be his earlier, excessive attempts to project an inauthentic British image.

Lynton, who viewed the British with ironic amusement and whose relationship to them was correspondingly more distant, reacted more pragmatically to the order to change his name. He did not wish to have an unwanted name imposed on him by 'some nameless antisemite or some titled country squire' in the War Office: 'I therefore spent an evening in the canteen with the Cheltenham telephone book and a couple of beers and gave birth to Mark Oliver Lawrence Lynton, which I have been ever since' (91). As the name change did not affect his underlying sense of his identity, it was of little consequence to him that his new name became permanent:

> I always only intended Lynton to be a nom de guerre in the most literal sense, and to become a Loewenstein again when it was all over. The war just lasted too long and everyone, myself included, became used to Lynton. (92)

Though justifiably proud of his service with the 3rd Royal Tank Regiment, Lynton retained the perspective of the outsider in his account of his period on active service, which juxtaposes satirical humour with the description of his unit's distinguished military exploits.

The 3rd Royal Tank Regiment landed in Normandy on 13 June 1944 and endured the costly fighting there before breaking out, taking Amiens, and liberating Antwerp before being beaten back in the attempt to relieve the 1st Airborne Division at Arnhem. It fought in the Battle of the Bulge, carried out assault crossings of the rivers Aller and Elbe, participated in the liberation of Bergen-Belsen, and finished the war at Flensburg, on the Danish border. Lynton served as a tank commander, a position that combined responsibility with a high rate of attrition: throughout the campaign, the tanks of the 11th Armoured Division were routinely in the vanguard of the advance and were regularly picked off by the German defences, with the loss of over two hundred tank commanders. Lynton shared the pride of the 'Desert Rats' who had fought and beaten the Wehrmacht, from the deserts of Libya across north-west Europe to the shores of the Baltic; he repeatedly depicts the unexpected heroism of such unlikely figures as the 'remote and sheep-like' medical officer Barry Whitehouse (147–48) or the improbably boyish Robin Lemon (128; he was twice decorated with the Military Cross). But his use of the distancing perspective of the humorist ensures that Lynton the narrator, and foreigner, always appears distinct from the British collective of the unit that he describes.

Lynton's fellow officers are set in the mould of the British upper classes, with their public school education and undemonstrative manners. The contrast between their seemingly casual and amateurish approach to war and their successes on the battlefield against a determined and experienced foe allows for unexpected comic effects. Examples include descriptions of the taking of Osnabrück by the 3rd Royal Tank Regiment 'by a combination of luck and poor map reading' (152) or the tricking of the German forces at Neustadt, north of Hamburg, into surrendering by means of the improvised 'telephone caper' (164). As Lynton's narrative makes plain, he served with distinction in the British Army but, unlike the Perry brothers, never wished to identify with its values and codes of behaviour.

Walter Eberstadt made a significant contribution to reconstruction in the British Zone of Occupation in Germany while still in his mid-twenties. Like Geoffrey Perry, Eberstadt was involved in the takeover and rebuilding of the German media. In late 1944, he was sent to Radio Luxembourg, from where SHAEF (Supreme Headquarters Allied Expeditionary Force) broadcast to Germany; when the war ended he was posted to Hamburg, the city from which he had been forced to flee ten years previously. There he played a key role in the setting up of Radio Hamburg, renamed Nordwestdeutscher Rundfunk, which was later divided into Norddeutscher and Westdeutscher Rundfunk and became the model for the system of German public-service broadcasting. Eberstadt was responsible for recruiting German radio journalists like Jürgen Schüddekopf and Peter Bamm; avoiding those tainted by association with the Nazis, he selected and was responsible for overseeing such renowned radio journalists as Axel Eggebrecht and Peter von Zahn.[10] He was also responsible for assisting Hamburg's first post-war mayor, Rudolf Petersen, with his broadcasts. Lynton was active in security, later moving into political intelligence, though his account of his activities in these fields should be treated with caution.

Unlike the Perry brothers, neither man was primarily influenced by British values and standards of conduct, for their memoirs reveal a sense of growing emotional distance from Britain and of frustration with the British authorities. The external impetus for their emigration to America was, in both cases, an early post-war visit to the United States: Lynton spent a month in New York in 1946 with his family, who had arrived there in 1941, and Eberstadt enjoyed his stay there in 1948. Eberstadt had returned to Oxford to complete his degree in law, but by 1950 had grown restless enough to emigrate. Both he and Lynton cite the refusal of the British authorities to grant them British nationality when they were officers in the British army as a prime reason for their dissatisfaction in post-war Britain. Lynton even claims — erroneously — that the Home Office did not count his period of wartime service towards the five years of residence in Britain required for purposes of naturalization (264–65).

In retrospect, Eberstadt was critical of his desire to integrate and to assume a British identity: 'Major Everitt posed as the newly retired army officer, not, I hope, to the point of making a fool of himself' (361). Lynton experienced no such emotional conflict. His naturalization, in March 1947, came too late to change his feelings towards Britain; unlike Peter Perry, he thought little of the official letter of thanks for his military service that he received from the War Office, and his demobilization proved to be another exercise in comic disorganization. Both he and Eberstadt found the United States more suited to their ambitions and to their expectations, which British society had always seemed unlikely to fulfil.

Refugees in the Ranks

Encountering a society as sharply delineated by class as Britain, many refugees (though by no means all) tended to reintegrate into British society at approximately the level of class and occupational status with which they were familiar from their native countries, replicating to a considerable extent the career and life expectations with which they had grown up. Those aspirations, in many instances, played a determining role in shaping young refugees' lives in Britain, as was the case with two men from lower-class backgrounds who were guided as a result towards a pattern of integration very different from that of Eberstadt and Lynton. Both Fred Pelican and Eric Sanders came from modest backgrounds; neither of them went to public school or university, neither was commissioned as an officer in the forces, and neither entered what might be termed 'establishment', upper-middle-class professions, though both did well in career terms; Sanders, a convinced socialist, rose to a senior position in the state school system. They came from families ambitious for their advancement, but the imprint of their social origins on both their professional and private lives was clear.

Fred Pelican was born as Friedrich (Fritz) Pelikan at Miastezko near Katowice, Poland, in January 1918; his family moved across the border to Breslau (Wrocław), so that he could attend a Gymnasium and study medicine. The family was not wealthy, and Pelican's father died when he was young. In the ethnically mixed region of Silesia, racial tensions were high even before 1933; Pelican encountered sustained and vicious anti-Semitism, culminating in his abrupt expulsion from his school and the desecration of his synagogue in November 1938. A conscious Jew, Pelican would have grown up to consider himself an outsider in German society, with little of the sense of entitlement displayed by his wealthier, more assimilated counterparts. After the pogroms of November 1938, Pelican attempted to leave Germany illegally, but was arrested at Monschau, on the Belgian border, and detained for over five months in Dachau. He was only released because he was granted a transit visa for Britain, on the strength of a ticket (purchased by his mother) for a ship departing from Liverpool for Shanghai on 28 October 1939.[11] The systematic abuse and humiliation that he endured in Dachau had a severe impact on the young Pelican, undermining his self-confidence and, at least in the short term, moderating further his expectations in life.

The contrast between his treatment in Dachau and the reception that he received in Britain gave rise in Pelican to a profound, almost uncritical admiration for his new homeland, as expressed in the foreword to his autobiography:

> I pay tribute to the heroic British people who at the most critical time of my life granted me refuge, and never showed malice or hostility towards us. They welcomed and embraced us on account of our exemplary conduct, because we respected the rule of law, and thus adjusted to freedom and democracy.[12] ('Foreword', unnumbered page)

The prospect of a new life in Britain, symbolized in his first sight of the White Cliffs of Dover, became for Pelican the opportunity for a fresh start, through which he could put behind him the humiliation and discrimination of the past. He was especially struck by the friendly and orderly process of his reception on arrival: 'This very first hour in Dover left in me a lasting impression to this very day, and made an impact never to be forgotten — that a real land of Hope and Glory was to follow' (34). Pelican was housed with other 'transmigrants' at Kitchener Camp at Richborough, near Sandwich in Kent, which he describes as 'like a large family' and where he settled contentedly (34–35).[13] There he was befriended by a resident of Broadstairs, Mrs Joyce Piercey. The kindness that he encountered overwhelmed Pelican and contributed to his development of a new sense of self-worth and identity:

> Has all this really happened to me? I couldn't have dreamed it up. I, who a few months ago went through a process of dehumanisation, kicked about and spat on, immune to dead bodies, had now experienced a reversal in a strange land, a sort of kindness and humanity completely strange to me and, above all, it came from a non-Jewish person. (37)

In the last summer of peace, Pelican was enthralled by the seaside resorts of Kent, with their spirit of spontaneous and unconstrained enjoyment:

> I was fascinated by the atmosphere of joy and hilarity, completely strange to me. I watched the scene intensely as ordinary members of the public seized the microphone to lead a sing-song, joined by the rest of the public in a spirit of happiness. That was the England I got to know and love in the year of 1939. (37)

When war broke out, Pelican promptly volunteered for the Pioneer Corps and was detailed to 74 Company, one of two companies formed at Kitchener Camp. For him, joining the Pioneer Corps was a matter of pride, irrespective of its lowly, non-combatant status:

> I was very proud of myself, very excited and ready to submit to whatever was required of me. I reflected upon the transformation that had taken place in a comparatively short time. Here was I, a fully-clad soldier in the British Army, while six months ago my young life had been in jeopardy in a German concentration camp — a remarkable transformation! (43)

Pelican's sense of gratitude to Britain found expression in his deep loyalty to his adopted homeland: 'The nation on the whole had my full admiration: war or peace, this was the greatest country on earth, I can repeat it a thousand times' (58–59). His account of his period of service consequently differs greatly from those of Eberstadt and Lynton, for whom service in the Pioneer Corps was a tedious and somewhat demeaning interlude.

After training, Pelican's company was sent in early 1940 to France, where, according to his account, they performed their duties admirably; but in May 1940 they were left dangerously close to the advancing Germans, an act of culpable neglect on the part of the military authorities. Pelican, however, chooses to stress instead the successful evacuation of his company and the morale-boosting nature of their reception back in Britain. This attitude of almost unreserved approval forms a pattern in his description of his service in the Pioneer Corps. On the one hand, any reprehensible or hostile behaviour by the British soldiers with whom they served is swiftly glossed over, as in the cases of an intemperate outburst of rage by his British commanding officer (96–97), or the poor conduct of a sergeant major at Bicester, who was rapidly replaced (92–95). On the other hand, the achievements of the Pioneer Corps are presented in a most favourable light. In autumn 1939, Pelican depicts his company as welded into an effective unit by their basic training: 'The training period almost complete, I was amazed how well we all had adapted ourselves to an entirely new way of life. An excellent understanding prevailed between the [British] sergeant and men' (43).

Pelican was subsequently stationed in towns and villages across southern England and south Wales, moving so many times that he himself admits to losing count (89). In almost all of these postings, the Pioneer Corps men acquitted themselves well: when Pelican, promoted to corporal, was in charge of a detachment constructing gun emplacements on the south coast, their work won the approval of several qualified officers (70–72). His unit even succeeded in enlivening the quiet Bristol suburb of Shirehampton by holding weekly dances, complete with continental pastries (73). By summer 1943, his company had become a physically fit and efficient unit, ready to play its part in the invasion of France:

> My 74th Company had come a long way from the time when we first joined up. A gradual process of transformation had taken place. The days when we were purely engaged in labouring of one kind or other, non-combatant and defenceless, had long gone. (89)

They were sent to Normandy on 11 June 1944, five days after D-Day, and supported the 21st Army Group in its advance across north-west Europe. In December 1945, Pelican was transferred to one of the War Crimes Investigation Units tasked with tracking down Nazi criminals; among those that he helped to bring to justice were

Hans Barr, responsible for killing some two thousand people by phenol injections at Neuengamme concentration camp, and Dr Bruno Tesch, whose company manufactured Cyclon B gas.

By the time he was discharged, in autumn 1946, Pelican had been promoted four times, rising to the rank of staff sergeant. Pelican's army service appears to have formed the foundation upon which he could construct a new sense of identity, secure in his own standing and abilities, to replace that of the abused and persecuted outsider that he had been in Germany. By joining organizations like the British Legion, he was able to consolidate his sense of belonging to British society, which he praises effusively throughout his autobiography, thereby indirectly confirming his own self-worth. But Pelican's life was also shaped by his origins in Germany. Coming from a modest background, he evidently did not strike his British superiors in the army as 'officer material', whereas German Jews from middle-class backgrounds were regularly commissioned as officers. His wife Gladys, whom he married in 1941, was a working-class woman from Stamford Hill, an area of Jewish settlement in the borough of Hackney, north-east London; her family still spoke Yiddish, a characteristic that distinguished the Jews from Eastern Europe, unassimilated, loyal to traditional Jewish practices, and often still working class, from the assimilated, educated, and middle-class Jews who had adopted the lifestyle of the western European cities. It would be hard to find a greater contrast in terms of class identity than that between Gladys Pelican and Vera von Kuffner, Walter Eberstadt's wife.

Eric Sanders was born as Erich Ignaz Schwarz in December 1919, into a family of modest means in St. Veit, a poor area of Hietzing, a western suburb of Vienna. The family faced a struggle to subsist; they formed part of the impoverished lower middle class living under the shadow of economic insecurity. Sanders's middle name reflected the problems of identity that he experienced as a Jew in Vienna: he should have been called Itzig or Isak, after his grandfather, but that was felt to be too Jewish, while he came to feel that Ignaz was too Catholic. Sanders was deeply attached to Vienna and would have liked nothing better than to be integrated into the society of his native city. Consequently, his brutal expulsion from Austria constituted a radical break shaping his later life, his sense of his identity, and his attitude to both Austria and Britain. Sanders was, however, resilient and optimistic by temperament. As the title of his autobiography, *Emigration ins Leben* [Emigration into Life] suggests, he overcame the adversities of emigration and built a new and fulfilled life for himself in Britain.[14] But as his subtitle, *Wien–London und nicht mehr retour* [Vienna–London One Way Only], implies, he was never able to effect an emotional reconciliation with his native city. The pain caused him by his marginalization in Vienna was already evident before 1938: when his classmates sang an anti-Semitic song, the impact on him was devastating. His description of the long and bureaucratic process of his forced departure for Britain, where his mother had family, is dominated by his distress at the separation from Vienna.

Britain was, however, a largely welcoming refuge for Sanders. In Vienna, a British consular official, Mrs Holmes, ignored regulations by issuing him with a visa so

FIG. 3.2. Eric Sanders in British uniform. Courtesy of Eric Sanders.

as to ensure that the maximum number of visa applicants reached safety (65). On board the ferry from Ostend, Sanders records, the sun broke through, his insecurity vanished and he felt that he was beginning a new and more promising life (71). The family settled in the East End of London, moving later to Kingsclere, Hampshire, where the father found work as an agricultural labourer. Sanders himself continued his studies and was then employed by one of the refugee organizations located first at Woburn House, later at Bloomsbury House. In that capacity, he showed his customary initiative by enabling the emigration to Britain of a young friend from Vienna, Liesel Kober, and her mother.[15] Although there was much about Britain that was strange to him, Sanders experienced a new feeling of freedom in London: people could walk on the grass, anyone, even a Jew, could say what he wanted in public, and the policemen were friendly and helpful. Like many refugees, he was also impressed by the orderliness and honesty manifest in public behaviour in Britain (74–75).

Sanders was nevertheless often depressed by the loss of future prospects entailed by his refugee status; he never achieved his goal of studying music. He was also conscious, as a foreigner and a refugee, of being restricted in his life chances (89). Throughout his adult life, he lacked a sense of secure national identity. Unlike his father, who was a native Viennese and remained so in Britain even after acquiring British citizenship, Sanders, who had begun life as 'ein echtes Wienerkind' [a true child of Vienna], lost that certainty with his emigration and was never able to become a 'true Englishman'. For his identity, he was forced to fall back on his own inner self: 'I am sufficient to myself, and I carry the roots of my identity inside myself.' He lost his externally rooted identity when he was 'thrown out' of Austria on 25 August 1938 (70). Nevertheless, Peter Pirker, the editor of Sanders's memoirs, is surely correct to see Sanders's life in Britain as, on balance, a successful emigration; the relative openness of British society allowed the refugees, who had been reduced by the Nazis to mere objects of arbitrary state power, to develop their potential and to take their lives into their own hands.[16] As his autobiography shows, Sanders was re-empowered in Britain, regaining a measure of agency over his own life.

In early 1940, Sanders was accepted into the British forces. Although he was allocated to the Pioneer Corps, this represented a considerable boost to his morale: 'Just to wear British uniform seemed to liberate us from the demeaning status of refugees' (104). His unit was sent to France, only to be hastily evacuated from St Malo on 16 June 1940. Sanders was embittered by this turn of events; that embitterment increased when he learnt that while he had been serving in the British army, his father had been interned. Only the generous behaviour of his British sergeant, who out of sheer goodwill visited Sanders's father in Huyton, re-established his trust in the British (118–19). His further service in the Pioneer Corps was uneventful, as he had no interest in promotion and wanted only to pursue his education. He was continually troubled by his loss of a secure identity, as demonstrated in a letter that he wrote to the *News Chronicle* when a British soldier had objected to his speaking German:

> Ich will Ihnen eine einfache Frage stellen: Was bin ich? Ich bin, wie mein Vater, in Österreich geboren. Ich wanderte aus, als Hitler das Land besetzte, und kam im August 1938 nach England. [...] Ich habe jetzt zwei Jahre und fünf Monate im Pioneer Corps gedient. Dass ich kein Engländer bin, hat man mir klargemacht. Es ist nicht einmal gewiss, dass ich je einer werden kann. Ich bin aber auch kein Österreicher, denn ich darf meine Muttersprache nicht sprechen. (150–52)
>
> [I want to ask you a simple question: What am I? Like my father, I was born in Austria. I emigrated when Hitler occupied the country, and came to England in August 1938. [...] For two years and five months now I have served in the Pioneer Corps. That I am not an Englishman has been made plain to me. It is not even certain that I can ever become one. But I am not an Austrian either, as I am not allowed to speak my mother tongue.]

He hoped to establish the basis for a new identity by joining the fight against the Nazis, a hope that seemed to be fulfilled when he was accepted into the Special Operations Executive (SOE) and was sent to Italy, expecting to be parachuted into Austria. In the event, he spent a frustrating year of inaction in Italy.

With the end of the war, Sanders, having anglicized his name, was faced with decisions about the course of his future life. Unlike some of his Austrian comrades in the SOE, socialists who were eager to return to Vienna, Sanders was under no illusion about the depth and persistence of Austrian anti-Semitism. He believed that the great majority of Austrians of all classes had welcomed the *Anschluss* and had participated in appalling crimes against the Jews. He concluded that he would never again settle permanently in Vienna, as all his links with his native city had been callously shattered. When he did return to Vienna in June 1946, after a spell working with German prisoners of war at a camp in Somerset, it was as a British soldier; now a sergeant in the British Army Legal Unit, Sanders behaved in a demonstratively British manner and was treated as a member of the British occupation forces by the Austrians he encountered. He recalls that he saw himself 'als vollkommener Engländer' [as completely English] in Vienna at that time (283), a conscious, resolute, and lasting reaction against his treatment in 1938–39.

On occasion, Sanders suffered setbacks, caused by xenophobia rather than anti-Semitism, which led him to question his status in Britain. Yet at the end of such self-questioning, he always reached the same conclusion, preferring Britain over Austria:

> Ich war nicht im Geringsten in Gefahr, verbittert zu werden. Der Platz für das Negative war in meiner Gedankenwelt bereits besetzt — mit Wien und mit Österreich. Im Vergleich dazu erschien mir das England, in dem ich lebte, als ein Paradies der Toleranz. (261)
>
> [I was not in the least danger of becoming embittered. The place for negative feelings in my mind was already occupied — by Vienna and by Austria. By comparison with them, the England in which I lived appeared to me as a paradise of tolerance.]

The problem of his nationality was resolved in 1947, when he was granted British citizenship. His decision to become British was motivated partly by his parents' unwillingness to return to Vienna and partly by the cutting of the personal links that had bound him to the city: he had become a stranger in the city of his birth (277). Sanders trained as a teacher, married an English wife, and, without entertaining any career ambitions, went on to occupy senior positions at North Paddington School and at Elliott School in Roehampton; both were comprehensive schools in the state sector. A visit to Vienna in 2003 at the invitation of the Volkshochschule Hietzing did much to repair relations between Sanders and his native city, but by then his decision to lead his life in Britain had long been irrevocable.

It should be said that not all accounts by refugees of service in the British forces were so positive. Charles Hannam, whose memoirs will be discussed in Chapter 6, spent nearly five years in the British army, described in often distasteful detail in the later chapters of the second volume of his memoirs, *Almost an Englishman*.[17] Hannam was among the small minority of refugees sent to fight the Japanese in Burma instead of joining the war against the Nazis. He never saw action: the one occasion on which his battalion was set to attack the enemy turned into a farce, as the Japanese had already fled. Consequently, the close bond that developed between officers and men in combat was absent; instead, the class antagonisms prevailing in British society were replicated and indeed intensified, as the men came to regard their officers with barely concealed hatred and contempt. The regiment was mostly engaged in keeping order during the last phase of British rule in India, a task not suited to developing battlefield camaraderie. Hannam was shocked by the deep-seated racism of his fellow soldiers, who showed nothing but hatred for the Indians and contempt for their culture, religion, and way of life, peppering their conversation with expressions like 'fucking wogs' and 'black bastards'. Hannam saw the army not as a liberating force from the tyranny of Nazism but as an instrument of colonial control;[18] he was dismayed by the contrast between the reality of British imperial rule and the democratic values that he had imbibed at his British school. This was a war greatly different from the anti-Nazi crusade experienced by most refugees in the British forces in the years after 1939.

By volunteering for the British forces, and especially by seeing active service, young refugees were able to assume a new identity, that of men who wore the uniform of the British forces. Whatever their experiences, they would have been conscious of having taken the decision to join up, regaining a measure of control over their lives and reasserting their ability to function as free agents. The sense of powerlessness imposed on them by internment and the blow that it represented to their self-image and self-esteem, which Walter Eberstadt felt so keenly, was often counteracted by service in the armed forces. Even those who had joined the Pioneer Corps and avoided internment were re-energised by the opportunity to join the fight against the Nazis. Those who served with the occupying forces in Germany and Austria after the war were concerned to behave towards the civilian population of the defeated country in a way that would reflect the values of democracy and fairness that they felt they had absorbed in Britain; national prejudices or feelings of revenge were, to a very considerable extent, subordinated to tolerance and humanity. That would have been at least in part the result of the assimilated

German-Jewish identity that most of them had acquired before emigration; British Jews often proved less forgiving.

Notes to Chapter 3

1. See, for example, Norman Bentwich, *I Understand the Risks: The Story of the Refugees from Nazi Oppression Who Fought in the British Forces in the World War* (London: Gollancz, 1950); Peter Leighton-Langer, *The King's Own Loyal Enemy Aliens: German and Austrian Refugees in Britain's Armed Forces, 1939–1945* (London: Vallentine Mitchell, 2006).
2. Louis Hagen, *Arnhem Lift: Diary of a Glider Pilot* (London: Pilot Press, 1945).
3. Hagen and his book are mentioned repeatedly in *AJR Information* (from 2000, the *AJR Journal*), the monthly journal of the Association of Jewish Refugees, which has represented the Jewish refugees from Nazism in Britain since 1941.
4. See 'Sergeant Louis Edmund Hagen', <http://www.pegasusarchive.org/arnhem/louis_hagen.htm> [accessed on 13 February 2016].
5. Peter J. C. Perry, *An Extraordinary Commission: The Story of a Journey through Europe's Disaster* (Bristol: published by the author, 1997); Geoffrey H. Perry, *When Life Becomes History* (London: White Mountain Press, 2002).
6. Walter Albert Eberstadt, *Whence We Came, Where We Went: From the Rhine to the Main to the Elbe, from the Thames to the Hudson* (New York: W. A. E. Books, 2002).
7. Mark Lynton, *Accidental Journey: A Cambridge Internee's Memoir of World War II* (Woodstock, NY: Overlook Press, 1995). Memoirs are always, to quote from the title of Clive James's, 'unreliable' to some extent. Lynton has come under attack on these grounds (see Victor Ross, letter to the editor, *AJR Journal*, September 2015, p. 6), though praise for his memoirs from Lord Noel Annan appears on the page facing the inside cover of the book; Lynton had met Annan during the latter's distinguished career in post-war Germany.
8. Eberstadt's sister Bridget (Brigitte) joined the Women's Auxiliary Air Force and married a husband from the British upper classes, opting, unlike her brother, to complete the process of integration into British society.
9. Like a sadly large number of Eberstadt's friends from Oxford and the army, Paget did not survive the war; he was killed in the Reichswald in 1945.
10. See Hans-Ulrich Wagner, 'Über alle Hindernisse hinweg: London-Remigranten in der westdeutschen Rundfunkgeschichte', in *'Stimme der Wahrheit': German-Language Broadcasting by the BBC*, ed. by Charmian Brinson and Richard Dove, Yearbook of the Research Centre for German and Austrian Exile Studies, 5 (Amsterdam: Rodopi, 2003), pp. 139–57.
11. Transit visas were granted by the British government to refugees from the Third Reich, often men released from concentration camps, on the understanding that they would subsequently re-emigrate. That understanding was frequently a polite fiction, as in the case of Pelican, whose passage to Shanghai was cancelled when war broke out and who was permitted to remain in Britain.
12. Fred Pelican, *From Dachau to Dunkirk* (London: Vallentine Mitchell, 1993).
13. For a detailed and more balanced account of Kitchener Camp, see Clare Ungerson, *Four Thousand Lives: The Rescue of German Jewish Men to Britain, 1939* (Stroud, Glous.: History Press, 2014).
14. Eric Sanders, *Emigration ins Leben: Wien–London und nicht mehr retour*, ed. by Peter Pirker (Vienna: Czernin, 2008). The subtitle alludes to the title of a history of the Austrian Centre in London, whose leading members returned to Vienna after 1945: Marietta Bearman and others, *Wien–London, hin und retour: Das Austrian Centre in London 1939 bis 1947* (Vienna: Czernin, 2004), published in English as *Out of Austria: The Austrian Centre in London in World War II*, trans. by Miha Tavčar (London: Tauris, 2008).
15. Liesel Kober married Richard Grunberger, the historian and editor of *AJR Information* from 1988 to 2005.
16. Peter Pirker, 'Vorwort des Herausgebers' in, Sanders, pp. 6–10 (pp. 9–10).

17. Charles Hannam, *Almost an Englishman* (London: Deutsch, 1979).
18. The resentment of the Burmese at British colonial rule was observed by Rudolf Kauders, a Viennese who described his wartime experiences in *Donauwalzer am Irawadi: Exil in England, Kampf in Burma, Rückkehr nach Wien* (Vienna: Mandelbaum, 2011).

CHAPTER 4

The Years of Settlement
1945–60

In the years following the end of World War II, the Jewish refugees settled, on balance relatively smoothly, into British society, becoming integrated into that society while developing a distinct identity of their own, part German (or Austrian or Czech), part British, and part Jewish. Although there were many refugees who were never able to live happy and fulfilled lives in Britain, for the majority the process of integration into British life took place more easily than might have been expected in the anxious and precarious years immediately after their arrival in Britain. After the war, attempts by those hostile to the refugees to have them repatriated to their native countries, if necessary against their will, came to nothing. When the process of naturalization resumed after the war, many thousands of refugees took advantage of the opportunity to take British nationality, thereby removing the last formal obstacle to their status as British citizens.[1]

The settlement of the refugees was concentrated in certain areas, in particular the borough of Hampstead in north-west London, where refugees had come to form at least a quarter of the population during the war; this was the area along Finchley Road, from Swiss Cottage and Belsize Park (postal district NW3) and West Hampstead (NW6) to Golders Green (NW11) in the neighbouring borough of Hendon. Refugee communities also sprang up in the larger cities with existing Jewish communities, like Manchester, Glasgow, and Leeds, as well as in cities like Oxford and Cambridge, where refugees had moved from London during the war to escape the bombing and where groupings of refugee academics developed around the universities. It is noticeable that this wave of Jewish refugees settled predominantly in middle-class neighbourhoods, unlike the preceding wave of Jews from Eastern Europe, poor, largely ill-educated, and religiously observant, who had settled in working-class areas like London's East End in the years before World War I. The differences in modes of settlement and integration pointed to underlying differences and tensions between the two groups of Jews that prevented relations between them becoming genuinely close, and led to the preservation of a distinct identity among the later wave of refugees that kept them separate from the rest of Anglo-Jewry. This was a further factor that contributed to the integration of the Jews from the German-speaking lands, and their British-born children, into British, rather than Anglo-Jewish, society.

Certain groups of refugees experienced particular difficulties in adapting to life in emigration in Britain. Foremost among these was the problem of language; for most refugees, except the very young, English remained a second language, and they retained the accent that, to their increasing irritation, prompted the question 'Where do you come from?' as soon as they spoke to a native speaker.[2] Many refugees never fully came to terms with the subtly encoded conventions of British manners, such as the practice of small talk with its complex interplay of approachability and distance. They struggled to adapt to the habits and customs of everyday life — the food, the clothes, the accommodation, the heating (or lack of it). This affected the elderly in particular, who were more set in their ways, making it difficult for them ever to integrate to any significant degree into British society. Many older refugees who had held senior positions in their professions were effectively unemployable in Britain and faced the dispiriting choice between undertaking menial work and remaining in enforced idleness, deprived both of income and of their status as breadwinners. The burden of earning the family living often fell on their wives; a feature of refugee life was the way in which many women rose to this new responsibility. In the austerity years of the late 1940s, the refugees, like the British population as a whole, struggled with the shortages and hardships of daily life in a war-shattered country.

By the end of the 1950s, however, with rapidly rising consumer prosperity, the refugees had developed into a predominantly middle-class community whose professional and occupational profile differed sharply from that of British society as a whole, in which the working class still formed the largest component. The refugees came to enjoy levels of prosperity and material security comparable to those of their British middle-class counterparts; but the emotional and psychological traumas that they had undergone continued to affect many of them, not least the children who had come to Britain on Kindertransports and had lost one or both parents, or the men who had suffered permanent damage during their incarceration in Nazi concentration camps. The majority of the refugees, however, succeeded in building new and happy lives for themselves and their families in Britain. They had shared the suffering and hardships of war, especially the bombing of Britain's cities, with the British civilian population, and had contributed to the best of their ability to the common cause of the war against Nazi Germany. In the post-war decades of peace, as they reacquired a professional and social status comparable to that which they or their families had enjoyed in their native lands, they established for the most part a settled and secure existence in a country that they perceived as predominantly benevolent and, though often eccentric in its ways, as their adopted homeland.

The texts discussed in this chapter reflect the process — not always easy — of adapting to British conditions experienced by the refugees from Nazism in the first period of settlement. Refugees frequently encountered problems in adapting to material conditions in Britain; of deeper significance, however, especially for the younger refugees, was the pressure to adopt a new identity consonant with their changed situation. After the Holocaust, it was not possible for them simply to resume their pre-war German or Austrian identities, but neither did they wish to abandon their heritage entirely, let alone to attempt to integrate without distinction into British society. The authors covered in this chapter embarked, mostly with courage and good humour, on the task of recording their impressions of their relationship to their new homeland.

The Immediate Post-War Years

The earliest period of the post-war settlement of the refugees in Britain is documented in detail in an informative collection of letters by the writer, theatre critic, and journalist Hermann Sinsheimer, covering the period from September 1946 to his death in August 1950.[3] The majority of the letters were addressed to a former classmate in Germany, Frida Schaffner, née Reibold, with whom he remained on friendly terms. Sinsheimer was born in 1883 in the small town of Freinsheim in Rheinland-Pfalz, in south-west Germany. Although he studied law, his attraction to the theatre proved greater; he moved first to Munich, where he rose to the position of editor at the famous satirical magazine *Simplicissimus*, then to Berlin, where he became editor of the *Feuilleton* (arts section) of the *Berliner Tageblatt* and one of Germany's leading theatre critics. In 1938 he emigrated to Palestine, where he declared in a lecture that he had come to sit in lecture halls at the university, not to stand at the Wailing Wall, a clear indication of the unsuitability of Palestine as a country of refuge for such a highly assimilated German-Jewish intellectual. He re-emigrated to Britain later that year, settling in London, where he also experienced considerable initial difficulties. He had emigrated alone because his first wife, Anny Balder, stayed in Germany and divorced him; he had arrived in Britain at an age where, like many refugees, he was unable to practise his profession and, partly as a consequence, he experienced a breakdown in his health in January 1940. Like Alfred Kerr, he was reduced to living in hotels that catered for refugees; the first letters to Frida Schaffner were written from the Carlton Mansions Hotel on Bedford Place, Bloomsbury.

Sinsheimer, however, proved resilient, re-establishing himself as a writer by acting as a reviewer for a range of literary publications, including the *Political Quarterly*, edited by Leonard Woolf, Virginia Woolf's husband, such prestigious titles as the *Times Literary Supplement* and the *New Statesman*, and numerous publications in Germany and Switzerland. Gollancz published his study of Shylock, in an abbreviated version, with a foreword by John Middleton Murry, a leading literary figure in London.[4] Sinsheimer was assisted immeasurably by his marriage to his second wife, Christobel Fowler, a Cambridge graduate in Modern Languages, who had become close to him during his illness and whose support and strength of character proved of inestimable value in helping him to adjust to British conditions. A remarkable woman, she had interrupted her studies during World War I to work as a nurse at the front; she continued to propagate her pacifist convictions fearlessly throughout World War II.

The couple married in February 1947, and Sinsheimer took British nationality in November 1948. In July 1947, they moved to Kensington High Street, a desirable, affluent area, though the flat that they occupied was situated on the fourth floor and had no lift, a considerable disadvantage for a man with a heart condition. For two years, from 1946 to 1948, Sinsheimer devoted much of his time and energy to the re-education of German prisoners of war, lecturing in prisoner-of-war camps across the country as part of the large-scale British programme of denazifying German prisoners of war and inculcating into them the principles of democracy, tolerance, and respect for others, irrespective of race, religion, or nationality.[5] The demanding speaking programme that he undertook for the Foreign Office testified to his commitment to the principle of re-education: in September 1946, he wrote that crisscrossing the country by car, train, and aeroplane was taking up three quarters of his time (246), while in August 1947 he lectured at six widely separated camps in the space of ten days (297). His lectures were, he reports, very well received, especially by those from his native region, who could more easily relate to him on a human level; but he was fierce in rebutting any expression of Nazi ideology or any attempt to excuse the crimes committed in the name of Germany, even when they came from Field Marshal von Brauchitsch (257). His espousal of British values was matched by the scattering of English words in his letters, like 'not so bad' and 'civil servants' (438, 439); he used the phrase 'boils down to' because he could not think of the German equivalent (431).

Sinsheimer's letters are characterized by humour, erudition, an exuberant delight in the use of language, and a deep-seated humanity. He was by nature an optimist who believed the best of human beings, despite the experience of the Nazi years.[6] He claimed to owe his democratic, humanist convictions to the beloved town of his birth, Freinsheim, with its liberal, Western-orientated intellectual climate.[7] Indeed, he maintained that the true German values were those he had imbibed in his native town, and that they had been corrupted and defiled by the Nazi regime but had survived among the Jewish refugee communities abroad; these had remained loyal to the heritage of the Enlightenment and the liberal tradition of the nineteenth century. That conviction provided Sinsheimer with a firm foundation for his continuing faith in the humanist values of liberty, reason, and democracy, ideas that performed an important function in British society. Nevertheless, Sinsheimer found many aspects of that society unfamiliar and alien to him. He complained about the food and still more about the beverages, expressing astonishment at the impossibility of having a drink in the capital city after 11 p.m. (335), and lamenting his fate in living in a country that produced no wine (305). The British weather became a metaphor for the unfamiliarity and unpredictability of conditions very different from those that prevailed in sunny Freinsheim, situated amidst the fertile vineyards of the Deutsche Weinstraße. How, asked Sinsheimer, could a Freinsheimer like himself, accustomed to the orderly progression of the seasons, come to terms with a country where it was warm in winter and wintry in summer? (356).

From Sinsheimer's humorous tone here, half ironic, half affectionate, one can infer both his resilience in emigration and his willingness to adapt to life in Britain. In his first letter to Frida Schaffner, he recounts the obstacles that he has overcome — illness, homesickness, and the language barrier — in becoming 'ein englischer Schriftsteller' [an English writer], adding the phrase 'daß Gott erbarm'!' [heaven help us!] (245–46). The heavy weight of his writing commitments, detailed in letters like that of 14 May 1947 (281), makes plain the degree to which he succeeded in that endeavour. Sinsheimer grew to like Britain, from historic cities like Lincoln to the picturesque village of Sedlescombe in East Sussex, which he visited while on holiday in Hastings in August 1948, when he commented admiringly on the architecture, the food, and even the weather (363). Like many refugees, he was pleasantly surprised by the relative helpfulness of British officials, notably less authoritarian than their German counterparts, when obtaining a travel permit for the first of his two post-war visits to Germany (393). He particularly appreciated the toleration of differing opinions and the freedom of ideas that he found in Britain, exemplified in the widespread publicity given to his wife's anti-war poems in the middle of World War II. 'Das ist England' [That's England] (276), he commented. The degree of his acculturation is demonstrated by his growing enjoyment of the English Christmas, which he had at first found strange: he soon came to participate happily in the celebration of the festival with his wife's relatives in Kent, overindulging in Christmas pudding and singing English carols (323–24).

Sinsheimer was able to construct an identity for himself in Britain, retaining as a lifelong Freinsheimer his deep-rooted loyalty to his native town and remaining true to the humanist ideal of being a European, unbound by narrow nationalism, but at the same time adapting those pre-existing loyalties to his situation in his new homeland. His pronounced internationalism could, he believed, flourish unhindered in Britain. Yet Sinsheimer remained an outsider and was never able fully to integrate himself into British society or to perceive himself as fully British. In his first letter during his first visit to Germany, dated 31 March 1949, he described himself as no longer belonging in Germany and not yet belonging in Britain, a feeling that dismayed him, and called himself a 'Zwischenmensch' [man in between] (397). But within three weeks he was confessing to missing London (405). A Munich newspaper proclaimed him an Englishman who could state without hesitation that he felt at home in England; he did, however, reject the epithet 'stolzer Engländer' [proud Englishman], declaring that he had neither been born an Englishman nor intended to be one (409). These confusions of identity naturally beset refugees who had arrived in Britain at Sinsheimer's age. But in his case they were eased by his ready acceptance of the qualities that he admired in Britain. An example was the pleasure that he took in amusing his audience at a lecture on Goethe by making gentle fun of England; one of the best things about the English, he explained, was their fondness for self-irony (425).

The issue of Sinsheimer's new identity crystallized around his acquisition of British citizenship. This was motivated in large measure by the purely practical reason that he needed a passport to travel to Germany, not because of any profound emotional commitment to his new nationality. He was proud to remain a Freinsheimer and a European, a 'Weltbürger' [citizen of the world] who rejected national or religious differences and put his faith in the fundamental oneness of humanity (364–65). Consequently, his naturalization appears to have left him cold; he reported that he felt more 'entdeutscht' [de-Germanized] than 'verbritischt'

[Britishized] (371). But in the end he joined in when British friends invited him to celebrate his naturalization, singing the well-known lines from Gilbert and Sullivan's *H.M.S. Pinafore*:

> For in spite of all temptations
> To belong to other nations
> He became an Englishman. (379)

One notes one small but significant change: in the original, the character 'remains' an Englishman, whereas Sinsheimer 'became' one. It was an accommodation which, though initially forced on him, he was ultimately content to accept.

A slightly later example of the refugee perception of Britain as a fundamentally friendly and benevolent environment, despite the cultural differences between its society and those of Germany and Austria, is a short story that appeared in August 1953 in *AJR Information*, the monthly journal of the Association of Jewish Refugees. The author, Fritz Ruhemann, was an architect, born in Berlin in 1891. Ruhemann, like many German-Jewish professional people, had a strong interest in literature and the arts, as is demonstrated by his active involvement over many years with Club 43, the refugee cultural discussion forum that was founded in 1943 and survived for nearly seventy years; his brother was a distinguished restorer of paintings. Ruhemann chose as his subject the experiences of an elderly refugee lady, widow of a German professor, as she walks from her rented flat in Belsize Park, northwest London, in the direction of Swiss Cottage and the Cosmo café on Finchley Road, a well-known haunt of refugees, offering Continental food and a congenial Continental atmosphere.

The view of relations between the British and the Jews from Central Europe conveyed in such texts reflects the refugees' general image of Britain as a haven of relative freedom, decency, and tolerance underpinned by habits of courtesy and consideration in day-to-day life. Ruhemann's story 'Vorfrühling in Swiss Cottage' [Spring Comes to Swiss Cottage] captures this aspect of refugee life in the post-war years.[8] The interplay between Continental and British manners forms a principal theme of the story, as it follows Frau Professor Oppenheimer, lonely and depressed, walking through London one spring morning, steadfastly ignoring the polite Englishmen who seek to brighten her mood with remarks like 'Nice morning, Madam'. Lost in thought, she stops next to a building site and blocks the way:

> Die Passanten quetschten sich geduldig an den Bauzaun und nahmen sogar die Schuld auf sich, die guten Engländer, indem sie 'sorry' sagten; manche sagten 'thank you'. Plötzlich riss sie ein Heimatklang aus ihrer verlegenen Verwirrung: 'You, my lady, you hold ze whole traffic up.' Ja, das verstand sie! Ja, sie war fast angenehm berührt von diesem vertraut irdischen Ton und stammelte 'Oh, sorry!'. (5)

> [The passers-by squeezed patiently up against the hoarding and even took the blame on themselves, good-natured Englishmen that they were, by saying 'sorry'; some said 'thank you'. Suddenly a voice from her native land roused her from her embarrassed confusion: 'You, my lady, you hold ze whole traffic up.' Yes, that she understood! Yes, she was almost pleasantly surprised by this familiar, down-to-earth tone and stammered 'Oh, sorry!'.]

In her confusion, she steps straight out into the road, nearly causing an accident, only for the driver to wave her politely across — 'After you, Madam' — while someone else takes her by the arm to lead her over the road, disappearing before she even has time to thank him. A workman from the construction site provides her with a seat, where she reads a letter telling her that her children overseas are coming to London. The story ends with an exchange between the lady, now much more cheerful, and the workmen; although this is conducted on her side in heavily German-accented English and on theirs in Cockney, the two parties communicate with friendly good humour across the cultural and linguistic divide. The change in atmosphere from the opening of the story is very marked. When Frau Oppenheimer sets out, she is aware only of the unseasonal chill and the remnants of a London fog. But by the end, when the workmen have resumed communication with her, advising her to see the Charlie Chaplin film *Limelight* that is playing at the Odeon cinema nearby, her mood has altered and she is aware of sunshine and birdsong: '"Haf you noticed sat se birds haf just started to sing?" "Just started, my foot. Them birds 'ave been twittering their bloody 'eads off, ever since early morning". "Reelly?" "Merkwuerdig, dass ich das die ganze Zeit nicht gehoert hatte [Strange that all this time I had never heard them]"' (5).

The harsh realities of exile are not ignored here: the lady is living in much reduced circumstances — she occupies one of the many cramped rented rooms, with shared bathrooms, into which the grand houses of Belsize Park, neglected and shabby, were then divided, and she is in poor health and lonely, her husband dead and her children overseas, while she struggles to adjust to unfamiliar British modes of social interaction. But the depiction of her British environment is, fog and damp apart, thoroughly positive. All the British characters, from well-spoken gentlemen to Cockney workmen, treat the lady with friendly politeness, and their courtesy comes so naturally that the lady hardly notices it; only the curt tones of a fellow refugee remind her of this difference between British and Continentals. In reality, such displays of polite consideration would not have been the rule, even in the London of 1953. But the repeated depiction of British society as characterized by fair play and kindly manners arguably fulfilled a need among the refugee readership: partly as a welcome contrast to the brutality and inhumanity of the society from which they had fled, and partly as an idealized vision, a *Wunschbild*, of the new society into which they could, by virtue of their qualities and abilities, hope to integrate, thus completing the process of integration that had been cut short in their homelands.

That process and the difficulties that the refugees encountered were charted in a number of articles in *AJR Information* by Kenneth Ambrose, born as Kurt Abrahamsohn in Stettin, who had come to Britain in 1936, aged sixteen, to study at King's College, Taunton. In 1940, Ambrose was interned and deported to Australia aboard the notorious vessel *Dunera*, returning many months later to serve in the RAF. Despite the disruption of his education in both Germany and Britain, Ambrose went on to study at university and later worked at the highly regarded, Jewish-owned retailer Marks & Spencer, as well as becoming a regular contributor to *AJR Information*. Ambrose's articles combined a narrative of personal experience with generalizing reflections on the development of the refugee community in Britain and its social and cultural identity.

In two articles on 'The Second Generation', written in 1949, Ambrose focused on those who had come to Britain as children or young people, standing awkwardly between the generation of their parents, still wedded to their Continental ways, and the anglicized generation born in Britain.[9] The alternative of trying to pass as English was not open to those caught midway between British and German social cultures, so Ambrose advised his generation of refugees to recognize that their sense of discomfort, of not being firmly rooted in either camp, was part of their identity. The older generation was rooted in Continental values, a strength but also a limitation in a foreign society:

> The majority of the older generation can of necessity only make a series of external adjustments to an established way of life acquired beyond the Channel. We admire them for the striking success with which most of them have adapted themselves under the trying circumstances with which we have all been familiar. At the same time we know that our way is different in nature and not only in degree. We are not as firmly grounded as they are in another culture and most of us could be absorbed almost entirely by our new surroundings. Yet as we grow up we become conscious of the fact that we are not entirely a part of either the old way or the new, but could only be more or less poor imitators of either.

The British-born generation, on the other hand, had largely lost contact with German social culture, and was rooted in that of Britain, taking little interest in the culture of its former homelands and preferring 'the types of entertainment which their English school mates enjoy' (February 1949, p. 5).

These articles presented an easily recognizable paradigm: the older generation remained tied to the values and lifestyle of its native society, the transitional generation sought uneasily to combine elements from both the old and the new societies, while the younger generation was largely immersed in the social culture that surrounded it in Britain. The possibility of holding out against the insistent pressure to integrate was not mentioned, only that of adapting to it according to the varying sociocultural patterns that had shaped the three generations. The second generation, whose members had lived within two cultural patterns and were familiar with both, faced the choice between them. Ambrose advised his contemporaries against jettisoning either completely, neither opting for a purely British style of life, nor following the example of 'our young Anglophobes, mercifully few', who rejected British society outright. Instead, he gave preference to an intermediate position:

> Those members of the second generation who believe that something of value is contained in both the old and in the new culture patterns have congregated there. They are not ashamed of the older generation and do not artificially dissociate themselves from their past, nor do they turn their back on their new home. They try to remember that in our effort to make life more worth living many English are on our side. (July 1949, p. 3)

This led Ambrose to conclude on the optimistic note that the second generation was well placed to act as a 'hyphen between two culture patterns' (July 1949, p. 3), an intermediary between two generations and two societies. His accommodation to British society continued and deepened during the 1950s, when he published articles praising aspects of British public life that refugees had previously dismissed as archaic or eccentric,[10] and preferring British children's books to *Struwwelpeter* [Shock-Headed Peter], the German classic, which Ambrose now saw as 'a horrid book' quite unsuitable for his small British son.[11] By the end of the decade, Ambrose was able to look back on his life in Britain, with satisfaction, affection, and some surprise in another article in *AJR Information*:[12]

> Twenty-four years ago to the day I arrived at my English public school in Somerset, with a good knowledge of English, but otherwise a fairly typical German middle-class teenager of sixteen, who happened to have the wrong religion for his country of origin. [...] Twenty-four years after my arrival I am by all appearances one of the British middle-class. I live with my family in a small house with a garden, I work for a large Anglo-Jewish firm, my boys go to or are entered for a good public school. [...] I march off to work in the morning with briefcase and rolled umbrella to catch my train just like my neighbours, and on Sundays I wash my car, if necessary, do the minimum of gardening, and enjoy my family and home. My children only understand the few words of German which they have learnt from 'Oma' and 'Opa' ('granny' and 'grandpa'). (June 1960, p. 11)

The touch of self-mockery in this middle-class, suburban idyll did not detract significantly from Ambrose's conclusion, expressed in the article's title, 'The Best of Both Worlds', that he belonged to the generation of refugees that was both well enough integrated to enjoy British life and still familiar enough with the German past to draw benefit from its legacy. In terms of his external lifestyle, he had adapted smoothly to Britain, having come to appreciate the advantages of orderly queuing, neighbourliness without prying, and a sense of social responsibility:

> I appreciate and have adopted many of the good characteristics of the British. [...] All generalisations are dangerous, and all countries have good and bad points, yet on the whole I feel that I would rather live here than in any other country I know. (June 1960, p. 11)

However, his abiding sense of the past and its legacy, his desire not to forget, or to allow the world at large to forget, how the Jews of Germany had lived, distinguished him from his British neighbours.

This later article is remarkable for its relaxed tone, its feeling of well-balanced normality:

> If I try to stand back and take a look at myself at the gateway to middle-age and after nearly a quarter-century in this country, it seems to me that I have turned out surprisingly normal. I have become used to being judged not for where I come from, but for what I am. [...] I am just a relaxed, ordinary citizen now, but one, I hope, who has a good understanding of both the older generation of refugees who were unable to outgrow the habits and thoughts of their earlier days, and of the younger generation to which these habits are strange. I am, it seems to me, getting the best of both worlds. (June 1960, p. 11)

While not minimizing the problems faced by groups like the elderly or ignoring the inevitable disappearance of the refugees' Continental, German-speaking culture among their British-born children, Ambrose depicts a broadly successful process of adaptation to British society, to which both conditions in post-war Britain and the qualities of the refugees themselves contributed.

Settlement in the 1950s

As might be expected, those who integrated most thoroughly into British society were the youngest of the refugees, like Ingrid Jacoby, who had arrived in Britain in 1939 aged only twelve. The first volume of her diaries, covering the early years of her life in Britain, has been discussed in Chapter 1. The second and third volumes cover the first post-war decade, beginning with her arrival in Oxford from Falmouth in autumn 1944 and ending in 1955, on the eve of her marriage and the birth of her first child.[13] Although she also moved in refugee circles in Oxford, Jacoby, growing up outside London, was confronted with a largely British social environment and perforce made the necessary adaptations to British everyday life. Her command of English, for example, was perfect. But as a child in Falmouth, with only her elder sister for family support, she had experienced the trauma of separation from her parents, the loneliness of emigration, and the isolation of the outsider. The death of her mother in the Holocaust, in particular, haunted her, recurring as a tragic motif in her diaries at the emotional low points in her life (III, 154). The two volumes, around four hundred pages each in length, give a detailed and perceptive picture of life in Oxford in the post-war years, as seen from the perspective of a teenage girl growing into a young woman; the insight that the diaries afford into the author's emotional and personal development, as she matures into independent adulthood, is one of their greatest qualities. They also record, sometimes very frankly, the turbulent course of Jacoby's love life; only when she met her future husband, a non-Jewish Pole called Stanislaw (Stan) Joseph (formerly Tkaczyk) did she find the happiness and stability that she craved.

Jacoby was first found lodgings by her father's cousin, the art historian Bruno Fürst, in the home of a refugee, Dr Beschorner, and his English wife. But when the Beschorners' marriage broke up, she moved to north Oxford, then home to a substantial refugee community that included both academics (like Mrs Labowsky, her next landlady, who had translated Dante in her younger years and whose daughter Lotte held a Research Fellowship at Somerville College)[14] and those with no connection to the University (like her following landlady, Miss Wulf, or her fellow tenant, the elderly Miss Lorch). Jacoby lived from March 1945 at 47 Lonsdale Road with Mrs Labowsky, then from December 1948 at 23 Lathbury Road, subletting from Miss Wulf, and from December 1951 in a flat on Kingston Road that she shared with her sister Lieselotte. Her sister had previously lived in Park Town, in the house of the distinguished biochemical pharmacologist Hermann (Hugh) Blaschko, and then in cheaper accommodation on Plantation Road. All these addresses were in the small area of north Oxford favoured by refugees, both for its academic connections and for its relative cheapness.

FIG. 4.1. Eric Doitch, *The Old Underground Station*.
Courtesy of Käthe Deutsch and the Ben Uri Gallery.

Her father had sent Jacoby to Oxford to take a secretarial course, but she soon abandoned that and found a job at Oxford City Library, where working with books proved to be more to her liking. After a spell working at Wolsey Hall correspondence college, she found a position in October 1947 with one of Oxford's best-known academic bookshops, Parkers', where she worked in the foreign department. Her ascent in the field of academic and specialist books reached its high point in January 1950, when she was engaged by the renowned firm of antiquarian booksellers A. Rosenthal Ltd., whose premises were at 5 Turl Street. She secured this position thanks to her connection with Mrs Wawerka, a Viennese who ran a typing agency; when Jacoby worked there, supplementing her weekly wage, it was not unusual for academics like the philosopher Karl Popper to bring in their manuscripts (II, 249–50).

Jacoby encountered a British environment in Oxford from the outset. Her fellow lodgers at the Beschorners' were two British girls with whom she became friendly, while her colleagues at Oxford City Library, who included the poet Elizabeth Jennings, were all British; she soon befriended her fellow junior library assistant Margaret 'Sandy' Sanders, who became part of her social life. One of her fellow lodgers, Prue Dixon, invited her to spend Easter 1945 with her family in Wiltshire, where the warmth of her reception moved her to tears: 'I will never be able to repay them for this wonderful weekend' (II, 42). Jacoby was attracted by the Englishness of her hosts: 'The family [...] sitting in front of an open fire with cups of tea at their elbows were as though cut out of a magazine to represent a typical English family' (II, 41). Her diaries continue to record her meetings with Prue Dixon, then with the other young English female friends that she made as neighbours, through work, through her baby-sitting, and through introductions; with these friends she shared lunches, visits to the cinema, and invitations to tea, building up a substantial network of acquaintanceship across north Oxford. She prided herself on mastering the intricacies of British social life and customs, like making tea correctly or striking the right level of small talk; she also became wedded to the radio programmes of the BBC. The entries in her diary often record an intensive round of social activities broadly typical of young women in Britain during the post-war years:[15] meetings in popular teahouses and cafés like Lyons, Fuller's, and the Cadena, or visits to the theatre to enjoy shows, like a dramatized version of the humorous history of Britain *1066 and All That* at the Playhouse (II, 380).

Yet Jacoby clearly did not integrate seamlessly into British life in Oxford. She frequently complained of acute loneliness and a sense of life unfulfilled, both closely related to her awareness of her status as a refugee and outsider. Even in her leisure activities, she differentiated herself from the ordinary run of young English women: her taste was for serious theatre (within a few weeks of her arrival in Oxford, she was seeing Shaw's *Candida*; II, 16–17), classical music (both on the Third Programme and at public concerts), and foreign art films (like *Les Enfants du Paradis* and *Bicycle Thieves*). In her daily life, she frequently encountered Mrs Labowsky's friends — Mrs Guttmann (wife of the spinal injury specialist Ludwig Guttmann) and Mrs Cosman (mother of the artist Milein Cosman, later to marry the music critic Hans

Keller), as well as Mrs von Hofmannsthal (widow of the Austrian writer Hugo von Hofmannsthal).

Through Bruno Fürst, through her work at Parkers', where the foreign department was largely staffed by Viennese refugees, and still more at A. Rosenthal Ltd., where she became close to Albi Rosenthal himself and to his associate Maurice Ettinghausen,[16] she came into contact with numerous distinguished refugee academics: the musicologist Egon Wellesz, the art historians Nikolaus Pevsner and Otto Pächt, as well as Rudolf Wittkower's son Mario. Those she met socially ranged from the Oriental Studies specialist Benedikt Isserlin to the young Peter Zadek, later one of Germany's greatest theatre directors. She was introduced to Yehudi Menuhin at A. Rosenthal Ltd. and even acted as temporary secretary for Isaiah Berlin. Two of her closest friends, both independent-minded intellectuals, typified the difference between her and her English peers: Fiammetta Olschki, granddaughter of the founder of a celebrated Florentine antiquarian bookshop, who invited her to spend a fortnight in Florence in August 1951, and Erica Spender, sister-in-law of the writer Stephen Spender, whose flamboyant lifestyle seemed designed to flout every social norm and convention.

These cultural differences that set Jacoby apart from her English peers reflected a deeper, more painful conflict in her sense of identity. Jacoby was powerfully drawn to British life and values, which she admired and sought to emulate in her own life. But at the same time she was profoundly aware that her status as a foreigner and refugee designated her as an outsider in British society. Conscious of her origins in Vienna, she was not willing simply to abandon that part of her identity, even had that been possible. The internal conflict between these two aspects of her identity is encapsulated in two contrasting diary entries. In the first, on 15 October 1944, she confided to her diary her anger at the authoritarian behaviour of her refugee landlord, Dr Beschorner, which prompted a wholesale rejection of her refugee identity:

> I thought to myself, 'He's only a refugee, like me. Why should I do what he says?' The Nazis threw him out of his country as they did me and my family and my friends. As far as the British are concerned he's no better than me. I despise him for his typical Continental character. 'How I should hate to be Continental,' I said to myself. Now you're staring. You can't believe you heard me right, can you? I come from Vienna, you say, and yet I don't consider myself Continental? Quite right. I'm British — British in spirit and behaviour. I speak their language perfectly and I love the British people. I no longer understand the Continental mentality and no longer identify with foreigners. I'm not their kind any more. (II, 11)

Yet only weeks after this impassioned embrace of Britain and the British, Jacoby experienced the full depth of her emotional commitment to her Viennese past. Invited to spend Christmas 1944 with the Urbachs, long-lost friends from Vienna, she was shocked to learn that their daughter, her childhood playmate, had forgotten their shared past:

> I wanted her to be a child again, a child in Vienna, my school-friend, romping and playing with me. I wanted to catch hold of her grown-up hair and uncurl

it and put it back into pigtails. I wanted to take her grown-up clothes off and dress her in her little girl's pleated skirt that I used to like. I wanted to squeeze her brain and crush out all her Englishness, her ideas poisoned by England. Poisoned? But England is my country — English is my language! But at that moment they were the murderers of my Viennese past. I longed for us all to be back in Vienna and that Hitler and the war had never happened. (II, 21–22)

Jacoby's sense of herself as the other, the outsider in British society was particularly marked at times of acute loneliness, as after her arrival in unfamiliar Oxford: 'I am so lonely! [...] Never in my life have I felt so much like the refugee I am; never before have I realised so clearly that I belong nowhere' (II, 9). Such outbursts became less frequent as she found her feet in Oxford, and were noticeably absent when she was absorbed in a relationship. Jacoby's admiration for the British, especially those from an upper-class background, was initially compounded by a sense of her own inferiority: she envied her friend Prue Dixon, who was 'not a Jewish refugee or a foreigner' and whose brother was 'the personification of an Englishman, with a nice sense of humour and a quiet reserved manner' as well as 'very upper class' (II, 12, 15). She was also gratified to be befriended by a colleague of Mrs Beschorner's, Daphne Hall, whom she described as 'enviably blonde and pretty and very upper class' (II, 25). But Jacoby gained in self-confidence as she established herself more securely in Oxford. By March 1947, it took an unexpected letter from a former Viennese friend to 'remind me with a jolt that I'm not really an English girl' (II, 186). She acquired British citizenship in October 1947.

Jacoby's identification of herself as British was reinforced by her alienation from Austria, which manifested itself on her first post-war return visit in July 1950. Yet she retained her love of the Viennese accent, atmosphere and cultured conversation that she encountered in refugee households in Oxford (III, 162). Contact with foreigners made Jacoby conscious of the extent to which she had, almost unnoticed, assumed a British identity and identified with Britain. She instinctively sprang to the country's defence: 'I feel very English with Fiammetta [Olschki], who often criticises English institutions and customs' (III, 76). During her visit to Florence, she felt uncomfortable, remarking that 'from this distance, I seemed to belong [to England] much more than I actually do when I am there' (III, 129). She even told an Italian admirer that her name was Jane, re-inventing herself as typically British and remarking: 'I may not be a real English girl in England but I've got to be one everywhere else' (III, 131).

By August 1952, the passage of time and the self-confidence that came with maturity had caused her to assume almost automatically that she was British. It came as a shock to her when, waiting for a bus on Banbury Road, an undergraduate suddenly asked her: '"You're not English, are you?" It felt as if an arrow had pierced me. My first instinct was to exclaim: "Of course I am!" Didn't I have naturalisation papers and a British Passport to prove it?'. It turned out that the student had merely intended his remark as a compliment to an attractive young woman: '"You're too pretty to be English," he said. I would rather he had said, "You're too English to be pretty!"'. Jacoby's assumption of her British identity, which she now valued and lived by, had been challenged (III, 251). But in the same diary entry she records a very different experience that confirmed her in her British identity. When her friend Sara Mostyn was castigated by her 'distinguished' grandmother for visiting a pub with a working-class man, Jacoby noted with satisfaction that she, a foreigner, was not classed as socially undesirable: 'Yet I, despite my so very different origins from hers, was fully accepted. I felt totally English and couldn't imagine that anyone would ever think of me in any other way' (III, 251, 252).

Jacoby's development of an identity of her own as she grew into adulthood in Britain was complicated by her difficult relationship to her Jewish origins and past. Coming from an assimilated family that had cut most of its ties to Judaism, she had little difficulty in adapting to the secularized Anglican environment of the Britain in which she lived. She had already converted to Christianity in Falmouth and went quite frequently to Christian services of worship in Oxford, especially at St Aldate's Church, where she arranged the baptism of her cousin Herta; she also acted as godmother to her friend Joan Beschorner's daughter, a practice unknown in Judaism. Significantly, she was always aware of the Christian religious festivals, but not of the Jewish ones; in consequence, she was on occasion irritated by the observance at A. Rosenthal Ltd. of Jewish holidays that she had not expected. She was also surprised by the practice of stopping work on Fridays in time for the Sabbath (II, 371). Jacoby frequently paraded her ignorance of Jewish religious practices, as if deliberately distancing herself from them. At a 'Jewish supper' she 'felt like a fish out of water' (II, 379), and on another occasion she confused circumcision with christening, amazing Mrs Ettinghausen by asking why the birth of a baby girl should spare the family the need for circumcision (III, 53–54).

Beneath this determination to keep her distance from everything Jewish lay deeper and more painful feelings of 'shame and inferiority' (II, 379) that Jacoby seldom allowed to intrude into her everyday life. As late as April 1953, she confessed that she had never discussed the fact that she was Jewish with her future husband: 'My embarrassment at being Jewish, even with S. [Stan], is something I can't conquer' (III, 307). It was for that reason that she was uncomfortable with Jews who were consciously Jewish, in particular orthodox Jews like the family in Portsmouth that had taken in her friend Ruth (II, 252), or with refugees who were all too obviously German Jews, like her friend Ilse Rosendorf (II, 44) — the term 'German' in this case extends to cover Jews from Vienna. Jacoby was easily disconcerted by displays of behaviour that flouted the conventions of courtesy governing British public etiquette, especially when they conformed to the stereotype of the Jewish refugee, as in her reaction to a 'pushy woman' who tried to jump the queue for a lift on Banbury Road: 'I could tell from her appearance and her accent that she was a Jewish refugee and I felt ashamed for her, and at the same time triumphant because I could never be like that' (II, 183). The shame that Jacoby felt was arguably shame for her own Jewishness projected onto an external object, while her sense of triumph at her own behaviour reflected both her determination to assume a British identity and an underlying anxiety that it might yet be disrupted by her Jewishness.

Jacoby's feelings about being Jewish probably owed more to her father than to any hostility or discrimination that she experienced in Britain. Her father's views can fairly be classed as Jewish self-hatred, as in his remarks on a group of elderly refugees from London sunning themselves in a garden in Surrey:

> 'Look at these people,' he said to me in a confidential tone. 'Aren't they ugly? What an ugly race we Jews are.' I had to agree. Centuries of suffering and being downtrodden must leave their mark, I suppose. In that brief moment my father and I were united in a longing not to belong to this race, to belong to the glamorous Anglo-Saxon one instead, in whose handsome features there is carved their age-old superiority. (II, 128)

Jacoby herself rarely gave vent to such comments. She was, however, well aware of the widespread suspicion and hostility towards foreigners in British society; that did not greatly affect her in her daily life, since she was well integrated, broadly accepted, and could pass as British. One of the friends for whom she babysat, Ted Hayes, had developed attitudes of racial superiority during his service abroad with the RAF. This casual, unthinking racism came out when Hayes called a wartime acquaintance 'black as this grate' and claimed that Jews were also 'inferior to us'; Jacoby, fearful of admitting her Jewish birth and compromising the friendship, did not argue (II, 282–83).

The only other instance of anti-Semitism recorded by Jacoby occurred when she was house-hunting in June 1954 and encountered an unnamed man who compared Jews to gypsies as transients (III, 348). But this isolated incident was far outweighed by the ease and contentment with which she settled with her future husband into their home in Bedford Street, off Iffley Road near the River Thames, adopting a pattern of life barely distinguishable from that of their neighbours. By this time, Jacoby had succeeded in constructing an identity for herself, asserting her autonomy and assuming agency in her own life; although conscious of her Viennese and Jewish origins, she would not allow the prejudices of others to dictate the terms of her relationship to her past or her present life.

A very different approach to the recording of the refugee experience in post-war Britain is to be found in *Basic British*, Victor Ross's humorous account of the problems and pleasures of integration into British society.[17] An example of the sub-genre of texts that gently ironize both refugees and native British in their attempts at mutual (mis)understanding, *Basic British* follows in the tradition of the Hungarian George Mikes's bestselling comic study *How to Be an Alien* (1946). Victor Ross (Rosenfeld) was born in Vienna in 1919, into a highly cultured Jewish family that numbered Sigmund Freud among its acquaintanceship. Arriving in Britain as a very young man, he was interned in 1940 and deported to Canada, before joining the Pioneer Corps and then the regular British forces, experiences that are humorously recreated in *Basic British*. After the war, Ross rose to become chairman of *Reader's Digest* in the United Kingdom and a witty and accomplished writer. The humorous effects in *Basic British* derive principally from the interplay between the fictionalized Ross as first-person narrator and his Uncle Bertie in their earnest but ill-conceived attempts to reconstruct themselves in the image of their British hosts, a goal rendered the more unattainable by the rapidly changing nature of British society in the 1950s.

Ross sets out his vision of the integration of the refugees and its limits with considerable comic verve in his prologue:

> This is the story of an arduous apprenticeship in the art of being British. It has extended over the past nineteen years, and now it is high time to report progress. The Britisher in me is threatening to gain the upper hand, although, like Achilles pursuing his tortoise, he will never quite make it. The gap gets smaller and smaller, but it will never close.

Being neither English, Welsh, Scottish, or Irish, Ross claims that he is '*quintessentially* British', but only as an 'elusive abstraction' (7); as numerous refugees have pointed out, it is possible for a foreigner to become British, by naturalization or sheer length of residence, but never English; one can only be English by birth. The barriers to full integration are the result both of British attitudes, customs, and practices and of those apparently ineradicable features and characteristics that set the refugees apart from their hosts. However, whereas there are many refugees 'who are doing their damnedest to embrace the British way of life', the reaction of the British is cooler: 'the embrace is not always returned with the same ardour by the other side'. Ross, a British citizen resident in Britain for nearly twenty years, can advance the self-ironizing paradox: 'today, unless you saw me or heard me speak, you would never guess that I am not a native' (8). He is at once British and, in his appearance and speech, foreign. Even when he believes himself to have mastered the delivery of English, he cannot pass as an Englishman; a lady declares that she knew at once that he was a foreigner because he spoke English too well (12). Try as he may, he cannot escape his foreign condition.

The prologue provides a telling example of the misunderstandings that divide the refugees from the British, despite their admiration for Britain and their pronounced willingness to conform to British practices. Ross recounts the story, telling though probably apocryphal, of a refugee of liberal persuasion who is impressed by the 'No Smoking' notices on British trains; as *Smoking* means 'dinner jacket' in German, he takes this as the democratic reservation of certain carriages for those sections of society too poor to afford evening dress. Much of the book's humour derives from Uncle Bertie's self-defeating efforts to prove his integration into British society by using English idioms: he states, for example, that he is only 'a drip in the ocean' (106), that he would like to own a cat or 'perhaps a tiny doggerel' (22), or that a lady who could not bear children was 'unbearable', then 'inconceivable', and finally 'impregnable' (16). But, as Ross recognizes, the problems posed to the foreigner by the English language extend beyond the narrowly linguistic into the field of social conventions familiar only to the insider brought up and educated in Britain. He advances something approaching a semiotic theory of language, positing a gulf between English words and their actual meaning in a given social situation:

> English is in fact an elaborate code masquerading as a language, bearing superficial resemblance to a language in that it uses words used by other languages, but in such a way that their ostensible meaning is no guide to what they really signify. (14)

This transformation of language into a subtly encoded network of social conventions is in large measure responsible for the failure of the refugees to grasp the inner workings of British society.

Basic British consists of chapters that depict key stages in the narrator's life in emigration, such as his internment, his service in the Pioneer Corps, and his naturalization, and chapters that describe certain aspects of British life which, gently ironized, epitomize the division between the refugees and the British. Chapter 3, which is devoted to the widespread suspicion of intellectuals in Britain and the concomitant cult of the amateur, is entitled 'If you're bright keep it dark' (27–39), while Chapter 6, 'A Ross by any other name', details the vain efforts of the refugees in the Pioneer Corps to select names that convincingly support their bearers' aspiration to be viewed as English (61–68). In some respects, life in Britain defies comprehension by the refugees, as in the case of food: 'The British cuisine has not reached its present state overnight. A thing like that needs planning and years of practice. The conversion of harmless ingredients into what is known as plain English fare is no hit-and-miss affair' (17–18). In other areas, the refugees have successfully infiltrated British society, as when one of the foreign-born experts designing the Festival of Britain appeals to his feuding colleagues: 'If we must quarrel about the British way of life, at least let us do so in Hungarian!' (105). Ultimately, however, the refugees' attempts at assimilation founder on the changes taking place in British society, which is increasingly Americanized and consumer-oriented. As a naturalized Briton, Ross feels proudly superior to any foreigner — 'After all, the poor devil can't help it' — but in the company of his British neighbours and British-born children, 'the full flowering of my patriotic fervour' is hampered by his consciousness of his own inalienably Continental origins (119).

The years between 1945 and 1960 represented a decisive stage in the development of the community of Jewish refugees from Nazism in Britain, forming, as it were, the bridge between their turbulent early years in Britain and the long period of mostly settled residence that followed. These years were marked by a process of adaptation to material conditions in Britain, but also by the gradual development of a new sense of identity in response to changed social conditions; at the same time, the refugees preserved parts of the social culture, predispositions, and attitudes acquired before emigration; as in many other areas, the degree to which these elements were combined varied widely, especially according to age on arrival in Britain. Although this period was by no means without difficulties for them, it was arguably then that the 'new British citizens' were able to consolidate their sense of emotional and psychological settlement into a more self-confident, re-empowered relationship to British society.[18]

Notes to Chapter 4

1. On the issues of repatriation and naturalization, see Grenville, *Jewish Refugees from Germany and Austria*, pp. 52–76.
2. The phrase supplied the title for the memoirs of Carl F. Flesch, *'Where Do You Come From?': Hitler Refugees in Great Britain Then and Now: The Happy Compromise* (London: Pen Press Publishers, 2001). Flesch, son of the famous violinist Carl Flesch, was born in 1910, arrived in Britain in 1934, and was still being asked where he came from over sixty years later. For Flesch,

this was part of a process of integration that had been for the most part successful, but where he retained, for better or worse, the last vestiges of a past Continental lifestyle and identity.

3. Hermann Sinsheimer and Christobel Sinsheimer, *Briefe aus England in die Pfalz*, ed. by Hans-Helmut Görtz, Gabriele Giersberg, and Erik Giersberg (Neustadt an der Weinstraße: Selbstverlag der Stiftung zur Förderung der pfälzischen Geschichtsforschung, 2012). On Sinsheimer, see Deborah Vietor-Engländer, 'Hermann Sinsheimers deutsch-jüdisches Schicksal', in *Zwischen Rassenhass und Identitätssuche: Deutsch-jüdische literarische Kultur im nationalsozialistischen Deutschland*, ed. by Kerstin Schoor (Göttingen: Wallstein, 2010), pp. 285–303.

4. Hermann Sinsheimer, *Shylock: The History of a Character; or, the Myth of the Jew* (London: Gollancz, 1947); published in full as *Shylock: Die Geschichte einer Figur* (Munich: Ner Tamid Verlag, 1960).

5. On the contribution of the German-speaking refugees to re-education, see Anthony Grenville, 'German-Jewish Refugees in the British Forces and the Re-Education of German Prisoners of War in Britain: The Case of Herbert Sulzbach', *Angermion*, 2 (2009), 143–57.

6. It was with good reason that his wife's young niece, unable to pronounce his German name, called him 'Dr. Sunshine' (217).

7. The title of Sinsheimer's memoirs, *Gelebt im Paradies: Gestalten und Geschichten* (Berlin: Verlag für Berlin-Brandenburg, 2013; original publication Munich: Pflaum, 1953), translates as 'Dwelt in Paradise'.

8. Fritz Ruhemann, 'Vorfrühling in Swiss Cottage', *AJR Information*, August 1953, p. 5.

9. Kenneth Ambrose, 'The Second Generation', *AJR Information*, February 1949, p. 5, and July 1949, p. 3.

10. Kenneth Ambrose, 'Your Newspaper', AJR Information, January 1950, p. 3.

11. Kenneth Ambrose, 'Struwwelpeter', *AJR Information*, February 1954, p. 8.

12. Kenneth Ambrose, 'The Best of Both Worlds', *AJR Information*, June 1960, p. 11.

13. Jacoby, II: *The Girl in and out of Love, Oxford 1944–1950* (2006), and III: *The Girl in and out of Love, Oxford 1950–1955* (2009).

14. See Regina Weber, *Lotte Labowsky (1905–1991): Schülerin Aby Warburgs, Kollegin Raymond Klibanskys: Eine Wissenschaftlerin zwischen Fremd- und Selbstbestimmung im englischen Exil* (Berlin: Reimer, 2012). This contains a brief description of the house where Mrs Labowsky let out rooms after her husband's death (92). Jacoby's rent was 35 shillings a week (£1.75), including breakfast and Sunday lunch.

15. For examples of Jacoby's social life, see the entries for 24 March 1945 (II, 37–38) or 11 February 1951 (III, 43).

16. Rosenthal's son Julian, whom Jacoby describes as a young boy, became the sports presenter Jim Rosenthal.

17. Victor Ross, *Basic British* (London: Parrish, 1956).

18. See *Britain's New Citizens: The Story of the Refugees from Germany and Austria: Tenth Anniversary Publication of the Association of Jewish Refugees in Great Britain* (London: Association of Jewish Refugees, 1951).

CHAPTER 5

Established Refugee Writers

As a destination for writers fleeing Nazism, the United States took pride of place, receiving a host of distinguished figures that included Thomas and Heinrich Mann, Bertolt Brecht, Alfred Döblin, Hermann Broch, Lion Feuchtwanger, Franz Werfel, and Erich Maria Remarque. Britain could not compare with the United States in this respect, but there were a number of noted writers who, having established themselves before 1933, left Germany or, later, Austria, and found refuge in Britain; the writers to be discussed here, including the artist-turned-writer Fred Uhlman, arrived in Britain as adults, unlike those to be discussed in the following chapter, who arrived as children. Such refugee writers, as already noted in the cases of Stefan Zweig and Alfred Kerr in Chapter 1, were dependent on the medium of the German language, in which they wrote and in which their works were read. They accordingly faced particular difficulties in adapting to the British market, where they were unknown when they arrived. This chapter charts the course of their attempts to confront these obstacles. Some of them never made the transition to publishing in English at all; others wrote and published successfully in English. The issue of language was related to the wider issues of their identity in emigration and their conception of their place in the society of their host country. Some resolved these problems by returning to Europe; others opted to settle in Britain. Although almost all of them are known as writers of fiction, the texts discussed here are all autobiographical or, in the case of Gabriele Tergit, based on close observation of the refugee environment in north-west London.

Writers Who Left Britain for Europe after 1945

Among the best known of the German-speaking writers who emigrated to Britain after 1933 was Hilde Spiel. Born in Vienna in 1911, Spiel came to Britain in 1936 to join her future husband, the German writer Peter de Mendelssohn; although she wished to escape from the authoritarian regime in Austria that had bloodily suppressed the Social Democratic Party in February 1934, she would probably have preferred France to Britain as a country of refuge. Spiel's ambiguous attitude to Britain, her sense of being torn between London and Vienna, is expressed in the title of the volume of her memoirs covering the years 1946–89, *Welche Welt ist meine Welt?* [Which World Is My World?];[1] the title of the volume covering the years 1911–46, *Die hellen und die finsteren Zeiten* [The Light and the Dark Times],[2] also points to a life sharply divided.³ Spiel stayed in Britain until early 1946, when she returned to Austria, the first of three periods she spent in Europe in the immediate post-war years, the longest being her stay in Berlin, where her husband had secured an important position with the British occupying forces; from 1948, she lived for fifteen years in the London suburb of Wimbledon, before returning permanently to Vienna in 1963. There she became one of the city's leading literary figures, renowned both as a writer and a journalist.

In the early chapters of *Die hellen und die finsteren Zeiten*, Spiel fashions a narrative from her early life that prepares the way for her later decision to return permanently to Vienna, despite the events of the Nazi years in Austria. She was born into a Jewish family, albeit one that had, as she emphasizes, previously converted to Catholicism; as a child, she was not even aware of her Jewish ancestry. She repeatedly stresses the extent of her family's assimilation into non-Jewish Austrian society, citing her father's membership of a student duelling fraternity and his easy assumption of a wartime commission in the Austro-Hungarian army, neither of which were institutions that welcomed Jews (27). She also relates proudly that her maternal great-uncle, a pillar of the established order, had been a professor of medicine and personal physician to a Habsburg archduke and Ignaz Seipel, the Catholic prelate and leader of the (anti-Semitic) Christian Social Party that governed Austria for much of the interwar period (19). Her abandonment of Jewish practices, religion, and identity plainly facilitated her reintegration into Austrian society after her return in 1963.

Spiel was educated at the renowned progressive Schwarzwaldschule and then studied philosophy at the University of Vienna. A highly gifted and ambitious young woman, she set out on a literary career and, already in her early twenties, was publishing and making a wide range of connections within Vienna's literary establishment. However, she felt it impossible on moral and political grounds to stay in Vienna under the *Ständestaat* (corporate state) of the 1930s. Spiel's decision to emigrate was thus at least partly an act of voluntary self-exile. She never experienced the full force of Nazi persecution after 1938 and did not witness the depths to which her Viennese fellow citizens sank. In later years, she adopted a notably complaisant attitude to the anti-Semitism that had tainted Austria under the Nazis, mixing with right-wing figures severely compromised by their past and making little mention in her memoirs of the anti-Semitism that was still widespread in Austria in the 1960s and 1970s; she claimed not to have become aware of it until the Waldheim Affair brought it out into the open in the 1980s.

Arguably, Spiel never truly perceived herself as a Jewish refugee, since she had fled from the Schuschnigg regime for political, not racial reasons. She also preserved a sense of distance from the racially persecuted refugees from Austria who fled the Nazis after March 1938; few of them would have shared her view that the brief Austrian civil war of February 1934 represented 'einen härteren Einschnitt' [a sharper break] than the *Anschluss* (102). Her attachment to her homeland, despite its record of fascism and anti-Semitism, influenced her attitude to Britain, leading her to dwell on the less happy aspects of her experiences as a refugee and thus helping to justify her eventual choice of Vienna in preference to London. When she first arrived in Newhaven in late 1936, seasick after the stormy crossing and feeling that Britain was separated from the Continent by a gulf wider than the Atlantic Ocean, she was greeted by irksome immigration procedures, then by Peter de Mendelssohn with the collar of his trench coat turned up against the elements.

The couple settled in a cheap, cramped rented flat at 59 Linden Gardens, near Notting Hill Gate. Spiel's description of her first months in London contains numerous features common to accounts of the city by bewildered, disorientated refugees: the rain and fog, the damp cold that penetrated through every crack and fissure into their flat, the gas meter that devoured the coins paying for the inadequate heating, the unfamiliar and inedible food, and the linguistic divide that hindered communication with the British. They were so poor, Spiel recounts, that they only survived by living on credit from a nearby branch of the Express Dairy. But from surviving on chance pieces of work that came their way, they gradually established a foothold in the literary and journalistic world of London; together with the money de Mendelssohn earned by working for Prince Hubertus zu Löwenstein's American Guild for German Cultural Freedom, this enabled them to move to better accommodation at Broadwalk Court, Palace Gardens Road, Kensington. At first, the couple were overawed by the size and the aura of power of imperial London. To belong to British society, to which they looked up with some admiration, was 'ein beglückender, ja erhebender Gedanke' [a gratifying, indeed an elevating thought] (151), even though their regular visits to Bow Street Police Station to renew their residence permits reminded them that they were in Britain only on sufferance.

Spiel embarked on the long and complex process of her initiation into British society and its way of life. She set about overcoming the language barrier by reading widely in English, learning to admire the succinctness, wit, and clarity of British essayists, which was greatly to assist her in her efforts to become an English-language writer. Her external adaptation to life in London proceeded relatively smoothly, but she found the process of familiarizing herself with the unspoken codes and rituals of English society more difficult, intangible and elusive as they were. Spiel was principally attracted to the educated, highly cultivated, liberal or left-leaning stratum of the British upper middle class, which she had already encountered in Vienna in figures like Hugh Gaitskell, future leader of the Labour Party, and Elwyn Jones, future Lord Chancellor. Much as she complained about her status as an outsider in Britain, she was in reality exceptionally fortunate in the contacts she made. Through D. N. Pritt, a leading left-wing Labour MP and barrister, she met important figures like the scientist J. B. S Haldane and his sister Naomi Mitchison, while at the PEN Club she met a variety of leading literary figures, becoming very friendly with Henrietta Leslie, PEN's wealthy patron.

As well as an enviable network of literary and journalistic acquaintances, she also had contacts with the British upper class, including her close friend Dorothy ('Dodo', no surname given), who introduced her to the manners and conduct of that class; within months of arriving in Britain, she records being invited for dinner on Tite Street, a highly desirable address in Chelsea, by hosts of impeccable social pedigree (157–58). But much as she appreciated the consideration shown her, on occasions when she committed a social faux pas, she sensed in it an element of condescension, deriving from the assumption of the innate superiority of the British to mere foreigners, from whom nothing better was to be expected. That feeling of being relegated to a subtly inferior status, that resentment at never fully being recognized as an equal, helped to fuel Spiel's later decision to leave Britain for Austria. Even before the war, she was evidently willing to make allowances for Austrians that she was unwilling to grant to the British: she records that she almost fainted with shock on seeing British Mosleyites demonstrating at Piccadilly Circus (175), but when describing her visit to Vienna in December 1938 she passes over the vastly more threatening presence of Austrian Nazis.

The outbreak of war changed Spiel's situation abruptly. She and de Mendelssohn had moved to Winchester Court on Kensington Church Street, a location that she loved, but after war broke out, when she was in hospital for the birth of their daughter, he moved the family home to Wimbledon, in the hope, vain as it transpired, of avoiding air raids. Spiel never forgave him, as she never ceased to compare suburban Wimbledon unfavourably with Kensington. The war also affected the situation of her parents, who had followed her to Britain. Her father was interned, then forced to undertake manual jobs to earn a meagre living. When he died of a heart attack, brought on by jumping into a cold bath on a hot day, she wrote that he had been killed by emigration, as surely as if he had been deported to a concentration camp, if more slowly and less brutally (205). But the war also transformed Spiel's feelings towards the British. Like most refugees, she greatly admired the calmness and resilience with which the civilian population withstood the nightly air raids. Buoyed up by the phlegmatic courage of the British, she was able to control her fear, drawing comfort from the radio programmes of the BBC, be it the sonorous tones of the newsreaders or the popular humour of *ITMA* (*It's That Man Again*), and joining in 'our' national anthem at the end of a cinema performance as the images of the royal family appeared on the screen. She grew confident that 'mit diesem Volk und seinem humanen Herrscherhaus könne man nicht untergehen' [with this people and its humane monarchy one could not go under] (197).

Spiel fell prey to sharply conflicting feelings towards Britain. On the one hand, she felt an instinctive sense of solidarity with the British people at war, having shared in their hardships (including the bombing of her house in Wimbledon in February 1944) and identified with their triumphs. She saw Britain as the home of democracy and admired its tolerance, openness, and humanity. She was also keen to establish herself as an English-language writer: her novel *Flute and Drums* was published as early as 1939, and by 1945 she was writing for such prestigious publications as the *New Statesman* and Cyril Connolly's *Horizon*. By the end of the war, she had spent the greater part of her adult life in Britain, her two children had been born there, and she had grown accustomed to life in London. Yet she also missed Vienna, on occasion admitting to a longing to return to Austria (194) — though she reacted very sharply when British people suggested that she might act on that feeling, assuming that they were yet again relegating her to the inferior status of foreigner and outsider. She never came to terms with life in Wimbledon, regarding it as 'groß- und spießbürgerlich' [wealthy and philistine] (187), a suburb where relations with her neighbours remained polite but distant. She also complained repeatedly that in Wimbledon she was cut off from the community of refugees from Nazism.

At the end of the war, Spiel participated in the victory celebrations on VE Day with wholehearted enthusiasm, joining the crowds that surged through London's West End and singing 'For He's a Jolly Good Fellow' when Winston Churchill appeared on the balcony at Buckingham Palace: 'Nie zuvor, nie nachher ein solcher kollektiver Glücksrausch! Nie wieder eine solche Gewißheit, hier und nirgends anders beheimatet zu sein' [Never before, never afterwards such a collective wave of happiness! Never again such certainty that our home was here and nowhere else] (203). But that heartfelt solidarity with the British people ebbed away. Three months later, in August 1945, when news came of the dropping of the atomic bomb on Japan, Spiel and de Mendelssohn were staying with Kingsley Martin, editor of the *New Statesman*, at his cottage in Essex. Martin commented that the war was now over, adding that his guests would surely return to their own country. That casual remark, which Spiel found devastating (207), confirmed her in her conviction that the British had never fully accepted them: 'Da wußten wir, und gestanden's uns doch nicht ein: neun Jahre der Einfügung in die englische Welt waren vergeblich gewesen' [Then we knew, even if we didn't admit it to ourselves: nine years of adapting to the English world had been in vain] (206). An invitation to stay with one of the great figures of British journalism was, apparently, insufficient proof of Spiel's acceptance into the British literary establishment.

The following chapter, entitled 'Der Sprung ins Festland' [The Leap onto the Mainland], opens with the anguished question 'Aber wohin gehörten wir?' [But where did we belong?] (207); this gives expression to the crisis of identity that had remained latent during the war, when Spiel had no doubt that she belonged in Britain, but been reactivated at the war's end, when it became possible for refugees to return to their homelands. Spiel's eagerness to follow her husband back to Europe, where historic decisions were being taken and the cultural world remade, caused her to become increasingly impatient to leave Britain. That feeling came to a head when her friend Dodo commented with mild scorn on the appearance at the Junior Carlton Club of another refugee, Peter Smollett (Smolka), wearing spats. These remarks infuriated Spiel, who saw in them further proof that behind their backs the British dismissively labelled all foreigners as 'Dagos' or 'Jerries'. She had, she states, hoped for 'eine gnädigere Akzeptanz' [a more gracious acceptance], but now she feared that the friendships that she had made, her familiarity with British intellectual life, and her contacts with the literary world all counted for nothing (121).

Spiel was consequently delighted when in January 1946 she was sent to Vienna as an accredited correspondent for the *New Statesman*, the first of three periods that she spent in Europe in the immediate post-war years. She perceived it as an escape from the narrow confines of insular Britain, yet, ironically, as a British journalist abroad, she spent much of that time among the army officers and civilian administrators of the British occupying forces in Austria and Germany. Here she could mix with the cultivated, liberal members of the upper class, like the academics Noel Annan and Michael Balfour, who had been her preferred social milieu in Britain: 'Alle haben vortreffliche Manieren und die erleichterte Gelassenheit von Menschen, die eine übermenschliche Anstrengung hinter sich gebracht haben' [They all have perfect manners and the relaxed calm of people who have come through a superhuman exertion] (223), she commented approvingly.

In Vienna, she was prey to 'den widersprüchlichsten Gefühlen' [the most contradictory feelings] (224) about a homecoming to a city to which she no longer fully belonged. Yet the principal divide of which she was conscious was not that between the Jewish victims of Nazi persecution and the Austrians who had perpetrated or acquiesced in it, but that between the vanquished Austrians and the Allied victors, to whom she perforce belonged. During her time in Berlin, Spiel declared herself unwilling to settle in Germany, on account of its people's support for Nazism and complicity in the Holocaust. This stands in sharp contrast to the absence of any such reflections on Austrian anti-Semitism, which was arguably more virulent and widespread; after Spiel bought a property in St. Wolfgang in the Salzkammergut in the 1950s, a prelude to her permanent return to Austria, her willingness to exonerate her fellow countrymen became yet more pronounced. That did not apply to Britain, however; Spiel refers frequently to the pre-war activities of Mosley's fascists, to their links to the British upper classes through such figures as Diana and Unity Mitford, and to the emollient line towards Nazi Germany prevalent among the Cliveden Set. These tendencies form part of Spiel's negative representation of the British establishment.

In *Welche Welt ist meine Welt?*, Spiel portrays her return to London from Berlin in 1948 as the transition from one of the most exciting to one of the loneliest and most monotonous periods in her life (100). She recoiled from the prospect of life as a housewife, bounded by the daily routine of household chores, and also from the genteel boredom of life in suburban Wimbledon, which she stylized as 'ein grünes Grab' [a green grave] (102), remote both physically and in its well-to-do philistinism from the intellectual and social dynamic of central London. Yet Spiel found the atmosphere of Wimbledon hard to resist, with its characteristically English aroma of damp, fog, autumn leaves, and garden fires, and its well-behaved, well-intentioned inhabitants (105). For over a decade, Spiel states in a chapter entitled 'Die Qual der Wahl' [Hard Choices],[4] she was tormented by an inner uncertainty, a conflict of divided loyalties to two countries and ways of life (174). She was bound to Britain by affection, habit, and routine, and by the fact that her children, British-born and -educated, were growing up there. But by 1963, when they were independent and her marriage to de Mendelssohn was failing, Spiel opted for Austria. She continued to visit Britain, to see her daughter, and spent a year in London in 1982–83 as a cultural correspondent, fulfilling her ambition of living in Kensington, albeit with no sympathy for the politics and values of Margaret Thatcher's Britain.

Born in Vienna in 1897, Robert Neumann first came to Britain in summer

1933, to work on a book on the armaments magnate Basil Zaharoff. He returned as a refugee the following year, fleeing from the fighting that shook Austria in February 1934. He was to stay in Britain for almost twenty-five years, until he left for Locarno, Switzerland, in 1958. Neumann had established his reputation in Vienna before 1933 with two successful volumes of parodies. His ability to absorb and replicate patterns of language may well have contributed to the success that his prose works, including *The Inquest* (1944) and *Children of Vienna* (1946), enjoyed in Britain; he was exceptional among refugee writers in achieving success at this stage with works written in English.[5] But as his memoirs, *Ein leichtes Leben* [An Easy Life], show, he neither wanted nor was able to adapt fully to British conditions or to establish a settled life in Britain.[6] Divided into three parts, each named after one of the women in Neumann's life, *Ein leichtes Leben* is an unusual combination of autobiography, reminiscences, family history, travelogue, and portraits of writers and intellectuals,[7] all artfully welded into a coherent whole by Neumann's narrative skills. Those skills make the text entertaining, though ultimately the reader may tire of Neumann's tendency to fashion an amusing story out of every minor incident and to place himself centre-stage even when, as in his claim that Winston Churchill himself ordered his release from internment in 1940 (81–82), a degree of exaggeration is apparent.

In Neumann's memoirs, Britain becomes a mere setting, a skilfully crafted literary milieu designed to throw into sharper relief the actions, qualities, and insights of the author. The image of Britain remains static throughout the text, barely changing between 1934 and 1958 and relying on standard features like British food and the British weather. In his first chapter, 'Kein Ehebruch in Richmond' [No Adultery in Richmond], Neumann (who was married four times) derives considerable comic effect from his portrayal of British attitudes to sex, through his description of the lengths to which a family hotel in Richmond, in south-west London, goes to prevent couples indulging in sexual relations (13–15). British prudery also features prominently when Neumann moves to the village of Cranbrook in Kent, where he has to introduce his future third wife, much younger than himself, as his niece. But the very fact that he is living with her causes his housekeeper to give notice, while the local men forbid their womenfolk to work in his house (291); he imagines with glee the outrage caused by his installation of a bidet, the first, he claims, in Kent, and previously reserved for French women of dubious repute (234). This strand of the text concludes with his account, in the chapter 'Nie wieder Shakespeare' [Never Again Shakespeare], of a night spent with an English girl during which she insists on reading him Shakespeare's sonnets, to the exclusion of physical relations (335–38). Neumann repeatedly dwells on those features of British life that baffle refugees from Europe, from the ceremonial drinking of tea to the ubiquitous suspicion of foreigners, from the emphasis on character-building, rather than learning, in education to the conventions that govern the empty exchanges between members at a gentlemen's club (231–33).

Neumann depicts the conditions that the refugees from Central Europe encountered in Britain vividly and with compassion, as in the chapter devoted to the fate of the fictional Herr Marcus (46–50), who undergoes the misery and tedium of life in a furnished room in one of the boarding houses in north-west London where refugee residents could eke out an existence of penury and social exclusion. Neumann, who craved recognition, was particularly wounded by this refusal to acknowledge the refugees and by the systematic belittling of their gifts and achievements. As the refugees are ignored in life, so their deaths pass unnoticed in emigration. Neumann's mother lies in an unmarked grave in Ramsgate, far from Vienna and forgotten by all except her son (289), while his sister and brother-in-law, like a number of his acquaintances, are ground down and destroyed by life as refugees. In this respect, *Ein leichtes Leben* takes on some of the bitterness of Neumann's earlier depiction of Britain in 'Melvale, or, The Smile of the Sleepers', one of the stories that make up *By the Waters of Babylon*, in which aristocratic young men, educated at Oxford, parade their fascist sympathies and contempt for the lower orders.[8]

Even Neumann's account of his internment, which, as Richard Dove has demonstrated in his masterly analysis of Neumann's internment diary,[9] had a devastating impact on him, is in his memoirs recounted with sovereign irony and turned into a series of entertaining incidents. Although Neumann rails against the injustice of his internment — he had been placed in Category B at his tribunal hearing partly because he was not yet married to Rolly Becker, with whom he was living — and although he describes the internment camp on the Isle of Man as the British equivalent of a concentration camp, 'KZ auf Englisch' (76–82), the bitterness that Neumann felt on his and Rolly's account evaporates into comic stories. Examples include the purchasing of the barbed wire surrounding the camp by a group of orthodox Jews or the prolonging of a religious service to avoid deportation to Canada. Neumann depicts himself as taking control of the situation, dictating terms to the camp commandant and even securing his own release by means of a furious letter to the Prime Minister. Much of the later part of his memoirs, before his departure to Switzerland, is taken up with that staple of comic caricatures of England, the haunted house. Neumann's account of his old house in Cranbrook tantalizes the reader with the complexities of his efforts to arrive at the 'truth', if any, behind the property's ghostly past. It can also be understood as an indication of the author's increasing distance from the reality of Britain in the late 1950s, as he prepared to leave the country.

Writers Who Stayed in Britain after 1945

Elisabeth Castonier, née Borchardt, was born in Dresden in 1894; her father, half-Jewish, was the hugely wealthy son of a banker, while her mother was the daughter of a Russian aristocrat and an upper-class Englishwoman. She was brought up partly in Paris, where the family lived in luxury in a mansion near the Bois de Boulogne, and partly in Berlin, where they lived in an apartment on the Reichskanzlerplatz, in the same building as Richard Strauss. Castonier's father was an artist who mixed in artistic circles at the highest level: as a child in Paris, Castonier records meeting Rodin and being taken to visit Monet, at whose house she encountered Renoir and his wife. Although her background was thoroughly cosmopolitan and although she travelled widely, she never visited Britain and had no inclination to do so until sheer desperation forced her to seek refuge there in autumn 1938. By then, Castonier, who had rebelled against her privileged background and broken with her parents, had participated in the bohemian world of the artists and intellectuals in Schwabing, Munich, in the years after the end of World War I. There she met her husband, Paul Castonier, a Danish sailor turned opera singer; they married in 1923 but divorced several years later. In Berlin, Castonier built up a large network of literary friends and contacts, which included Theodor Wolff, Oscar Bie, Franz Blei, and Alfred Kerr; as she made her literary career as a journalist, reviewer, and independent author, she wrote for such noted editors as Wolff and Hermann Sinsheimer, and after 1933 for Georg Bernhard and Leopold Schwarzschild.

Castonier was forced to flee Germany in 1933 when Hitler's assumption of power put an end to her burgeoning literary career there. She settled first in Vienna, fleeing again in March 1938, after which she spent some six months in Italy, mostly in Positano on the Amalfi Coast. But when it became impossible for her to remain in Mussolini's Italy, she left for Britain, in part for the purely practical reason that she had deposited the remnant of her inheritance at a bank in the City of London. From this unpromising beginning, Castonier was to develop a deep and lasting relationship with Britain, where she lived for the rest of her life, and an affection for the English countryside; she lovingly portrayed Mill Farm in Froyle, Hampshire, where she lived and worked for ten years, and its inhabitants, human and animal, in *Mill Farm: Menschen und Tiere unter einem Dach* [Mill Farm: People and Animals under One Roof].[10] After her pampered, privileged childhood and her years as a progressive writer and journalist, Castonier spent most of the last thirty years of her life in close and happy communion with the English countryside, finding fulfilment in her work as a farm labourer, which she maintained until she was sixty.

However, the image of Britain presented in the earlier instalment of Castonier's memoirs, *Stürmisch bis heiter: Memoiren einer Außenseiterin* [Stormy to Fair: Memoirs of an Outsider], was far from positive.[11] There, Britain appears as the source of antiquated attitudes and recondite social rituals aped by wealthy Europeans like Castonier's parents; she refers dismissively to the ceremonial drinking of tea and consumption of English biscuits as well as to her English grandmother's exhortations not to display emotion. The British people that Castonier met on her travels were likewise unsympathetic, as were those who observed unmoved the spectacle of desperate Jews being insulted, robbed, and manhandled by Nazi thugs as they sought to escape to Italy from Vienna's Südbahnhof (267–70). In Italy, Castonier gained an insight into the kinder side of the English through the generosity of a Mrs Lynn, a complete stranger who offered to help Castonier's friend Alice Berend, impoverished and terminally ill in exile (271–73).

Castonier's first impressions of Britain on crossing the Channel were unfavourable: the coldly impersonal immigration officers and the cool indifference of the British to the 'aliens' anxiously queuing for admission at the height of the crisis that preceded the Munich Agreement of autumn 1938. But once on the train to London, her mood was transformed: at the sight of the green fields and the small red-brick houses with their colourful gardens, her anxieties evaporated. From the countryside, verdant and peaceful, emanated a sense of stability and security, the atmosphere of an intact world utterly different from the Continent about which the British understood little, but against whose menace Britain was to act as a bulwark. Castonier realized with bewilderment and relief that she was in a country where football matches and horse-racing made newspaper headlines while Hitler was dismissed as a Continental troublemaker (282–83). The British attachment to cherished values and rituals proved stronger than the fear provoked by the Nazi threat: her gas mask was presented with the same elaborate ceremonial as the cooked breakfast served to her on her first morning in Britain (283–84).

Castonier's first lodgings consisted of a spartan attic room in Maida Vale. She earned little to ease her financial situation, as she had only occasional articles accepted by the *New Statesman* and by émigré papers, but her network of British contacts grew, in part thanks to the singer Audrey Mildmay, wife of John Christie, the founder of the Glyndebourne Festival. During the war, she had five animal stories for children published by Collins, while *Eternal Front*, her riposte to Lord Vansittart's *Black Record*, came out in 1942. This enabled her to move to a flat on Baker Street. But after the pioneering female conductor Kathleen Merritt, whom she had met through Audrey Mildmay, invited her to join her on a visit to Jane Napier, who farmed at Mill Farm, she decided to leave London and, aged fifty, abandoned writing for a decade of work as a farmhand.

Castonier had already developed a deep affection for the English countryside, describing its landscape in poetic terms: 'Sie besteht aus gedämpften, verschleierten Bildern, die deutlich zu erkennen und zu genießen man sich nur allmählich gewöhnen kann' [It is composed of muted, veiled images, which one can accustom oneself only gradually to seeing clearly and enjoying] (289). The beauty of this landscape reveals itself only to the patient, perceptive observer: 'Man muß Geduld haben, um das Gesicht dieser Landschaft zu erkennen, dann schweben die opalfarbenen Vorhänge, die sie verhüllen, empor, die weißen und gelben Schleier lichten sich, enthüllen die eigenartige, zurückhaltende Schönheit' [It takes patience to come to know the face of this landscape, then the opal-coloured curtains concealing it lift, the white and yellow veils clear, revealing its characteristic reticent beauty]. Castonier relates these features of the English landscape to the character of its people, the congruence between them forming a central theme in her depiction of Britain:

> Wesen und Gestalt von Mensch und Tier sind vom Klima beeinflußt, in Rhythmus und Reaktion abwartend, gelassen, genau so, wie die Landschaft friedlich-geruhsam ist. Die Zartheit der Farben, die kühlfeuchte Luft, die stets ein wenig verschleierte Sonne, die zurückhaltenden Menschen stehen in völligem Einklang mit dieser Insel, auf der jeder Engländer sein eigener Gärtner ist. (290)

> [The being and the form of man and beast are influenced by the climate, cautious and calm in their rhythms and reactions, just as the landscape is peaceful and restful. The delicate colours, the cool, moist air, the permanently slightly veiled sun, the reserved people are in complete harmony with this island, where every Englishman is his own gardener.]

Castonier attributes the British people's relaxed and self-assured stability to a long process of historical evolution, undisturbed for centuries by any invader who might have imposed alien practices and customs on them. Instead, they were free to develop their own traditions over a long period of time; hence the respect for tradition that differentiates the British from 'Continentals' like herself:

> Dies Volk ist eine Seefahrernation, eine Nation seefahrender Gärtner ältester Tradition, fest auf einer Insel verwurzelt, seit tausend Jahren niemals von einem 'bösen Nachbarn' gestört, die Landschaft wurde nicht von fremden Horden verwüstet, Dörfer und Städte nicht zerstört, die Bewohner nicht gezwungen, andere Sitten anzunehmen. Von Generation zu Generation durch die Jahrhunderte entwickelte sich ungestört althergebrachte Tradition, an der zäh festgehalten wird. Wir, die Kontinental-Hastigen, können uns nur schwer an die Gelassenheit von Landschaft und Mensch gewöhnen. (290)

> [This people is a nation of seafarers, a nation of seafaring gardeners of ancient tradition, firmly rooted in their island, never disturbed for a thousand years by any 'evil neighbour', the landscape not devastated by foreign hordes, towns and cities not destroyed, the inhabitants not forced to adopt other customs. From generation to generation across the centuries, long-established traditions developed, to which they hold fast tenaciously. We hasty Continentals can only accustom ourselves with difficulty to the calm of landscape and people.]

Castonier's experience of Britain at war greatly enhanced her respect and affection for the attitudes and behaviour that she considered characteristic of the British. As war became inevitable, she discerned a new determination to resist Hitler, a new confidence in confronting the evil that he represented, and an all-embracing spirit of solidarity that was to inspire the British people throughout the war: on learning that she was born in Germany, a veteran of World War I assured her that she was nevertheless 'all right' and shook her hand (300). The chapter 'London unter Feuer' [London under Fire] (301–16) depicts the behaviour of Londoners during the Blitz, united in their resolve to fight the evil of Nazism, but to do so without hatred or hysteria; the resulting spirit of solidarity expressed itself in the willingness of the normally reserved British to speak to strangers in public places. They proved indomitable: from Waterloo Bridge, Castonier observed the armada of small ships setting out in May 1940 for France, where defeat was turned into the legendary, morale-boosting evacuation from Dunkirk.

At the height of the bombing, Castonier was admitted to London's University College Hospital for major surgery. At first, she met with some hostility as a German, but was rapidly accepted into the community of the ward; one woman assured her that foreigners were welcome, while the woman who had insulted her apologized. Castonier awoke from her operation to feel her bed shaking from the exploding bombs and to see a line of stretchers with casualties from a direct hit on nearby Tottenham Court Road. But the women in the ward made light of the air raids: when a midwife brought in a newborn baby, they suggested that it be named Blitzy. The sangfroid of the British, their good-natured humour under fire, and their refusal to capitulate inspired the refugees: 'Krieg in diesem Land war nicht so schwer wie in anderen Ländern [...] immer wieder war es gut, inmitten dieser lächelnden, durch nichts zu erschütternden Gelassenheit zu leben' [The war in this country was not as hard as in other countries [...] it was always good to live amidst this smiling, unshakeable calm] (315–16).

Castonier found relief from the strains and stresses of war when she went to live and work as a farmhand at Mill Farm. This represented not only a remarkable change in her life — from writer and intellectual to agricultural labourer — but also a personal transformation. Her description of her first visit to Mill Farm (316–21) highlights the healing qualities of the English countryside; its tranquil peacefulness on a beautiful spring day, the delicate blue of the sky, the green of the hills, and the gentle sunlight create the conditions for an organic unity that encompasses humans, animals, and the inanimate elements of nature. Life on the farm displays the unchanging rhythms of seasons and harvests as well as the natural cycle of life; the rhythmical murmur of the millstream that had powered the long-disused wheel of the farm's mill reminds Castonier of the transient span of a human life (320).

Contact with the land brought about a renewal of life for Castonier; when Jane Napier set her to work driving a tractor to plough a field, she felt no need or desire to do anything else. This was no flight, she states, but the beginning of a new life, a complete physical and mental change. As if she had, through some mysterious transformation, been born again, she forgot her career as a writer, devoting herself instead to the farm and its crops and animals. They and the dilapidated old farmhouse made a new person of her and imbued her with a 'tiefe Freude an der Schöpfung' [deep joy in creation] (324); this quasi-religious element in her love of nature was reflected in her later conversion to Catholicism. When a serious injury forced her to give up farm work a decade later, she returned to her typewriter, determined to remain active to the end. She reflected in her memoirs on a life lived out against the background of the pastel shades of the English countryside and surrounded by people and animals who shared her joy in it. The trajectory of her life had taken her from a privileged childhood and a career in Germany to the haven of Mill Farm, where the traditions of life in the English countryside held sway in harmony with the natural order.

Another German-Jewish writer whose career was disrupted by the advent of National Socialism but who enjoyed a long and productive life in Britain was Gabriele Tergit, the pseudonym of Elise Reifenberg, née Hirschmann. Born in Berlin in 1894 and married to the architect Heinrich Julius Reifenberg, Tergit worked as a journalist and made her breakthrough with her novel *Käsebier erobert den Kurfürstendamm* [Käsebier Conquers the Kurfürstendamm] (1931), before being forced to flee Germany in 1933. After a period in Czechoslovakia, she and her husband went to Palestine, but, finding conditions there intolerable, left for Britain in 1938. In London, Tergit continued to work as a journalist and to write novels, but could never entirely fulfil the promise of her earlier years. In Britain, she wrote a novel about a German-Jewish family, *Effingers*, published in Hamburg in 1951, but both this and her other less substantial publications, *Das Büchlein vom Bett* (Berlin, 1954) and *Kaiserkron und Päonien rot* (Cologne, 1958), failed to reach a wider public either in Britain or in Germany.

Tergit was active in a number of organizations working on behalf of the refugees from Nazism in Britain, sitting on the Board of the Association of Jewish Refugees and playing a leading role in the London-based PEN-Zentrum deutschsprachiger Autoren im Ausland [PEN Centre of German-Language Writers Abroad]. Her husband designed the building for the New Liberal Jewish Congregation, now Belsize Square Synagogue, the only synagogue founded by the refugees from Nazism in London. As this commitment to institutions representing the refugees permanently settled in Britain indicates, Tergit continued to champion the values that had characterized assimilated German Jewry before 1933, while also depicting Britain as a congenial environment for the preservation of those values. In the numerous articles that she wrote for *AJR Information*, the monthly journal of the Association of Jewish Refugees, Tergit repeatedly stressed the wealth of culture and the respect for books and learning that the refugees from Nazism had brought with them to Britain; she also insisted that they had remained true to the traditions of that section of German Jewry that had been assimilated into German society while remaining consciously and loyally Jewish. These refugees had experienced a reasonably smooth transition into British society, where they established a flourishing presence, though in reduced circumstances and, in the case of the more elderly, unable ever to adapt fully to British values and practices; it is to be noted that Tergit herself continued to write mostly in German.[12]

An example of this view of German-Jewish emigration to Britain is to be found in her article in memory of the distinguished artist Julius Rosenbaum (1879–1956).[13] Tergit chose to present Rosenbaum as an exemplar of the assimilated German Jew who maintained a balance between his German national identity and his allegiance to the community of his birth: 'Julius Rosenbaum was a refugee artist who was an upright Jew in the sense this expression had in the former life of our community.' After a period in Paris studying with the French Impressionists, Rosenbaum had returned to Berlin, where he worked for many of the noted illustrated papers of the day. He refused to change his name, considering it as 'a confession every day of his life', 'a stamp of his German Jewishness' (10). That persisted even after 1933, when he devoted his energies to the cultural life of the embattled Jewish community until his emigration in 1939. Life as a refugee in London was initially hard; he had to work as a mechanic, a painter, and a fitter in a small factory. But Hampstead, where he settled with his wife, the artist Adele Reifenberg, supplied the conditions for a resumption of his artistic career. They established a flourishing art school, a circle of devoted students exhibited their work as the Belsize Group, and Rosenbaum spent the last seventeen years of his life in the area.

As a cultural artefact, books functioned as the emblem of the transfer of German-Jewish culture to Britain, where a substantial number of refugee publishing houses, antiquarian booksellers, and specialist bookshops sprang up. Tergit celebrated this notable addition to culture in Britain in an article marking the sixtieth anniversary of the founding of Martin Breslauer's firm in Berlin.[14] The title of this article, which translates as 'The People of the Book and the Jubilee of Martin Breslauer', points to the deep veneration for books that characterized German Jewry. Breslauer was forced to flee to London in 1937; although he was killed in the Blitz in 1940, his son, who succeeded him, maintained the continuity of Jewish culture and tradition in Britain. Tergit also celebrated Libris, the best known of the bookshops specializing in rare and academic German books;[15] located on Boundary Road, St John's Wood, Libris was run by Joseph Suschitzky from Vienna. She describes the bookshop, in its antiquated premises, with loving attention to the delights that it offered to the bibliophile. This article, whose title translates as 'Books on Their Travels', recounts the stations in Suschitzky's emigration: from the concentration camps of Dachau and Buchenwald to an unwelcoming Britain where he was first denied permission to work, then interned on the Isle of Man, to a first menial job in a catering establishment, then to a job at Foyle's bookshop, and finally to the founding of his own business.

Suschitzky's journey mirrors that of his books and of the German-language culture that he and the other Jewish refugees brought with them to Britain; escaping from a regime that burnt books and persecuted their authors and readers, the books so prized by the Jews of Central Europe were at first coolly received in Britain, but eventually found security in a new, if unexpected home. In her concluding paragraph, Tergit evokes the image of the thousands of German books that had vanished from Germany but which survived at Libris; it is as if the 'Urschöpfung' [original model] (8) of an entire culture has been preserved in amber, allowing that part of German culture, destroyed in its native lands, to live on in Britain.

The principal carriers of the traditions, values, and heritage of German Jewry in Britain are, however, the refugees who people Tergit's articles. 'Große Generation' [Great Generation] is written as a piece of reportage on her visits to three elderly refugee ladies in their homes in north-west London.[16] These ladies belong to the generation before Tergit's, born early enough to have experienced the flowering of German Jewry in the decades between the unification of Germany and World War I. When married, they had all enjoyed the security of great wealth; but equally important was the stability of the age, which allowed them to feel secure in their assimilated German-Jewish identity and in their community's standing within German society. The ladies come from a range of backgrounds, all highly cultured. Frau Guttmann from Berlin has, like all three widowed ladies, experienced the disappearance of her fortune in the great inflation of the early 1920s, which was followed in the 1930s by her forced emigration. Yet she has coped admirably with that rupture in her life and has settled contentedly, though in humbler circumstances, in rented accommodation in Swiss Cottage, still the proud possessor of her fine crystal and porcelain.

Frau Schindler, from Upper Silesia, comes from a strictly orthodox Jewish family that had become wealthy, assimilated, and non-observant over little more than a generation, while maintaining a deep-rooted allegiance to the German-Jewish community. She exemplifies that section of German Jewry for which education, art, and culture had filled the space left by the lapsing of religious faith. Frau Kristeller brings the refinement and artistic taste of Hamburg's *haute bourgeoisie* to north-west London — qualities which, Tergit claims, were lost to later generations that came of age during World War I, the Weimar Republic, and in emigration. Yet the article concludes with the reassuring image of Frau Kristeller knitting and reflecting contentedly on her life while corresponding from London with no less than sixty-six family members — the embodiment of the perpetuation in Britain of the cultural tradition of German Jewry.

Fred Uhlman, born in Stuttgart in 1901 into a prosperous, assimilated, middle-class Jewish family, was forced to flee to France in March 1933, as much for his political activities on behalf of the Social Democratic Party as for his racial origins. Unable to continue practising as a lawyer, he found that he had a gift for painting, and it was in the visual arts that he first made his name, in Paris and subsequently in London, where he arrived in August 1936. Only late in life did he establish himself as a writer, most notably with the short novel *Reunion*, which was published in 1971 and became highly successful on its republication in 1977 with a foreword by Arthur Koestler.[17] Uhlman also published his autobiography, *The Making of an Englishman*, in 1960.[18] Covering his life up to 1945, this contrasts the very different experiences of growing up in Stuttgart and then, following the interlude in Paris, of adapting to Britain, which he nevertheless describes as 'a heaven and a haven' to anyone coming from the Continent (203). Despite the wry irony of the title, which suggests the impossibility of a man of Uhlman's background ever becoming truly English, the outstanding feature of the latter sections of the book is the author's love of Britain, expressed with passion and conviction. Given Uhlman's negative experiences in Britain — the resistance of his wife's father to their marriage, his internment in 1940, and the crass anti-Semitism that he encountered among his wife's upper-class connections — this may at first sight appear surprising.

Uhlman, however, possessed a resilience and optimism that enabled him to surmount such setbacks. In his youth, he had developed a profound attachment to Stuttgart and to Swabia, his native region. His family, who were not observant, were not primarily defined by their Jewishness before 1933; indeed, his father was resolutely hostile to religion, considering himself first and foremost a proud German patriot. Consequently, before 1933 the family had felt that they occupied a solid and well demarcated position within German society, even if their fellow Germans did not always regard them as equals. Uhlman carried this sense of a secure identity with him into his emigration to Britain, where it helped him to make light of the blatant anti-Semitism among his wife's older relatives. He was particularly incensed by the failure of British right-wing Conservatives to take a stand against Hitler, a critical attitude that placed him in a position of superior understanding, not of inferiority, in relation to them. It was on this firm basis that, according to *The Making of an Englishman*, Uhlman came to define Britain by all that he saw as positive in the country where he had settled and to form a lifelong attachment to it; he remained conscious of his Jewishness, but felt able to assimilate, largely because he was more than willing to do so. That eagerness to embrace Britain arguably shaped his autobiography as a literary text.

Like Ruth Feiner, Uhlman instrumentalized his time in France to create a foil against which to depict Britain. Although he was at first attracted to the artistic

Fig. 5.1. Fred Uhlman, artist and writer. Courtesy of Caroline Compton.

culture and refinement of Paris, he soon came to value Britain, with its humanity and quiet courtesy, more highly: 'I know that all big towns are savage and cruel, but London seems to me gentle compared with the cruelty and corruption, indifference and selfishness of Paris' (145). He owed his admission to Britain to a stroke of good fortune. Unable to make a living in Paris from his paintings, Uhlman went to Spain in 1936, but found himself trapped there by the outbreak of the Spanish Civil War. In the (then) small fishing village of Tossa del Mar, he met Diana Croft, daughter of the aristocrat Sir Henry Page Croft, who was touring Spain with her friend Betty Sackville-West. Through her, Uhlman was able to enter Britain; they married in November 1936. Diana Croft was in rebellion against her upper-class background; she could hardly have expressed her rejection of the beliefs and prejudices of her father, a Conservative of outspokenly reactionary views, more clearly than by marrying Uhlman, a German, a Jew, and a Socialist.

Uhlman describes at length his initial ignorance of Britain, its culture and customs: 'I arrived in England on the 3rd September, 1936, but if it had been China I could not have known less about the country which is now my second home' (196). With comic vividness, he depicts the strangeness of life in Britain as it appeared to an educated German: 'I had no clue to the strange taboos and customs which make the English such strange and often exasperating people' (200), among which he cites the class divisions that rent British society, the preference for understatement over self-promotion, and the reluctance to express passionate opinions in public. But this attitude rapidly modulates into admiration, for notable by their absence are such phenomena as inflation, civil war, arbitrary arrest and detention in concentration camps, or racial persecution: 'England — or so it seemed to me — was a paradise, a country without suffering, changeless, excluded from the common lot of mankind, a happy isle of lotus eaters.' Uhlman dwells on the admirable features of British society like the police: 'There were — most amazing of all — policemen who carried no guns, called you "Sir" and asked you to sit down when you went to report a change of address' (201). Significantly, he glosses over the burdensome regulations that required 'aliens' to report repeatedly to the police.

Marriage to Diana Croft marked the end of Uhlman's financial difficulties. In September 1938, the couple moved into a house at 47 Downshire Hill, a street in Hampstead fashionable among artists and intellectuals; among their neighbours were Roland Penrose and Lee Miller. It was there that in autumn 1938 the Free German League of Culture (FGLC), one of the most important organizations of the German refugees in Britain, was founded; Uhlman's relations with the Communists who came to dominate the FGLC later deteriorated severely, another factor that distanced him from his native German culture. Uhlman, who had at first experienced Britain as 'a stranger country than any I had known before, as far away from Europe as Peking', rapidly 'fell in love with the people', who compared all too favourably with his former fellow countrymen: 'What a change from the open rudeness of the Germans and the thin varnish of politeness of the French. These people were tolerant, kind, helpful, good-mannered, disciplined, friendly, and less selfish than people anywhere else. Rudeness was exceptional, violence rare' (202).

Uhlman, however, also experienced the more unpleasant aspects of life as a refugee in Britain. He was exposed to grossly offensive expressions of anti-Semitism: a cousin of Diana Croft reported to her mother — Diana's aunt — that she had seen Diana with 'a little Jew' in Kew Gardens, eliciting the response that 'she knew always when a Jew was in her room because she had an uncanny feeling, "just like touching a grass snake"' (204).[19] Sir Henry was always coldly polite to Uhlman, but he never forgave his daughter for what he regarded as her misalliance; he came to see his grandchildren, a girl born in 1940 and a boy born in 1943, only once a year, on his way to spend Christmas with what Uhlman pointedly calls 'the rest of his Anglo-Saxon family' (209). Uhlman's internment, on 25 June 1940, ten days before the birth of his daughter, represented the low point in the treatment of the refugees by the British authorities. The stupidity of the policy of internment is conveyed when 'a dear old lady, an intimate friend of ours', telephones him to inform him of the necessity of his detention as 'a German'; internment, she assures him, will be 'really rather fun. You can play tennis all day and you won't need to worry about the war' (223–24). In reality, Uhlman was arrested at Ware, Hertfordshire, where his wife was visiting a relative, transferred to Watford and then to temporary accommodation in the winter quarters of the Bertram Mills Circus at Ascot, before being sent to Hutchinson Camp on the Isle of Man, where he was detained for six months.

Like Robert Neumann, Uhlman presents the experience of internment in a considerably milder light in his autobiography than in the diary that he kept at the time (223–43).[20] To dwell insistently on the harsher aspects of internment would have run counter to the positive depiction of Britain that otherwise dominates *The Making of an Englishman*. Yet he does not ignore the poor physical conditions endured by the internees, or, more importantly, the psychological impact, especially the refugees' resentment at the injustice of their imprisonment as potential Nazi agents. Uhlman also highlighted the mental stress inflicted on the internees by what he called 'a special torture known as "release"' (227); the uncertainty of the duration of their detention, and the difficulty of discerning the criteria according to which they might be freed, added a special dimension to their suffering.

Uhlman's account of his arrival on the Isle of Man conveys the incongruities and contradictions of internment:

> When we arrived at Douglas, Isle of Man, surrounded by soldiers with fixed bayonets, many people turned up to see the prisoners from the victorious battles of Hampstead and Golders Green. We passed the war memorial and every one of us took our hats off. One of the soldiers shouted, 'Faster, faster'. I told him that the man in front of me was seventy — and he stopped at once. (230)

The absurdity of treating harmless civilians as if they represented a military threat to be warded off at bayonet point is reflected by the ironic tone in which 'the victorious battles of Hampstead and Golders Green' are celebrated by the parading of the detainees through the streets. As a sign of their loyalty to Britain, all the 'enemy aliens' take their hats off before the war memorial, only to be ordered curtly to march faster. Yet British military harshness towards civilians has its limits: the shouting soldier, once informed that the detainees include elderly men, desists, and an element of humanity is restored.

That element of humanity is maintained after Uhlman's release on New Year's Eve in 1940, when he returned to his wartime home in Bambers Green, Essex, as 'a bearded German who could hardly speak English'. Yet: 'I met with nothing but kindness and friendliness and was not once made to feel that I was more of an outsider than any other newcomer' (244), despite at least one of his neighbours, appalled at the wartime alliance with 'the Bolsheviks' (245–46), pronouncing that he would rather be governed by Hitler than by Clement Attlee. In his conclusion, Uhlman details the failures in his life, but balances them against his achievements:

> I have found not only a refuge but a real home in England, which I love more than any other country in the world. I believe that if tolerance, kindness, political maturity and fairness are the touchstones of civilisation, Great Britain is the most civilised nation on earth. (249)

What life in Britain lacks in excitement and intensity, it gains through decency and humanity: 'instead of getting scorched by the fierce, devouring flame of France, I am warming my hands at a steady, moderate fire, which, I hope, will keep me warm for many more winters' (250).

This chapter has examined the ways in which the older generation of refugee writers engaged with the conditions that they encountered in Britain and the strategies that they developed to cope with those conditions. Their experiences and reactions varied widely, from the abiding sense of distance between Neumann or Spiel and British society, to the deep affection for Britain demonstrated by Uhlman and Castonier. Although they all flourished professionally in Britain at least to some extent, it is probably fair to say that they were never able to make good the damage to their careers caused by the rupture of forced emigration; Elisabeth Castonier did, it is true, derive new and unexpected inspiration from her relationship with the English countryside, but she wrote about it in German, published in Germany, and achieved little resonance beyond the German-speaking world. The older refugee writers mostly found Britain a congenial country of refuge, but they struggled to make a lasting mark on the British literary scene. Only Fred Uhlman, who took to writing when well-settled in Britain, wrote in English, and could be considered as much an English as a German writer, found a readership in both languages.

Notes to Chapter 5

1. Hilde Spiel, *Welche Welt ist meine Welt?: Erinnerungen 1946–1989* (Munich: List, 1990).
2. Hilde Spiel, *Die hellen und die finsteren Zeiten: Erinnerungen 1911–1946* (Munich: List, 1989).
3. See Andrea Hammel, *Everyday Life as Alternative Space in Exile Writing: The Novels of Anna Gmeyner, Selma Kahn, Hilde Spiel, Martina Wied and Hermynia Zur Muehlen* (Berne: Lang, 2008).
4. The phrase derives from the saying *Wer die Wahl hat, hat die Qual*, expressing the agony (*Qual*) of having to make a choice (*Wahl*) between alternatives.
5. Neumann's writings in Britain have been expertly analysed in Dove, *Journey of No Return*.
6. Robert Neumann, *Ein leichtes Leben: Bericht über mich selbst und Zeitgenossen* (Munich: Desch, 1963).

7. Neumann's comments on his contemporaries are remarkable for their sheer malice. See, for example, his dismissal of the literary merits of George Orwell's *Animal Farm* (143), or his highly offensive characterization of his female fellow writers (392).
8. Robert Neumann, *By the Waters of Babylon*, trans. by Anthony Dent (London: Dent, 1939), pp. 35–52. The German version was not published until after the war.
9. Dove, *Journey of No Return*, pp. 173–84.
10. Elisabeth Castonier, *Mill Farm: Menschen und Tiere unter einem Dach* (Reinbek bei Hamburg: Rowohlt, 1976).
11. Elisabeth Castonier, *Stürmisch bis heiter: Memoiren einer Außenseiterin* (Munich: DTV, 1967).
12. See, for example, her memoirs: Gabriele Tergit, *Etwas Seltenes überhaupt: Erinnerungen* (Frankfurt a.M.: Ullstein, 1983).
13. Gabriele Tergit, 'In Memory of a Refugee Artist', *AJR Information*, October 1956, p. 10.
14. Gabriele Tergit, 'Das Volk des Buches und das Jubilaeum von Martin Breslauer', *AJR Information*, October 1958, p. 12.
15. Gabriele Tergit, 'Buecher auf Wanderschaft', *AJR Information*, April 1971, p. 8.
16. Gabriele Tergit, 'Große Generation', *AJR Information*, August 1957, pp. 10–11.
17. Fred Uhlman, *Reunion* (London: Adam Books, 1971; republished London: Collins & Harvill, 1977).
18. Fred Uhlman, *The Making of an Englishman* (London: Gollancz, 1960).
19. The aunt in question would have been Sir Henry's sister, Lady Edward Pearson, a member of Oswald Mosley's British Union of Fascists.
20. On Uhlman's three accounts of his internment, see Charmian Brinson, Anna Müller-Härlin, and Julia Winckler, *His Majesty's Loyal Internee: Fred Uhlman in Captivity* (London: Vallentine Mitchell, 2009).

CHAPTER 6

The Child Refugee's Perspective

The younger generation of refugee writers — those who arrived in Britain as children — created a rich legacy of texts, mostly autobiographical in nature and written in English, which record their experiences in Britain and their reactions to their new country of residence. Although they were by virtue of their age better able to adjust to British conditions than the older generation of refugees, their very youth rendered them more vulnerable to the dislocation of forced emigration, especially if they were separated from their parents, and to the emotional and psychological shock of abrupt exposure to a new and unfamiliar environment. Texts written from the perspective of a child, both autobiographical and predominantly fictional, occupy an important place among the narratives depicting the experiences of the refugees from Nazism in Britain. This may in part be due to the large number of children involved, in particular the unaccompanied children who came to Britain on Kindertransports in 1938–39. In part, it is also due to the special quality of the child refugee's perspective, which, less encumbered by adult preconceptions and expectations, is capable of giving an unsparingly honest account of Britain as a country of emigration and of highlighting the features and qualities, both positive and negative, that characterized British society in its reception of the newcomers. The naive innocence of the child's-eye view adds to the effectiveness of such accounts when read through the prism of an adult reader's understanding.

Young Girls as Refugees

Among the best-known such texts is Judith Kerr's *When Hitler Stole Pink Rabbit*, which, with its sequel *The Other Way Round* (reissued in 2002 as *Bombs on Aunt Dainty*), recounts the flight of nine-year-old Anna and her family from Berlin in 1933, first to Switzerland, then to France, and finally, in 1936, to Britain.[1] The narrative follows in thinly fictionalized form the experiences of Kerr's own family: her father, the celebrated theatre critic Alfred Kerr (see Chapter 1); her mother Julia; and her elder brother Michael, called Max in the text. The subtle shifts in narrative perspective reflect the narrator's evolution from the bewildered child of 1933, to the insecure teenager of 1940, to the young woman of 1945 on the threshold of adulthood. After her arrival in Britain, conditions in her new country of residence play a crucial part in Anna's gradual development of a new, self-confident identity in place of that of the refugee and outsider. At the end of *When Hitler Stole Pink Rabbit*,

Britain appears as a pleasant change from the increasingly hostile and anti-Semitic environment of France. The family's first hours in their new country of refuge set the tone for the narrative, in which misadventures are softened by humour and the plight of the refugees is made more tolerable by the basic decency of the British.

In spring 1940, at the beginning of The Other Way Round, Anna, now aged fifteen, is all too aware of her otherness in Britain and of her status as a refugee dependent on the goodwill of others. At the girls' boarding school to which she had been sent, she, the 'clever little refugee girl' (280), had been made painfully conscious of the divide between her and the beefy, sports-loving English girls around her. Now, living with an American family in an exclusive part of Kensington, Anna depends on the charity of her hosts, wearing their daughters' cast-off clothes. With her carefully polished, borrowed shoes and her stockings from Marks & Spencer's — not the cheaper ones from Woolworth's (279) — she is indistinguishable in appearance from an English middle-class girl; but she is not accepted as such and is frequently treated, kindly but unmistakably, as a foreigner, living on sufferance in London and seemingly destined to become at best a secretary. She is deeply concerned for her parents, who live in shabby-genteel poverty at the Hotel Continental in Bloomsbury among other refugee guests, similarly poor and uprooted, struggling to adapt to life in a strange country. Over and above the feelings of insecurity common to girls of her age, Anna knows herself to be an outsider in Britain, fearing that 'perhaps it was simply that England didn't suit her' (301). But already at this stage, she speaks English without an accent (285), and is rapidly accustoming herself to everyday life in London.

The process of Anna's integration into British society is cast into relief when her brother invites her for a weekend at Cambridge, where he is studying law. More than any other family member, Max is driven by the desire to assimilate. He is desperately eager to be treated as British: 'After four years of public school and nearly two terms at Cambridge, Max looked, sounded and felt English. It was maddening for him not to be legally English as well' (291–92). Anna's weekend begins badly, with a rare encounter with narrow-minded xenophobia. On the train to Cambridge, she meets a 'tweedy woman', the incarnation of middle England, who at first takes her for a young girl bound for the social delights of Cambridge. She is disconcerted to learn that Anna is German: 'I could have sworn that you were just a nice, ordinary English gel.' Unable to understand how Anna could wish '[her] own country' to lose the war, the woman buries herself reproachfully in Country Life, the magazine of the rural gentry (308–10). But Anna greatly enjoys her weekend in Cambridge, where Max's friends entertain her with their wit and banter, while she observes how thoroughly her brother has integrated into undergraduate life: 'Anna watched them admiringly. How witty they were, she thought, and how handsome, and how English — and how strange to see Max virtually indistinguishable from the other two' (313). To be taken for English is for Max the supreme accolade; when George, his friend from public school, declares that he often forgets that Max was not born in Britain, Max is deeply gratified: '"Sometimes I almost forget myself," said Max so lightly that only Anna guessed how much it meant to him' (316).

However, Max's studies at Cambridge are interrupted by his internment. He bears the physical discomfort with fortitude, but finds it hard to accept his enforced reduction to the status of 'enemy alien': 'He hated being imprisoned and he hated being treated as an enemy, and most of all he hated being forced back into some kind of German identity which he had long discarded' (348). Max has adopted a British identity to the extent of rejecting his former German identity outright. He did not, he believes, belong among the interned 'aliens': 'I know it sounds arrogant to say so, but I know I belong in this country. I've known it ever since my first year at school — a feeling of everything being suddenly absolutely right' (372). As he has come to consider himself British, he demands to be treated on an equal basis with those whom he now sees as his fellow countrymen: 'All I want [...] is just to be allowed to do the same things as everyone else. [...] I'm sick to death of always having to be different!'. Even his fear during air raids is mitigated by his pleasure at sharing the hardships of war with the community around him: 'It's a relief just for once to have the same worries as everyone else!' (373). Convinced that he is under an obligation to face the same dangers as his British peers, Max succeeds in having himself accepted into the RAF. Refused permission to fly in Bomber or Fighter Command, lest he be shot down over German-held territory, he discovers a loophole in the regulations and, displaying the mastery of fine print that will make him a highly successful lawyer, joins Coastal Command; his posting to an operational squadron is the fulfilment of his wartime ambition, the indicator of his new identity as an officer in the RAF.

Anna, less confident than Max of belonging in Britain and less secure in her acceptance of a new identity, is also less confident about the outcome of the war. In summer 1940, her hosts leave Kensington for the safety of the United States, obliging her to move to the Hotel Continental. Every success of the advancing German armies fills her with fear, until in summer 1940, with invasion apparently imminent, she is haunted by nightmares in which Jew-hunting parachutists land in Russell Square (347). But her fears are dispelled by the resilient spirit of British resistance to Hitler, evident first in the evacuation of Allied troops from Dunkirk, then in the defeat of the Luftwaffe in the Battle of Britain; a memorable passage in *The Other Way Round* describes the reaction of the assembled refugees in the Hotel Continental to the BBC news bulletin that reports the decisive victory of the RAF on 15 September 1940 (363–64). Thereafter, despite the continual air raids, including a direct hit on the hotel that forces the family to move to an establishment in Putney, Anna gains strength from the courage and good humour with which the civilian population of London confronts the Blitz. As her fears recede, so her identification with the British deepens. She secures a job with a branch of the British Red Cross, a pillar of the establishment, and commences a course of classes in art, which will become her first chosen profession. *The Other Way Round* shows how important a function the experience of war played in the integration of the refugees from Nazism into British society, both through their contribution to the war effort and through their emotional and psychological identification with the British people in their struggle against Hitler.

The adjustment to life in Britain proves more difficult for the older generation. A combination of linguistic difficulties, poverty, loss of status, and unfamiliarity with his new environment turns Anna's father, a celebrated literary figure in Germany, into a marginalized, unemployable figure whose decline is reflected in his threadbare, distinctively foreign-cut clothes and shabby living conditions. One of the saddest passages in the text describes the reading that he gives at an international writers' meeting before an audience consisting of refugees, who appreciate the quality of his writing but are more interested in the free food, and of English intellectuals, whose good intentions do not extend to understanding German texts (303–07). In a reversal of traditional gender roles, responsibility for providing for the family falls on Anna's mother, requiring her to undertake demeaning secretarial work and putting her under constant nervous strain. The spectre of poverty looms over the parents throughout, while the children, better adapted to life in Britain, gradually assume the role of adults — a reversal of generational relationships articulated in the title of the book. By its end, Anna's father has already suffered the first of the strokes that will kill him soon after the war; shortly before his stroke, he attends a Beethoven concert and is moved to tears at being able to enjoy the culture of which he has been deprived during the long years of emigration.

The Other Way Round ends with Max and Anna walking through London in May 1945, participating in the victory celebrations in the same way as the tired but exultant British people around them. Max, in the uniform of a British officer, is the object of salutes and admiration, while Anna for once feels comfortable in Britain. In Piccadilly Circus, in the heart of the capital, the scene bursts into colour as the sun comes out, its rays falling on a sleeping soldier, exhausted but triumphant. Anna begins to sketch him, in an act of solidarity that foreshadows her life in Britain; there, as depicted in the third volume of the trilogy, *A Small Person Far Away*, she embarks on a career as a writer and Max becomes a leading barrister. In their different ways, both have fulfilled their father's hopes for their professional success. Anna has found a more secure identity through her marriage to an Englishman, which has in turn contributed to the integration of an erstwhile outsider into British society.

Lore Segal, née Groszmann, who arrived in Britain in December 1938, aged ten, on the first Kindertransport from Vienna, did not settle in Britain; unlike Judith Kerr, she emigrated via the Dominican Republic to the United States on graduating from university in 1948. Like Kerr, Segal came from a cultivated, prosperous, assimilated Jewish family; her father was chief accountant at a Viennese bank. Although Segal's parents were able to follow her to Britain, they could only gain admission on domestic service visas; the humiliation of the unaccustomed menial tasks to which her father was reduced undermined his health and ultimately his will to live, while her mother, more adaptable, slaved away as a domestic skivvy. Segal herself was, in the words of the title of her autobiographical volume, *Other People's Houses*, passed from household to household, in painful contrast to the warmth and security that she had enjoyed at home in Vienna.[2] Her book is an unflinching and unsparing depiction of life in Britain as a child refugee.

The shock of separation from her home and her parents dominates the opening sections on Segal's life in Britain. From the moment when her father tells her that she will be sent to England, which causes in her a sensation 'as if my insides had been suddenly scooped out' (25), the narrative is determined by the isolation and helplessness felt by an uncomprehending child thrust into unfamiliar, unwelcoming, and potentially hostile surroundings. On arrival at Harwich, Segal is sent to Dovercourt, a reception camp nearby, where she remains resolutely isolated among the other Kindertransport children. All the efforts of the British adults around her to help and engage with her, some well-meaning and some coldly unfeeling, are ineffectual. Her loneliness, longing for home, and sense of disorientation are powerfully conveyed by the narration of her experiences and emotions as if she were observing them from outside herself, a narrative perspective that mirrors the sense of self-alienation induced by the trauma of emigration and separation. Retreating into herself, she attempts to strike poses meant to please or impress the adults around her, but which all pass unnoticed, whether by the reporters who come aboard ship at Harwich (35) or by the local mayor on his visit to Dovercourt (44–45). The distorting perspective of this child's-eye view of unfamiliar people and events whose significance the narrator is too young to understand creates a disturbing and unsettling narrative mode. It conveys the impact of the abrupt transition to life in strange surroundings, in a strange country, and in the homes of strangers, of the loss of the protective parental presence, of language, identity, and security.

Segal is first sent to an orthodox Jewish family in Liverpool, the Levines, but only because, in her eagerness to please, she has said that she is orthodox without even knowing what it means; the song sung on the Jewish festival of Chanukkah, for example, is unknown to her (48). This creates the conditions for a fundamental misunderstanding between her and her first host family. They are disappointed that she (like her parents, when they arrive) is an assimilated Viennese who fails to conform to their image of the observant, Yiddish-speaking Jew, while she finds the routines of everyday life in their household baffling and bewildering. From the moment when she is handed over to Mrs Levine by the ladies of the refugee committee, Segal is afraid of the new adults in her life and of her new surroundings. Her behaviour becomes correspondingly more difficult; away from her parents, Segal appears as an awkward, argumentative, and occasionally tiresome child. Even when she is shown affection, as when Mrs Levine, moved to tears by her account of the discrimination suffered by Jews in Vienna, embraces her, she does not respond. It is Mrs Levine who utters the rebuke that gives the book its title: 'You don't do that when you live in other people's houses' (69). It comes as no surprise when the Levines use her absence on a visit to her parents in Kent as a pretext to get rid of her, an act that belies the appearance of solidarity between British Jews and refugees. Even worse is the behaviour of their co-religionist Mrs Rosen, who sends the orphaned Helene Rubichek away to an uncertain fate, aged seven (74).

Segal's parents are first taken on as servants by the Willoughbys, an affluent family in a village in Kent. Mrs Willoughby treats Franziska Groszmann with an exquisitely judged combination of surface kindness and patronizing condescension, making sure to impress her inferior status on her, and refusing to believe that members of the servant class, especially foreigners, can be as educated, cultured, and in every way as middle class as members of the British middle class. The fine irony with which the arrival of Segal's parents at the Willoughbys' house is depicted brings out all the principal features of the relationship between the British family and the Viennese servant couple (76–78). Mr Willoughby collects them from the station and drives them 'through a wide, open gate up a gravel drive toward a handsome, gentle house' — only to deposit them at the back (servants') door. Avoiding the carpeted part of the house (reserved for the family), Mrs Willoughby meets them in the kitchen and leads them along a flagstone passage and up narrow wooden stairs into an attic bedroom that lacks even the privacy of a door; 'Groszmann', says Mrs Willoughby, denying him the 'Mr' that would make him her equal as a human being, 'could put up a curtain tomorrow'. She then asks solicitously whether they are hungry — and offers 'to set out an egg on the kitchen table' for their supper (77).

When Franziska asks if she can read the family's copy of *The Forsyte Saga*, Mrs Willoughby is nonplussed, replying that she can borrow it 'so long as she brought it back when she was finished'. Undeterred by this estimate of her honesty, Franziska, on seeing the family's piano, informs Mrs Willoughby that she had studied music at the Vienna Academy; this prompts a heavily qualified offer of generosity: 'In that case you must come in and play when everyone is out' (78). While the energetic and versatile Franziska settles into her work as a housemaid, her husband Ignatz's career as a butler lasts only three days before he is demoted to the rank of gardener. The combination of manual labour and social degradation affects his health, leading to the final stroke that causes his death in summer 1944; well before that, he has become a shambling shadow of his former self, unwanted by any British employer and apt to quarrel with his fellow refugees. While the provision made for young refugee children in Britain appears inadequate, that made for the elderly, especially away from the larger urban centres, is non-existent. Franziska is left to struggle with her ambiguous feelings towards her British hosts, as when her gratitude to Mrs Willoughby for giving her the day off to fetch Lore from London is tempered by her host's request that she be back in time to prepare the Willoughbys' dinner (85–86).

When Segal cannot return to the Levines, accommodation is hastily found for her with the Hoopers, a working-class family in a nearby town, then with the Grimsleys, though both are plainly unsuitable; the Hoopers are content for her to go to the school attended by working-class girls like their daughter Gwenda, whereas Segal, preserving the middle-class aspirations of her Viennese background, insists on a grammar school. In summer 1940, Kent is declared a protected area and Ignatz Groszmann is interned; the family then settle in Surrey, where Segal is taken in by two wealthy sisters, Mrs Dillon, a widow, and her sister, Miss Douglas, who behave in a more kindly way to her mother and, insofar as he will accept it, her father. Segal is not blind to the element of condescension in the sisters' attitude to her parents and the other objects of their charitable activities, nor to their automatic assumption of their superiority to everyone foreign or lower class. Yet she is attracted by the gracious style of living of the English upper middle class, by the refinement of their manners, and by the elegance of their houses and furnishings. As she is initiated into the mentality and leisure activities of that select class, Segal becomes alienated from the refugee adults around her parents, who now seem to her 'underbred', talking too loudly, dressing in the wrong style, and 'drinking coffee from the tablecloth in the kitchen, instead of tea from the knee in the drawing room' (162). Returning to Mrs Dillon's house from a visit to her parents, she consciously re-adjusts her expression, posture, and mental attitude, assuming those that suit the conventions of her English hosts (163).

Given her assimilation into the English middle class, Segal is also uncomfortable with the Anglo-Jewish family to whom she is sent on Jewish religious holidays, finding them vulgar and her religious instruction uninspiring. But at the same time she rebels against what she sees as Mrs Dillon's attempts to 'make a Christian out of her' (147). Feeling 'a sudden furious loyalty to myself' (154), she senses the conflict between her original identity as a Viennese Jew and the assumed veneer of her British identity. That conflict comes to a head with her intention to study at Oxford, motivated at least in part by that university's associations with the British upper middle class and its secure self-confidence: 'Oxford seemed everything that I was not: at ease with itself, at one with its own past — upper class, English' (167). When she has to accept instead a place at Bedford College, then a highly regarded women's college in the University of London, she attributes the pain that she suffers to the conflict in identities that has arisen inside her as a result of her hosts' desire to anglicize her:

> I lay it to Miss Douglas and Mrs. Dillon, who wielded their influence for five years, when I was impressionable, trying to bring a new soul into the Church of England, and, instead, turning out a temporary snob and an Anglophile forever. (168)

This painful ambiguity in her feelings towards Britain dominates her brief account of her none-too-successful studies at Bedford College and her departure for the Dominican Republic, where she 'disembarked in the New World' (186) to start a new life.

Vera Gissing, née Diamant, who arrived in Britain in June 1939, just short of her eleventh birthday, on one of the transports of children from Prague organized by Doreen Warriner, Trevor Chadwick, and Nicholas Winton, experienced a very different conflict of identities. As a Czech, Gissing was never classed as a German national or 'enemy alien' in Britain; she could also attend a school that catered for children like her, the Czechoslovak State School. As a citizen of an allied country, she faced no difficulties in supporting the British war effort against Germany and could take pride in the contribution made by her fellow Czechs to the Allied cause; in contrast to her counterparts from Germany and Austria, she was under no threat from the hostility directed indiscriminately against 'Germans'. Unlike some Czech Jews, Gissing's first language was Czech, not German; after a German officer spat in her father's face, she never spoke German again. As the Czech people were under German occupation, she felt no conflict between her Jewish and Czech identities: both groups were perceived as victims of German oppression. Only after the war, when she returned to Czechoslovakia, did the anti-Semitism that she encountered create such a conflict, which she resolved by returning to Britain and taking refuge for a second time in her adopted British identity; this, too, would change when she travelled to Czechoslovakia again in 1968 and laid the foundation for a new balance between the three ethnic identities laying claim to her allegiance.

Gissing was in some respects fortunate as a child refugee in Britain, firstly in the external conditions of her life. She was accompanied to Britain by her elder sister Eva, who looked after her; she was taken in by an exceptionally kind and loving foster-family, the Rainfords, who treated her like a daughter; and she underwent most of her education at a school for Czech children. But Gissing was also able to confront the trauma of emigration and of separation from her parents on the basis of a secure sense of herself and her identity. A happy and resilient child, she was proudly confident in her Czech identity. That she was Jewish cast no shadow over her early life, at least until the Nazi occupation of Czechoslovakia in March 1939. As her family was not observant and religious differences played little part in the life of Čelakovice, her home town, she felt no distance between herself and her non-Jewish peers. As she wrote in *Pearls of Childhood*: 'To me then, being Czech mattered far more than being Jewish, for I loved my country and I was fiercely proud of being born a Czech' (23).[3] For her, Czechoslovakia was the country of democracy and freedom; she made sure to take 'my little Czech flag' with her to Britain (32). When she came to Britain, her Czech nationality could even be an advantage, as when her foster-sister Dorothy, 'bursting with the excitement of having a Czech refugee as a new sister' (44), introduced her to her new schoolmates, winning her a reception that could hardly have been accorded to a German or Austrian child.

On arrival in Britain, Gissing suffered painfully from homesickness and from the unfamiliar surroundings: the inedible food, the monotonous rows of apparently identical red-brick houses, and the strange language. But the warmth of the welcome extended to her by her foster-family in their home in Bootle, near Liverpool, greatly eased the transition to life in Britain. Even when she had to be evacuated to Southport, she discerned the kindness beneath the more severe exterior of her new host, whom she called Auntie Margery. After a spell at a council school, she was fortunate to be sent to Birkdale Central School in Ainsdale, where the headmaster, Mr Hughes, took a special interest in her; she was able to turn for him for advice long after she had left. Gissing's pride in her Czech identity was always present, even when listening to the radio: 'Whenever any Czech music was played, I almost wept with joy. Whenever Czechoslovak forces were mentioned, my heart swelled with pride' (68). There was no conflict between her feelings for her native land and her gratitude to Britain, as the Czech forces fighting alongside the British were also fighting to liberate her homeland and to allow her to return, as she hoped, to her parents. When Gissing learned that President Beneš would be the guest of honour at a special musical performance held in Liverpool in summer 1941, she resolved to attend at all costs. Her patriotism was richly rewarded, for it was her meeting with Beneš that paved the way for her admission to the Czechoslovak State School, then located at Hinton Hall, a somewhat dilapidated building near Whitchurch in Shropshire.

The school, which had been founded in 1940 after the fall of France, afforded children like Gissing the rare opportunity to continue their education in a Czech environment, as well as vital psychological and emotional support: 'Moreover, it gave us an anchor, a sense of belonging and security when we needed it most. It was our home, we were a family, and the closeness which grew out of adversity survived distance and time' (10). The school not only aimed to keep its pupils in contact with Czech culture. 'It also', she wrote, 'taught us to love and admire Britain; in a time of tremendous adversity for her own people, this country nevertheless had taken us in and offered us shelter and support' (85). On the basis of the security provided by what was in effect a surrogate Czech family in the form of the school, Gissing was able to approach British society with confidence; her interaction with the British appears to have been almost entirely positive. Despite the poor material conditions at the school, Gissing immediately felt 'at ease and at home' there (86), and, surrounded by her beloved Czech language, made numerous friendships, many of them lasting over the decades between the closure of the school in 1945 and the reunion that took place in 1985. In 1943, the school moved to Llanwrtyd Wells, a small town in Breconshire in mid-Wales, where a special relationship was forged between the pupils and the town's inhabitants; that relationship was memorably recreated on the occasion of the 1985 reunion, when the former pupils returned to '"our" village which had opened its doors and hearts to us' (9).

Although Gissing was happy at the Czechoslovak State School, anxiety about her parents cast a constant shadow over her life. In July 1945 she received a letter from her sister Eva, informing her of their mother's death in Belsen. In the letter, Eva attempted to make even this news less painful by emphasizing its British dimension, in the hope of casting a ray of light even into the darkness of the Holocaust:

> Mother lived to see the liberation of Belsen by the British army, she lived to see the end of the war and she rejoiced in our victory. She was not in Nazi hands but in kind British hands, in their hospital, when she died of typhus. (131)

In August 1945 Gissing returned to Prague, but met with indifference and even outright hostility: at school, her teachers discriminated against her, and at university her boyfriend was nicknamed 'Jew-lover' (166). After a particularly appalling display of casual Czech anti-Semitism (166), she returned to Britain in January 1949, declaring with relief: 'It was good to be back in Britain, which was, after all, my second home. I felt more of a native than a foreigner here' (169).

Determined to integrate fully into British society, Gissing resolved 'to close the door firmly on the past and to concentrate on putting down roots for the future' (169). She married a non-Jewish Englishman and raised three children. But when she returned to Prague in 1968, a visit to a small Holocaust museum next to the old Jewish cemetery proved to be a turning point in her life. There, she wrote, 'my search for my identity ended':

> I realised at long last that by shutting out the past I had closed the door on my inner self — that I would never find peace and true happiness unless I accepted myself for what I was: Jewish by race, Czech by birth, and British by choice. (171)

In Gissing's account, the reunion of 1985 set the seal on that new threefold identity. It gave her the strength to write *Pearls of Childhood*, at the end of which she declares her task completed (175), in the sense both of having finished her life story and of having come to terms with her past selves.

Two Young Male Refugees in Britain

The autobiographical trilogy by Charles Hannam (Karl Hirschland) provides a particularly clear example of the nexus between identity and agency in accounts of life in Britain by Jewish refugees from Nazism. The titles of the three parts of the trilogy, *A Boy in That Situation*, *Almost an Englishman*, and *Outsider Inside* (cited here as volumes I, II, and III respectively),[4] reflect the struggle of Karl Hartland (as the author calls his autobiographical persona) to find a settled place and identity for himself in British society; only when he has done so can he regain agency by asserting control over the direction of his life. Born in Essen in 1925, Hartland arrives in Britain on a Kindertransport in May 1939, following his elder sister, who has come on a domestic service visa, but leaving his father, a respected Jewish banker, behind.

At this stage, Hartland is hardly a defined character with a fixed personality, outlook, or temperament, but rather a developing personality, and one developing under particularly adverse conditions at that: he is a Jewish boy in Nazi Germany who then has to leave his home and family and find his way in a strange country where he understands neither the language nor the social forms and conventions. The systematic denigration and humiliation of Jews by the Nazis also impacts on the development of Hartland's personality and identity, since he partly internalizes the Nazi image of the Jew and seeks to distance himself from anything or anybody too obviously Jewish. This fracturing of his self-confidence creates yet more difficulties for him as he seeks to establish a secure identity on the basis of which he can confront his new environment in Britain. The three volumes record Hartland's development towards independence, and in particular his struggle to avoid being, as he repeatedly puts it, 'beholden to' others, a major problem for a child refugee who is of necessity dependent on the charity of others. This has a decisive effect on the course of his life, as when, unwilling to risk becoming dependent on his sister and her future husband, he refuses to emigrate to the United States with them:

> He could not afford to be beholden to anyone because that would have meant he could not be a person in his own right. What Karl wanted most was security, love and affection but when he was shown any he could not accept it without suspicion or resentment. (II, 11)

Only when he is able to decide for himself who he is can he escape from the pattern of revolt against those on whom he depends and determine autonomously the course of his life and career.

In Britain, Hartland is first sent to a hostel in Ramsgate, where conditions are tolerable and where he is among other German-speaking refugee boys. The warden is kindly, but there is little education and almost no training for any future employment corresponding to the boys' expectations and potential. From their position as outsiders, they view Britain favourably:

> The boys used the word 'fair' a lot, even when they were talking in German which they did most of the time; but they said 'fair' in English. They had a strong impression that England was a place where justice and fair play meant something. (I, 159)

But much as Hartland may desire to resemble an English boy, he is cut off from the English by barriers of language and convention. Although he is welcomed with great friendliness by a troop of English Boy Scouts, communication between them proves impossible. On Ramsgate beach, he can but gaze longingly at the British people around him, eager to belong among them but aware that he cannot. After the outbreak of war, the hostel closes and Hartland is sent to an agricultural training camp near Wallingford in Oxfordshire, in reality an approved school (an institution for young male delinquents), where conditions are extremely poor and where the boys are restricted to mindless and menial agricultural labour. The months that Hartland spends here represent a low point in his life in Britain; his account is an indictment of the at times wholly inadequate care provided for Kindertransport children.

Hartland is rescued from the camp by the intervention of his sister, who persuades the headmaster of a grammar school in Sussex, called Elmfield by the author, to accept her brother as a boarder. Hartland is unusually fortunate in his new school. He lodges with one of the teachers and is encouraged and supported by the headmaster, Mr Steven, a man of progressive convictions and ideals. As a result, Hartland, a mediocre student in Germany, applies himself to his studies to such effect that he wins a place at Cambridge. Just as important as his academic progress is his exposure at Elmfield to progressive ideas and democratic practices, such as the house meetings where the boys can express their views, demands, and complaints on an equal basis with the headmaster. It is here that Hartland acquires the egalitarian and democratic outlook which, in a radical break with the entrenched conservatism of the British upper and middle classes, is to make him a left-wing socialist. The reception that Hartland experiences is for the most part friendly; he is accepted into the school community, appointed a house prefect, and cheered when he leaves, though not as loudly as those of his peers who enjoy success at sports. However, some of the boys dislike him as a foreigner, while the traditionalist faction among the staff remains hostile to the intelligent Jewish refugee boys, whom they regard as interlopers, clever enough, in the pejorative sense of the word, to encroach on the privileges that were previously regarded as the rightful preserve of the British upper classes.

Hartland undergoes a process of socialization at Elmfield, as he is initiated into the rituals and practices of school life, and into the value system of middle-class British society. He is still subject to mockery and minor discrimination, but when he reflects on his German school, where a teacher had warned him of the dangers facing 'a boy in your situation', the phrase that gives the book its title, he recognizes that his situation at Elmfield, even as an outsider, is preferable by far (I, 207). Outside school, he meets with both kindness and hostility, understanding and indifference. When he is summoned before a tribunal in summer 1940 to be assessed as a security risk, he wins its members over by his freely admitted inability to comprehend cricket and by his willingness to volunteer for the army; they allow him to go free, joking that they 'hope you mean our army' (I, 211). But he is also aware that other young refugees are being interned and deported to Australia, and he hates the designation 'enemy alien', which reinforces his sense of exclusion and threatens his adoption of a British identity. When he volunteers for the RAF, the joke about his national allegiance is turned against him in a hostile and discriminatory manner, to justify his rejection: 'we can't take the risk that the Germans get a present of a bomber, can we?' (I, 214).

Hartland is immensely discouraged and demoralized by the obdurate refusal of the British to understand the situation of a German-Jewish refugee boy and his attitude to Germany. Yet he longs to adopt a British identity and to be absorbed into British society: 'More than anything he wanted to become an Englishman, to disappear for ever into a new identity, a new language, and clothes that in no way distinguished him from other boys' (II, 21). He feels free and happy in Britain, even though he has not yet achieved any stability of identity:

> But there were many confusions — he wished more than anything that he need not be a foreigner any longer. He wanted to disguise himself with a perfect Oxford accent, a pipe and a commission in His Majesty's forces, a lovely uniform and perhaps the spread wings of a pilot on his chest. (II, 33)

Instead, he ends up as a sergeant in an undistinguished regiment in the Far East. He is also shocked by the snobbery and class prejudice prevalent in sections of British society. British philistinism and scorn for the intellect go hand-in-hand with xenophobia and anti-democratic and anti-egalitarian attitudes, like the unthinking hatred among the possessing classes for socialism and for the welfare state introduced by the post-war Labour government to benefit the majority of the population.

By the time he embarks on a career in teaching, Hartland has learnt to cope with such features of refugee life as constantly being asked where he comes from. Once his English has improved, he evades the question by saying that he was brought up in Sussex; this 'seemed to satisfy the social mine detector the English middle classes carried before them' (III, 20). But the underlying dilemma of his identity has not been resolved, since his German origins make him an enemy, even though he is Jewish:

> Every time he talked to anybody they would say, 'And where are you from?' and he would say, 'From Germany,' and they would look puzzled as if to say, 'but are we not at war with them?' And he wanted to add, 'But I am Jewish, you see, and they threw me out.' (I, 205)

This exposes yet another level of internal conflict, as Hartland, who comes from a highly assimilated family and has also internalized some of the Nazi hatred of the Jews, has a highly ambivalent relationship to his own Jewishness:

> How could he come to terms with the two sorts of society in which he moved? One was the new school which accepted him unquestioningly and made him

want desperately to be an Englishman and the other was the world of Jewish refugees, his own people, but from whom he felt increasingly alienated. (II, 9–10)

When he stays in London during school holidays with his sister and her refugee friends, he feels a stranger among them, disliking their faulty English, foreign clothes, and demonstrative expressions of feeling. But at the same time, Hartland retains a profound attachment to his own people and their culture, to their humour, their food, and their conversation studded with Hebrew and Yiddish words. Only when he has finally achieved a measure of balance between the different aspects of his identity can he appreciate the qualities of the refugees he encounters in wartime Britain. At the same time, their attitude to him is ambivalent: they mock him for his 'posh' Englishness (II, 82), yet covertly admire him for being able to cast off his German-Jewish manners. The next phases in Hartland's life, after leaving school, in a sense represent his attempts to resolve these deep dilemmas of identity once he has opted to volunteer for the army instead of taking up his place at Cambridge; he does not wish to be beholden to anyone for paying his university fees: 'I don't want allowances made; I want to be accepted either because I am me, or because I am so good that they recognize it' (II, 113).

During his four years in the army in Burma and India (discussed in Chapter 3; see p. 81), Hartland witnesses viscerally racist attitudes towards colonial peoples that he compares to Nazi anti-Semitism. This causes him deliberately to conceal his Jewish origins, lest the racial aggression be directed against him. Yet he also experiences a new sense of solidarity among his 'mates' in the army, who support him with their friendship:

> And yet I found happiness in the army. I had mates: 'they may not have been very choice, but they were my mates', and they accepted and tolerated me with a generosity which I still find moving. For the first time in my life it seemed to me that I belonged somewhere. (II, 12)

Hartland then takes up his place at Corpus Christi College, Cambridge; his army service allows him to study free of fees. His degree at Cambridge helps him to consolidate his sense of British identity, as, in its way, his army service has also done.

Nevertheless, Hannam is still less than confident of his identity and standing in the eyes of British society, and he takes teaching positions at two private schools, before and after Cambridge, to overcome the stain of his 'tainted past' (III, 98): 'Coming to Sodenham [the name he gives to the school where he taught before going to Cambridge], a school for the young of the better sort of people, was an attempt to eradicate an unfortunate past' (III, 5). Yet he is totally out of place there and at Wolsey (the name he gives to the school where he teaches after Cambridge), as he encounters reactionary political prejudices and intolerant, regressive social attitudes; one of his colleagues at Sodenham, a former member of the Palestine Police, is a rabid anti-Semite, but Hartland lacks the self-confidence to confront him. At the end of the third volume, at a low point in his life, he makes the crucial decision to act independently, refusing to allow his future to be dictated by the opinions and expectations of others, and thus assuming agency over his own life: he leaves Wolsey, abandoning his attempts to pretend to be what he is not, a middle-class Englishman. In a break with his previous life, he embarks on a teaching career in the state sector, eventually becoming professor in the School of Education at the University of Bristol. Reflecting on his youth in his introduction to *Almost an Englishman*, Hannam regrets his failure to appreciate the qualities of his fellow refugees, the more so because British society, to which he aspired to belong, looked askance at him for his foreign birth. By becoming true to himself, he can admit to his German-Jewish origins while also embracing the other layers of identity that he has acquired in Britain:

> Only many years later was it possible to accept *all* aspects of my personality, the Jewish, the refugee and the English part. It took much time before I could say 'look, I am what I am, not what you want me to be'. (11, 12)

In contrast to Karl Hartland's achievement of agency and a balance of identities, hard-won as it is, stands the story of Wolfy Helfgott, the protagonist of Zvi Jagendorf's novel *Wolfy and the Strudelbakers*, who fails to establish himself securely in Britain and emigrates to Israel.[5] Wolfy arrives in Britain from Vienna as a young boy in 1939 with his parents, Chaim and Frida Helfgott, and his aunt and uncle, Mendl and Rosa Gold, with whom he lives after his mother's death and whose devotion to the ritual of baking strudel gives the novel its title. Wolfy's acute child's-eye observation captures the strangeness of Britain, the barriers — social, cultural, and religious — that separate his family from British society, and the great difficulties that they experience in adapting to it. For they are Eastern Jews, Yiddish-speaking, orthodox by religion, never assimilated into Western society, and far more marked by the traditional customs, values, and mentality of their ancestral home in Yablonicza (Yablunytsia, Ukraine), in the remotest reaches of pre-1918 Austrian Poland, than by the social culture of Vienna. In this they differ fundamentally from assimilated Jewish refugees, whose prospects for at least partially successful integration into British society were considerably better. Wolfy's father becomes known as Harry Halfgo by his British workmates, who cannot cope with foreign names. Consequently, Wolfy embarks on adult life in Britain as Will Halfgo, a name that expresses the indeterminacy besetting his identity and his situation in Britain; he exchanges the surname Helfgott, with its overtones of secure trust in God, for Halfgo, an articulation of liminality, impermanence, and the transitional nature of Wolfy's place in Britain.

The plight of the older generation of the family reflects the profound otherness of the unassimilated, Eastern Jewish refugees in Britain. That otherness applies equally to their pre-emigration life in Vienna, as expressed in the story of Kalman Gold, Wolfy's maternal great-uncle, who had died while travelling on a Viennese tram, carrying no identification:

> Kalman Gold's identity was in the emptiness of his pockets, which meant the fullness of his religion and the strangeness of its practice in a Christian city. The absence of a [house] key was heavy with significance but it couldn't be read by the conductor or the ambulance crew, just as Kalman could never comprehend the real presence of the body of Christ in the communion wafer. (9)

Fig. 6.1. Zvi Jagendorf and friend at a wedding. Courtesy of Zvi Jagendorf.

Wolfy's family, Diaspora Jews in the full sense of the word, carry their displacement with them to Britain, where their sense of uprootedness — social, psychological, and cultural — is exacerbated by the problem of language: they have become, Wolfy dimly gathers, 'refijees', sometimes 'bloody refijees' (13), in the trilingual patois of English, German, and Yiddish spoken in his family. The older generation of the family are simply incapable of coping with an environment that they view through the prism of their own incomprehension and helplessness: 'They were all miserable because they were refugees. Some people even thought they were spies but they were really more like orphans' (10).

The inability of the refugees to engage with British society in everyday life is made plain in the chapter 'Refijees', in which Rosa visits Mendl in the seaside town where he is being detained in a camp. Mendl is so afraid of the alien British environment that he would prefer to stay in the camp, but Rosa, more courageous, prevails on him to look round the town and even to enter a public house. They meet with suspicion, hostility, and an attempt at sexual harassment — as a smartly dressed foreign woman, Rosa is presumed to be 'easier' — but also with a measure of kindness and helpfulness, especially, to their surprise, from policemen, a combination that reflects the mixed reception extended by the British to the bewildered newcomers. Mendl, however, remains convinced that they are hated in Britain. When Rosa asks him why the British should have taken them in, he replies: 'To make us Christians' (21). This all-consuming fear of conversion to Catholicism, plainly a relic from the Polish past, is a major feature of the mentality of the older family members, though it is wildly misplaced in Britain, where the prevailing religion is the milk-and-water brand of Anglicanism that Wolfy encounters at Holloway Grammar School in north London. Nevertheless, his father persists in teaching him the 'magic phrases' that he had chanted to protect himself whenever he passed a church: 'In the dark spicy air behind the door the enemy in a black robe hovered ready to jump out and baptize you' (116). Conversion by a Catholic priest (clad in black and redolent with incense) would entail the abandonment of the traditional Jewish beliefs, practices, and values that are central to the family's identity; the absolute interdiction on any such interaction with Christian society follows them to Britain.

There is ample evidence of British anti-Semitism in the novel, though it seldom goes beyond obscenities and racial stereotyping. The most serious incident occurs when friends of Rosa's take Wolfy for an outing on the River Lea; they encounter a group of louts who insult them and push their boat into the overhanging trees. The fear of anti-Semitism, however, is omnipresent among the older family members, though it appears to be out of proportion to the hostility that they actually encounter. Their attitude to Britain is primarily determined by the Eastern Jews' projection of their ancestral memories of persecution and pogroms in Poland onto any Christian environment; this is a more potent factor even than fear of Nazism, which the family had only experienced for about a year in Vienna and which they understood as little as any other aspect of Austrian life. So powerful are these ingrained fears from the Polish past that anti-Semitism becomes a reality for the older refugees even when it exists only in their imagination; Wolfy's parents lock their front door in terror lest their harmless neighbour, the aptly named Mr Motherway, expelled from his flat by his wife for getting drunk on Christmas Eve, should batter down their door like some Polish peasant (136). It is the memory of Polish pogroms, not of the Nazi terror, that dominates the folk memory of these Jews from the East; those memories continue to resonate in Britain, while the Nazis are seldom mentioned.

Wolfy and his cousin Bernard are caught in a clash of cultures as they grow up in the Jewish area of settlement around Stamford Hill and Stoke Newington in inner north-east London. Earlier, during his family's wartime evacuation to Oakengates in Shropshire, Wolfy experiences that conflict painfully at first hand, when he is given a Christmas card at school by the Bishop of Lichfield, only to see the prize on which he prides himself burned by his father, appalled at the Christian images. While the cousins are interested, like their British peers, in football, war films, and, in Bernard's case, girls, Rosa and Mendl are above all concerned to preserve them from anything more than a necessary minimum of assimilation into their environment. But their efforts are laughably misdirected: they fear that Bernard's visits to the West End of London to attend Hebrew conversation classes may expose him to the risk of conversion, but fail to notice the risk of his sexual initiation at the hands of Soho's professional ladies. In adulthood, the rebellious Bernard converts to Buddhism, abandoning his Jewish faith in reaction against his parents' unrelenting pressure to conform to their conception of Jewish identity.

Wolfy, more tractable, never rejects his Jewishness, but neither does he remain unaffected by his socialization in Britain. He meets with considerable kindness in Britain, though it is almost always accompanied by a measure of incomprehension; the mentality of the British is too restricted to encompass the apparently exotic Eastern Jews, or even to make much effort to do so. This is the case with the kindly Mr Palmer, with whom the family lodges in Oakengates, and with Reverend Taylor, who teaches Religious Instruction at Wolfy's school. Taylor, who is 'fair and sympathetic' to Jewish boys, sees Jesus as a model of English fair play and courtesy, and regards the Old Testament as 'an adventure comic trailer to the real Bible' (107), stands opposed to Mr Willoughby, the beefy, somewhat sadistic Physical Education teacher, who dislikes Jews, more on account of their lack of sporting prowess than out of pure anti-Semitism (106–10). When Taylor helps Wolfy to retrieve his lost tsitsis (ritual fringes), he is surprised to learn that Jesus, like any devout Jew of his time, would have worn such a garment; Wolfy remarks that it may have helped Jesus walk on the waters of the Sea of Galilee, and they laugh 'for religious reasons which they, for a change, shared' (110). The qualifying phrase 'for a change' points to the relative lack of genuine contact between Wolfy and this representative figure in British social culture.

In the final chapters, a disorientated, middle-aged Will Halfgo returns, divorced and still insecure, to the vastly changed London of 1990.[6] But the homelessness, transience, and rootlessness that have since the Diaspora informed Jewish identity, at least in that part of Jewry that remained attached to such a conception of Jewish identity, have not lost their power:

> Will and Rosa, still alive, sat in a hot tunnel under the heavy weight of the city to which they had all fled fifty years before. Once they had been refugees, then aliens, then evacuees, always transients with suitcases on the way to somewhere else. Now they were commuters but neither would ever get home again. Home had been taken away by armies of looters, by a fading and falsifying memory, by restlessness and unease and in the end by the ghosts who dispossess the living and who will inherit the earth. (183)

Reinforced by generations of discrimination and marginalization in Poland, and underscored by Nazi persecution, that sense of otherness has never eased in Britain, which remains alien, potentially hostile territory. The book ends with the image of Will endlessly wandering the streets of London: 'Mostly, they had no claims on him. London left him alone to walk its A to Z, fighting with each step to put down the rebellious hope of finding, in the end, his way back home' (187). Their past has largely deprived this group of Jewish refugees of the capacity to arrive autonomously at a new and secure identity in Britain and thus to accept it in their hearts as their homeland; conversely, their otherness ensures that it will never fully accept them.

The texts discussed in this chapter record, often very vividly, the struggle of child refugees to cope with the challenges of forced emigration to a strange country and of separation from the parental home and its comfortingly familiar surroundings, as well as the long and painful process of adaptation to British conditions that they had to undergo. Unlike the older refugees, whose acquired predispositions, values, and social culture were already largely set when they arrived in Britain, the child refugees were not yet old enough to have developed to the same degree the elements of a stable and fixed identity. They were painfully aware that they did not share the British identity of their peers, but they also knew that it was impossible for them to maintain the identity of a German or Austrian child, especially given that they were Jewish; the identity of the Jewish refugee that was all too often imposed on them brought with it the threat of discrimination and marginalization. Consequently, these narratives often focus on the struggle of the children to establish a balance between these conflicting claims and pressures; the texts demonstrate the extent to which their authors were able to determine their own sense of identity and thus to assert agency in this key regard.

Notes to Chapter 6

1. Kerr's texts are cited here following Judith Kerr, *Out of the Hitler Time* (London: Collins, 1995); it contains *When Hitler Stole Pink Rabbit*, *The Other Way Round*, and *A Small Person Far Away* (first published in 1971, 1975, and 1978 respectively).
2. Lore Segal, *Other People's Houses: A Refugee in England 1938–48* (London: Bodley Head, 1974; original edn New York: Harcourt Brace, 1964).
3. Vera Gissing, *Pearls of Childhood* (London: Robson, 1988).
4. Charles Hannam, *A Boy in That Situation: An Autobiography* (New York: Harper & Row, 1977); Hannam, *Almost an Englishman*; Charles Hannam, *Outsider Inside: Volume III of the Hartland Trilogy* (Brighton: Alpha Press, 2008).

5. Zvi Jagendorf, *Wolfy and the Strudelbakers* (Stockport: Dewi Lewis, 2001).
6. The film that Will takes Rosa to see is *Truly, Madly, Deeply*, dir. by Anthony Minghella (BBC Films, 1990).

CHAPTER 7

A Wealth of Memoirs: Autobiographies of the 1990s and 2000s

The past quarter-century has seen a proliferation of memoirs and autobiographies in which Jewish refugees from Nazism have sought to convey their experiences and life stories. The reasons for this sudden surge in the number of such texts are not entirely clear. They may have been inspired by the fiftieth anniversaries of landmark events, from the pogroms of November 1938 to the end of the war in 1945; they may have been the result of the refugees' increasing need to communicate, either because of their awareness of advancing age, or because of interest from younger family members, especially grandchildren eager to learn about their origins; or, once retired, the authors may simply have had the time to write. A further significant factor has been the ease with which 'ordinary' refugees, as opposed to those with literary ambitions or outstanding achievements, have been able to publish in recent years, thanks to advances in technology; many of them have published books that are largely intended for personal satisfaction and private consumption. It is certainly true that since 1990 the Holocaust and the Nazi persecution of the Jews have assumed a place in the public consciousness that they never previously had.

Narratives of Integration

Many of these autobiographical texts tend to follow a similar pattern. A mostly stable and secure childhood or youth in Germany, Austria, or Czechoslovakia is disrupted by the advent of National Socialism, which leads to the narrators' flight to Britain. In Britain, they encounter initial difficulties, often severe, including their classification as 'enemy aliens' in 1939. During the course of the war, however, a process of integration and adaptation sets in, which enables the narrators to build new lives in Britain, on which they look back several decades later with a measure of pride and contentment, though never forgetting the losses and suffering inflicted on them and their families.

One such memoir from the early 1990s is Irene White's *I Came as a Stranger*.[1] White had little if any public profile, though she was widely popular among the refugee community for her charitable work; in particular, she read the content of *AJR Information*, the monthly journal of the Association of Jewish Refugees, onto cassettes for the benefit of its visually impaired members. She was born as Irene

Fig. 7.1. Irene White. Courtesy of Joan Arton.

Michelsohn (anglicized to Michelson) into a cultivated, well-to-do family; she had two brothers, and her father was a doctor who died when she was a child. White provides few details of her childhood in Germany, finding it too painful to write about; this leaves an empty space in her text, and by its very absence highlights the traumatic divide between a stable, happy childhood and the disruption caused by persecution and forced emigration. White emigrated to Palestine in 1934 to join her family, but in 1938 she left for London, enrolling as a student nurse at St Mary's Hospital in Paddington. Having initially expected to stay only for the period of her training, she spent the rest of her life in Britain. White's text is straightforward, lacking in literary artifice; it consists of thirty-five short chapters, only one of which, entitled 'Marriage and the Birth of My Children', exceeds five pages in length. The memoir aims to be a factual, truthful account of the author's life, as she claims in the acknowledgements: 'All the stories in this book are absolutely true' (unnumbered page).

As the book's introduction makes plain, however, it has a clear overall vision of the British environment against which most of its author's life story unfolds. White explains that her title was inspired by an elderly lady whom she visited as a welfare officer. When she left, the lady told her: 'You came as a stranger, and you left as a friend.' White continues: 'These were exactly my feelings when I came to England, with only a slight variation. I came as a stranger, and I stayed as a friend. May it remain a country of freedom and fair play for ever' (unnumbered page). White began to develop a warm attachment to Britain while she was still in Palestine. She met Colonel John Henry Patterson, a distinguished military man with connections to the highest social circles in Britain. It was 'Colonel Pat' and his wife who persuaded her to take her nursing diploma in Britain and ensured that she was accepted at St Mary's. She spent her holidays at the Pattersons' house in Iver, Buckinghamshire, and retained the fondest memories of them and their efforts to familiarize her with her new British surroundings.

On arrival in London, White was confronted with a strange city (22–26). Her English was 'practically non-existent' (22), she was alone, and her skills for navigating this apparently alien environment were very limited: she could find her way on the Northern Line of the London Underground only by following the black line of its colour coding. But White was very favourably impressed by the friendliness she encountered, which extended even to the formidable figure of the matron under whom she worked at St Mary's: 'When you are alone and very young with no friends or relations, do not know the language well and have no money, the slightest kindness is like a gift from heaven. Altogether, England seemed like a sanctuary to me' (22). She cites an incident when, asked by the matron what task she was performing in the operating theatre, she replied that she was 'washing the bloody sheets', only to be gently but firmly corrected: '"Blood-stained, Nurse, blood-stained." Well, that is how I learned English' (24).

As was the case with many refugees who were young adults in 1939, the war transformed White's life and in particular her relationship to her new homeland. She was thrust into the midst of the wartime emergency in May 1940 when, as a nurse at Park Prewitt Hospital near Basingstoke in Hampshire, she helped to care for large numbers of wounded men who had been evacuated from Dunkirk, often in an appalling condition. She was transferred to Hampstead General Hospital, where she treated the casualties of the Blitz; she grew accustomed to the almost nightly bombing, to the air-raid shelters and the danger, but also to the spirit of solidarity and comradeship that bound the civilian population together. This internalization of British wartime values was to underpin the life that she chose to lead and the identity that she adopted in later life. In 1943 she met her husband, Allan White, a fellow refugee, at a dance at the Brent Bridge Hotel in Hendon, a place of entertainment popular among refugees. When they married, the celebrations were modest in the extreme: as government regulations decreed that no more than five shillings (twenty-five pence) per person could be spent on a meal, the couple and their two witnesses enjoyed a meal for one pound at the Cosmo restaurant in Swiss Cottage, before White was called into the hospital, where she spent her wedding night treating air-raid casualties. But the Whites were happy, secure in the knowledge that the hardships and privations of war were shared by the population of London and that they were playing their part in the common cause.

Allan White joined the Royal West Kent Regiment and later transferred to No. 3 Troop, 10 Commando, an elite unit mainly composed of German-speaking refugees.[2] His wife, who had to leave hospital nursing on marrying, continued to nurse privately, later supplementing her earnings by letting out rooms. From a small flat in Golders Green, they moved to a larger rented house in nearby Temple Fortune, then to Hendon, where they bought a property. For both of them, building up a new and secure family life was a priority after the loss and disruption that they had suffered: 'We both came from the same background. Two people who had lost everything, a sense of belonging — we fell in love, determined to build up a new life together, hoping for a better world' (33). To White, Britain offered suitable conditions for their new life, irrespective of the economic difficulties of the years of austerity. They had two children, a daughter born in 1944 and a son in 1946. After the war, Allan White was employed in a pharmaceutical business, thanks to a connection to a fellow refugee; he later established his own company, the Veterinary Drug Company, a very successful business venture.

In the later post-war period, the Whites plainly enjoyed both financial security and happiness as a family, at least until Allan White's death in 1982. But, for both of them, the experiences of the wartime period and the subsequent post-war years of austerity shaped their attitude to life in Britain, providing a key part of the foundations on which they rebuilt their lives. Irene White came to share the values and standards of behaviour that she observed in British society during the war and its aftermath, frequently harking back to them with affectionate nostalgia. Her final chapter, 'This Book Tells the Story of Survival …', compares the prosperity and technological advances of later decades unfavourably with the simpler pleasures of her earlier years in Britain (111–12). She was able to observe the process of successful integration a second time, when her mother arrived in England in 1947; she intended to stay for a year but, like her daughter, stayed for the rest of her life. Margaret

Michelson also found England strange and disconcerting at first and, being older than her daughter had been on arrival, struggled to come to terms with her new surroundings. But within a few months, she had become used to the vagaries of the climate and had learnt that in Britain queues of men indicated a popular sporting event rather than an imminent revolution (45–46). *I Came as a Stranger* is written as a tribute to the country that had taken its author in as a foreigner and into whose society she was pleased to assimilate.

A far more problematical case study of integration is provided by Martha Blend's *A Child Alone*.[3] Born as Martha Immerdauer in Vienna in 1930, Blend came to Britain on a Kindertransport in June 1939, aged nine. Her memoirs demonstrate very clearly the importance of the factor of age at emigration: whereas Irene White was a young woman on arrival in Britain and was equipped to some extent to cope with a new country, Blend, like most unaccompanied child refugees, had fewer resources on which to fall back, lacking even a young adult's developed identity and feeling herself to be helplessly cast adrift in strange surroundings. The traumatic disruption of what had been a happy and stable family life in Vienna affected Blend profoundly, destabilizing her emotional and personal development, at least until her marriage and the birth of her children. Blend was the only daughter of assimilated but observant Jewish parents, who, though not poor, were by the 1930s living in straitened circumstances. Blend was an intelligent child whose parents were concerned to give her a good education; but she was also a solitary child who was to experience loneliness and marginalization in accentuated form in emigration. Being transported to a new home in a foreign country had a devastating impact on her:

> When I saw the unfamiliar furniture [...] the full realisation of what had happened to me hit me with overwhelming force. I was by myself at the age of nine in a strange house in a strange country with a strange language and worst of all, utterly separated from the parents I loved deeply and might never see again. (48–49)

The foster parents who took Blend in, Will (Woolf) and Annie Greensztein, were Yiddish-speaking Jews from London's East End who had, thanks to Will's earnings as a taxi driver, moved to the less impoverished area of Bow. Although they were kindly and caring, their lack of education created a sharp cultural divide between them and their ward. Blend was familiar with the weekly routine of their religious practices, but the voluble, demonstrative behaviour of women like her foster-mother was alien to her, as was Annie's deep-seated suspicion of all non-Jewish people and her unwillingness to interact with them unless necessary, part of the heritage of her Polish past. At first, Blend had little contact with her British environment. Until she mastered the language, she could not read the newspapers, listen to the radio, or join in conversations; at primary school, the schoolwork was incomprehensible to her, and even her decimal-based arithmetic was inadequate for British non-metric measures. The disruption caused by the outbreak of war added to her difficulties; the family left London for Paignton in Devon, returned, but left the capital again to avoid the air raids, spending two years in Paignton as a result. Back in London again, the bombing forced them to move several times. At primary school, Blend

Fig. 7.2. Martha Blend in 1988. Courtesy of Jon Blend.

was made aware of her status as an outsider: 'To my recently acquired title of "the refugee" was now added another: "the evacuee". I hated both heartily, wishing only to be a normal member of the class' (72).

As her knowledge of English improved, however, she made friends and participated in class activities, assuming at least externally the identity of a British schoolgirl: 'Soon I became fluent in English to the point where I stopped thinking in German. With straight brown hair, fair skin and small features, I was outwardly indistinguishable from my English classmates' (74). But the trauma of separation from her parents acted as a block to any deeper psychological integration:

> What had happened to me was so painful that it was quite beyond my powers to talk about it. There were hints of sympathy from my aunt [foster-mother] and her friends, but I hated these and found them a burden rather than a comfort. Incredible though this may seem, I never talked about my Austrian past or my real parents to my English school-friends.

Unable to integrate it with the British present, Blend instinctively suppressed her Viennese past: 'For me the past was like a cupboard on which I had firmly turned the key' (75). She remained prey to a painful internal conflict, most obviously between the competing claims of her Jewish and Christian British identities. During her years in Paignton, Blend was adopting the habits and, to some extent, the identity of a British schoolgirl, but she still felt a sense of guilt at the Christian practices like hymn-singing in which she participated, harmless though they were. At school she also began her 'lifelong love affair with the English language' (82), which led her to a degree in English at Queen Mary College, University of London; but she was troubled by the anti-Semitism expressed in some of the literary texts that she read, and recoiled from the overtly Christian elements in poets like Donne and Herbert.

At Torquay Grammar School in Devon, Blend had coped with the competing Jewish and Christian elements in her life by 'keeping them in separate compartments of my mind, telling my Christian friends nothing about my Jewish experiences or the Jewish adults about my Christian ones' (76). Although she 'had a strong sense of identification with the Jewish tradition as a continuation of part of my upbringing in Austria', she had also been affected by the pernicious effects of National Socialism, in that she 'could not help the unconscious feeling that there was something wrong and shaming about being Jewish' (76–77). To make matters worse, she began to feel embarrassed by the behaviour of her foster-mother, who spoke Yiddish in the street and indulged in 'expansive gestures' unlike those of the restrained and undemonstrative British, to whom Blend in part looked up: 'I could have wished for a mother in the mould of Mrs Miniver complete with upper-class English accent instead of this dumpy foreigner.' As she accurately concluded: 'Integrating these conflicting strands of culture, language and religion would have taxed the intellect of a mature philosopher, let alone a nine-year-old child' (77).

Blend excelled academically, both at Torquay Grammar School and, after the family's return to London, at Dalston County School. But as she grew up, she also came increasingly into conflict with the attitudes and values of her foster-parents, which were characterized by a consuming mistrust of gentile British society. To Blend, for whom a measure of integration into British society held out the promise of security from discrimination, fair treatment, and acceptance by her peers, this represented a threat that 'made me choke with fury' (102). She was 'being socialised into a confusing mishmash of English, Jewish and Polish ideas and standards' (102). Blend's relationship with her foster-mother deteriorated sharply in her adolescence, and not only because Blend was old enough to understand that her affections were divided between two very different sets of parents. She also became aware of the gulf in culture and education that separated her from her foster-parents and their social circle: she loved to listen to classical music, while her foster-mother referred to 'sympathy music [symphony]' and thought that a concerto was a musical instrument (84).

As the war came to an end, Blend was forced to contemplate the fate of her parents, which brought the conflict between her Viennese past and her British present sharply into focus. Until then, she had largely been able to suppress her memories of Vienna and to take refuge, at least superficially, in a new, British identity: 'On the surface, it was as though I had shed my Austrian language and personality as a snake sheds its skin and had grown a protective English covering' (104–05). The provisional nature of that arrangement with her situation in Britain had its parallel in her relationship with her foster-parents: even after the confirmation of her parents' death, she did not wish to be formally adopted by her foster-parents, so 'by tacit agreement' she continued the relationship on the existing basis, since 'by then I had the feeling that, kind though they were, I was not of their kind' (120). Yet at the same time she was acutely aware of the divide that separated her from comfortable, secure, British middle-class life, as in her recollections of the well-kept houses in Paignton's wealthier quarters: 'I used to walk past these smug citadels [...] and feel they were giving me the message "Keep out! You don't belong here!"' (110).

During her university studies, as she was embarking on the transition to adulthood, Blend's lack of a stable sense of her own identity continued to affect her. While her appearance and her command of English made her indistinguishable from her English peers externally, the childhood past that shaped her inner being prevented her from sharing their English identity: 'In my mind I had half-yielded to my teachers' well-meant suggestion that I was an ordinary English girl, without realising the chasm that separated my experiences from those of my classmates brought up in conventional English families' (142–43). At the same time, she avoided any knowledge of the Holocaust or any contact with survivors, feeling it to be beyond her strength to confront the reality of her pre-emigration past.

> This meant that my hold on reality was brittle and my identity blurred. I managed to survive by concentrating on the present and shutting out painful topics [...]. The 'I' who entered Queen Mary College was the sum of many horrific experiences and confusing sets of values, as well as the recipient of much that was kind, positive and enlightening. (143)

By her own account, being a 'closet refugee' (149) made Blend a difficult companion, even after she graduated and completed her teacher training course at the Institute of Education, London. Following a career break, during which she married and had two sons, Blend returned to teaching, working for twenty-three years at The Skinners' School in Hackney, and set about the rediscovery of her past: she studied the Holocaust, undertook a return journey to Vienna, and visited the sites of the camps where her family had been murdered. After spending much of her life struggling both to come to terms with the disruption of her childhood — or, in her youth, to avoid doing so — and to establish an identity for herself amidst the competing claims of her Viennese, British Jewish, and British environments, Martha Blend succeeded in later life in reaching a fragile equilibrium between them, to which the writing of *A Child Alone* bears witness.

That painful and problematic process of achieving a resolution between competing national, racial, and religious identities is illustrated with particular clarity by the memoirs of Lisl Klein, *Nobody Said It Would Be Easy*.[4] Klein, born in 1928 in Karlsbad (Karlovy Vary), Czechoslovakia, was the only daughter of comfortably prosperous, assimilated Jewish parents, both of whom came from families long resident in the Egerland, the area of the Sudetenland around Karlsbad. Her uncle Luis (Alois) was a wealthy man; he came to own the Richmond Hotel (also called the Richmond Park Hotel), which was to play an important part in his niece's later life. In the interwar period, Jews like the Klein family were exposed to the national and racial antagonisms that rent Central Europe, divisions that played a decisive role in shaping Klein's early formative years. It is arguably for that reason that in adulthood she attached great importance to the reaching of a synthesis in various aspects of her life, not least in her sense of identity. She articulates this concern in her reflections on memoirs that describe life in a new country after the Holocaust:

> First there is, pervading absolutely everything for ever after, the question of how do you live what other people regard as a normal life in the light of what has happened? It is not only hard to do, it is also hard to put into words. Also, the threads begin to go in many different directions and it becomes difficult to hold them together. But I'm going to try. Perhaps this need to synthesise has been the sub-text of my adult life. (83)

Klein's family was Jewish, and was defined as such. But they were thoroughly assimilated, German-speaking Jews who had previously considered themselves to be fully and equally integrated into the life and society of the Sudetenland; as Klein's uncle Luis put it: 'It was Hitler who made us into Jews' (6). Although they spoke German and had adopted the culture associated with that language, they were, by the 1930s, largely excluded from the non-Jewish German-speaking community. They were loyal to the state of Czechoslovakia, but, not speaking Czech, they could not belong to the Czech community either, since language was the defining element in the intensifying conflict between Czechs and Germans. Unlike Vera Gissing (see Chapter 6 above), who spoke Czech and could carry her Czech identity with her to Britain, Klein and her family were deprived of any national identity. The family were also Social Democrats. In Britain, they belonged to that faction of the Social Democrats which maintained its loyalty to Czechoslovakia, not to

Fig. 7.3. Lisl Klein at work.
Courtesy of Ken Eason, Executive Director, Bayswater Institute.

that which was orientated towards a non-Nazi Germany; but when the post-war Czech government expelled all Germans, it was borne in upon those who were intending to return to Czechoslovakia that, not speaking Czech, they were no longer welcome in their home country.

The experiences of Lisl Klein and Martha Blend demonstrate the differing forms that life as a refugee child in Britain could take and the differing hardships and losses that it could impose. Klein was not, like Blend, abruptly separated from her parents before her emigration: she accompanied her mother aboard the *SS Baltrover*, which arrived in Britain from the Baltic port of Gdingen (Gdynia), near Danzig (Gdańsk), on 28 November 1938, her father having preceded them. But that parental security was not to last: Klein's father, who was already nearing sixty when he emigrated, died in 1943, worn out by the demands of life without money in a foreign land, and her mother's mental condition began to deteriorate. Whereas Blend was able to stay with her foster-parents throughout her childhood and adolescence, Klein only lived with her parents for a very short time, spending most of her first four years in Britain in the houses of a variety of strangers, all of whom, with the notable exception of the Day family, were either unsuitable or emotionally remote, often both. It was only in spring 1943 that Klein was able to rejoin her parents in a cramped, primitively furnished flat in Hammersmith, which her parents could afford to rent on the meagre wages they earned from the lowly jobs open to them. But within six months, this 'kind of equilibrium' (76) was destroyed by her father's death.

The problems that emigration was to create for the Klein family became evident as soon as their ship arrived at Tower Hill Pier in London, where Klein's mother refused at first to disembark: she would not set foot in Britain, which she held responsible for her family's predicament, on account of its betrayal of its Czechoslovakian ally in Munich. A legacy of that bitterness remained with the older refugees; it was to cause a rift between mother and daughter as the latter became 'more absorbed and assimilated and British' (58), while the older family members failed to integrate. The family was first accommodated in a hostel in West Hoathly, where the 'idyllic surroundings' (58) of the Sussex countryside contrasted with the miserable plight of the Czech refugees, disorientated by their new environment, struggling to master a new language, and consumed by anxiety about relatives left behind. They were bewildered by the system of heating by open fires, by the food, by the ignorant suspicion of foreigners, and by the value placed on 'polite' manners. Yet they were received with great generosity in Sussex and learned to appreciate, as Klein's father said, that 'this is a country where you can leave your bicycle outside the door' (59).

By a stroke of good fortune, Klein was offered a place at the highly regarded Grey Coat Hospital School in Westminster. But this meant leaving her parents to live in Tooting, in the first of the many 'billets' that 'were to be my homes for the next four years'. Almost all of them — especially those forced to take in evacuees once war had broken out — were grievously inadequate for a young refugee girl, and 'even the nicest was not home'. The years of living apart from her family left Klein with the lasting sense of being a marginalized outsider:

> In your own family you count as an individual. Without it, you may get good and fair treatment but it is because you are one of a category. In England I have never been able to shake off this feeling of only being one of a category. [...] In any case, refugee-dom and war-time evacuee-dom fed into each other, and the combination has left a permanent mark. (63)

When her school was evacuated to Brighton, Klein lived with two families in that area, then in three houses in the Farnham area. To keep herself occupied on Sunday afternoons, while one of her hosts, a Miss Tombs, enjoyed her nap, Klein took to attending religious meetings, converted to Christianity, and was baptized and confirmed; she subsequently retained her affection for the Church of England, though not her faith (68). She lived for a short time in the house of a general, whom she never met, as she was restricted to the servants' quarters; when her mother came to visit and rang the front doorbell, she was sternly rebuked and dispatched to the rear entrance.

It was therefore a pleasant surprise to be welcomed at the front door of the Days' house, where Colonel Day offered to take Klein's case and showed her to her room. Her stay with the Days, which lasted for three years, marked a significant stage in Klein's acculturation (70–73). She was accepted into the family, to the extent that, more than fifty-five years later, the Days' children organized a celebration to mark her seventieth birthday. At the Days', Klein was exposed to 'the best side of the other culture — or at any rate one of them, for there are many British cultures'. She observed 'the renowned English stiff upper lip', but saw that it 'came not from insensitivity but from a strength based on I don't know what, certainly in part on Christian belief'; and she observed 'the renowned class distinctions', 'but tempered by grace' (72). The combination of gracious behaviour, elegance, and 'a strength that comes from custom and tradition' inspired admiration in Klein. When the Days decided 'to show the flag' in the darkest days of the war by holding a dinner party, the guests, in evening dress, feasted on warmed-up fish and chips served on a silver dinner service by Klein (who had volunteered to act as waitress, complete with cap and apron): 'And I thought that nowhere else in the world would such a thing happen. I think this is why we won the war' (71).

Yet Klein could not rid herself of her status as an outsider in this most British of families: 'At the same time I was never really part of this life, with my permanent school uniform, my pocket money that was a charitable gift from the school, my parents with their foreign accents, and my too-good school results.' The gulf in culture that separated the Czech refugee from the insular British was illustrated by a letter that Mrs Day wrote to Klein after the war, informing her that she had bought 'something called salami' in 'a new shop [...] called a Delicatessen'; she had served it to her husband, grilled, for breakfast (73). The stability of the Days' household and the ease of their British manners contrasted sharply with the situation that Klein encountered when she returned to her parents' care in 1943. Inevitably, she suffered from their poverty and failure to integrate into British society; after her father's death, her mother, her hopes of returning to Czechoslovakia dashed, fell into an unhappiness and inability to cope that contributed to serious mental instability. Although Klein was awarded a scholarship to read Modern Languages at King's

College London in 1946, her life in the small flat that she shared with her mother was dominated by the difficult relationship between a deeply depressed, anxiety-ridden mother and a daughter emerging into an adulthood for which she had been poorly prepared. It was not until some ten years later that Klein, by then in her late twenties, moved into a flat of her own in Chiswick.

The story of Klein's adult life is dominated by her remarkable ascent into the front rank of Britain's social scientists, specializing in the analysis of industrial organizations, in questions of productivity, and in the impact of the introduction of new technology on the workforce. She became an expert in industrial organization; her studies in this field, from *The Meaning of Work* (1963) to *Working across the Gap* (2005), often focus on the practical application of the social sciences. This involved an unusual combination of the academic with the practical:

> My professional life and work, it turns out, has been about synthesis. Research *and* practice, technical change *and* the human aspects that shape it and arise from it, putting together organisational understanding *and* technical understanding *and* psychoanalytic understanding [...] 'not either/or, but both/and'. (84–85)

But in her university years she was not yet able to achieve the integration of the disparate strands that made up her personal life and identity:

> Is it too fanciful to think that this striving for synthesis has its roots in the desperate inability to synthesise what was happening to me at this turning point? Or perhaps in the scattering and loss of a family which I hadn't been able to hold together? (85)

After two dead-end jobs as a librarian, Klein experienced something of a revelation when she was employed as a factory hand in a small pharmaceutical company in Hammersmith. The work was mundane, but Klein found the workings of the company and its component departments 'totally fascinating' (96); it was here that she began her 'life-long love affair with industry' (97). She took a course in personnel management at the London School of Economics, then became personnel officer for a small factory in Bermondsey manufacturing paint tins for the Metal Box Company. She moved into research, entered the political sphere by joining the Fabian Society, and took the first of a series of important positions in industry by joining Esso Petroleum as an industrial sociologist. In 1971, she joined the Tavistock Institute and, when her career there was cut short, founded her own Bayswater Institute in 1990.

The desired synthesis in her private life took longer to achieve, but was accomplished, after the fall of the Communist regime in Czechoslovakia, by the reintegration of her Czech past into her acquired British identity. This came about when, as heir to her uncle Luis in the process of restitution, she acquired the Richmond Hotel in her native Karlsbad and set about restoring it. Initially, Klein found it very difficult to return to the setting of the childhood that had been taken from her, the family that she had lost, and the Czech and Jewish origins from which she had become alienated. Her first return visit to her home town proved emotional and disturbing:

> Arriving in Karlovy Vary was momentous: the tantalising familiarity of buildings and configuration of trees, light and shadow, alongside the absence of familiar people. I stood on one of the little bridges over the Tepl, the tears pouring down my face. (197)

But over the five years of the restitution process, Klein re-established her ties to her home town; her restoration of the hotel in particular acted as a catalyst, a healing act of reconciliation between her past and her present. After the sale of the hotel, she arranged a house party for some twenty-five relatives and close friends, through which she achieved something approaching a synthesis of the various aspects of her life and identity:

> For the only time in my life I had managed to bring the different parts of my life together — old friends from Karlsbad, young friends from the street where I live now, colleagues, clients, a trustee of the [Bayswater] Institute, staff from the Richmond, even two real relatives. And they all got on together as if there was no problem in having disparate aspects. I remember thinking this is as near as I am likely to get to being happy, I could die now. (223)

As she had taken control over the fate of the Richmond Hotel, Klein succeeded in asserting agency in her own life, by acknowledging and embracing the Czech-Jewish past of her childhood alongside the adult identity that she had created in Britain.

Integration across Two Generations

Age on arrival in Britain was one of the most important factors determining the degree to which a refugee could integrate and the relative success or failure, often subjectively perceived, of a refugee's adjustment to British society and conditions. Refugees who came as unaccompanied children, like Martha Blend, frequently struggled to adapt to a strange environment after the trauma of separation from their parents. On the other hand, younger refugees who came with their parents, were educated and brought up in Britain, and spoke fluent English, were plainly at an advantage in the process of integration and identity-formation over those who came later, since the latter had been educated in their native countries and had already formed a sense of their identity as German, Austrian, or Czech Jews. The memoirs of two male refugees, Cäsar (C. C.) Aronsfeld and John Izbicki, demonstrate in detail this generational effect.

Aronsfeld published his memoirs, *Wanderer from My Birth*, in 1997.[5] He was born in 1910 in Exin (Kcynia), in what was then the Prussian province of Posen, an area with a majority of Polish inhabitants that became part of Poland after 1918. Growing up in a region of competing nationalisms where Germans, Jews, and Poles were pitted against one another, Aronsfeld experienced at an early age the destabilizing impact of rivalry between ethnic groups. Even before 1918, Exin's Jews had occupied what he terms 'an unenviable middle ground' (8) between Germans and Poles; although attracted to the former by German culture, they were victims of the anti-Semitism that was widespread among Germans in the eastern regions,

Fig. 7.4. Cäsar (C. C.) Aronsfeld. Courtesy of the Wiener Library.

while they kept their distance from the supposedly uncultured Poles, with whom they had little in common. Aronsfeld's family were nevertheless ardent German patriots and had little hesitation in leaving Exin once it came under Polish control. When the family moved to Berlin in 1920, Aronsfeld experienced his first forced emigration; even as a boy, he came to consider his family as 'expatriates' (17). Their patriotism was that of the assimilated German Jews, who were strongly and proudly aware of their Jewishness, but who also cherished their German culture and identity. Aronsfeld emphasizes the fact that his family spoke German, not Yiddish, which they regarded 'as little better than a fancy jargon, a sorry counterfeit of the German we spoke, the German of Mendelssohn and Heine' (2).

Aronsfeld was educated at the Prinz Heinrichs-Gymnasium, a school for aspiring middle-class German boys. But at home his upbringing was strictly Jewish. His family were 'middle-of-the-road Jews, taking our Judaism as much for granted as our Germanism' (39). That secure sense of German-Jewish identity was destroyed by the advent of National Socialism. After his forced emigration, the destruction of German Jewry, and the Holocaust, Aronsfeld lost his sense of identification with Germany and became a Zionist, though he spent the rest of his life after 1933 in Britain (bar a short period in the Netherlands in 1938–39). He remained, however, attached to the cultural values of assimilated German Jewry, and he adapted to some extent to British values and social culture. But, as the title of his memoirs, *Wanderer from My Birth*, shows, Aronsfeld styled himself as the permanent exile, a spiritual descendant of the Wandering Jew, the symbol of Diaspora Jews destined to wander homeless and rootless down the centuries.

This self-stylization as an exile is a prominent theme in Aronsfeld's memoirs. The memory of the painting *Golus* [Exile] that had hung in his parents' house, depicting 'the trek of the Russian Jews as they wander across the wintry wastes — without a home, almost without a hope', leads him to reflect: 'I then probably thought little of it, but now I seemed to be one of them, on a trek without end' (40). He also describes how Homer's *Odyssey*, which he had studied at school, became 'something like a *leitmotif* of my life', adding that, unlike Odysseus, he was to travel from land to land without ever finding a home (47). But his determination to accept — and thus, to some extent, to regain control over — the fate that events have forced on him is a key factor in Aronsfeld's construction of a new life and identity after the destruction of his existence in Germany. Although he was aware of his powerlessness in the face of the events that had overtaken him, calling himself in his preface 'a scrap of flotsam that was whirled around bits of Europe', he was also aware of the fact of his survival, both physically and psychologically — 'no mean achievement perhaps if I may say so' (ix). By creating a new identity for himself in Britain, Aronsfeld also reassumed agency in his life; he enjoyed a successful career and a stable family life in Britain.

Aronsfeld would have emigrated to France if a British friend, whom he had met on a hiking holiday in the Rhineland, had not offered him temporary accommodation. Abandoning his law studies without great regret, he arrived in Britain on 19 May 1933, when the 'somewhat drab and prosaic sight' of Parkeston Quay at Harwich contrasted with his vision of the White Cliffs of Dover, 'on which my mind saw emblazoned the word *Freedom*' (74). He was also disconcerted by the reception he received from the immigration officer, who grudgingly granted him permission to stay for one month, on condition that he entered no employment, paid or unpaid (74–75). Aronsfeld's image of Britain as a bastion of resistance to tyranny was also contradicted by British reactions to Hitler's regime, which he considered at best as weak and gullible and at worst as displaying sympathy with National Socialism, mostly from a position of crass ignorance. Aronsfeld was also trenchantly critical of Anglo-Jewish relief organizations like the Jewish Refugees Committee (JRC) at Woburn House, describing with some bitterness the eagerness with which Anglo-Jewry sought to persuade the refugees from Nazism to leave Britain swiftly and the ungenerous treatment that he received from wealthy Anglo-Jewish relatives. He compares the reception of the Jews from Germany in Britain to that accorded by the German Jews in earlier decades to immigrant Jews from the East: 'This was another chapter of the *Ostjuden* [Jews from the East] story, and the German Jews were now tasting the medicine they once dispensed to their fellows from Russia and Poland' (82).

In June 1934, Aronsfeld left London for Leeds, where he was employed — or exploited — as a sewing machine mechanic by the Jewish-owned Bellow Machine Company. He took this wholly unsuitable, poorly paid position under pressure from the JRC, which was seeking to train unemployed refugees in manual skills that might qualify them for entry into Palestine, a venture which in Aronsfeld's case proved to be a total failure. Instead, he attempted to hone his writing skills by sending letters to the *Yorkshire Post*. In this, he was more successful; a number of his letters, warning of the true nature of Nazi intentions, were published, as was one in the *Daily Telegraph*. But when the chairman of the JRC's local committee in Leeds learnt that an article by Aronsfeld on fascism in Britain had appeared in a Jewish publication in Berlin, he summoned the author to appear before him and informed him that, as a mere factory hand, he had no business writing articles for the press; in a furious tirade, the chairman, a Jew, went so far as to threaten Aronsfeld with deportation to Germany (123–24).

Aronsfeld soon became convinced that his future lay not in Leeds but in London. When his efforts to gain a foothold in journalism there came to nothing, Aronsfeld worked for the German-Jewish industrialist Salman Schocken, through whom he met Alfred Wiener, founder of the Jewish Central Information Office, a centre for the dissemination of information to be used in the struggle against the Nazis, then located in Amsterdam and now known as the Wiener Library in London.[6] Aronsfeld was to work for the Wiener Library for nearly thirty years, gaining recognition as a writer, scholar, and researcher in the fields of Jewish history and the Holocaust. He worked in Amsterdam until he was expelled by the Dutch authorities in July 1939. The Wiener Library also moved to London; during the war, its importance as a resource in the struggle against National Socialism was recognized and Aronsfeld's expertise protected him from internment.

Aronsfeld rose to become Assistant Director of the Wiener Library, acting as editor of the respected *Wiener Library Bulletin* for twenty years, and writing and publishing widely. In 1966, he joined the Institute of Jewish Affairs as Senior

Research Officer, editing the quarterlies *Christian-Jewish Relations* and *Patterns of Prejudice*. Aronsfeld's interest in relations between Jews and Christians led him to found the Wembley branch of the Council of Christians and Jews with a Christian friend; the branch held meetings for thirteen years. Although Aronsfeld cast himself as something of an outsider, entitling Chapter 15 of his book 'The Loner', he did not allow this to impact negatively on his sense of identity. After he moved to Harrow, near Wembley in north-west London, with his wife Helga and their young daughter Esther, his involvement in interfaith relations led him to reflect on his own ethnic and religious identity. He refused to attribute his status as an outsider to his emigration to Britain alone; he cited other factors that had disrupted the course of his life at an earlier stage, including the uprooting of his family from Exin, his maternal grandmother's interventions in his upbringing, and an unhappy relationship with an older woman.

It was thus with a sense of stability, security, and pride that he reflected on his 'strong roots' in the Jewish religion, which he had never considered abandoning, 'if only because such a change would have involved more than a change in religious faith', a change in the foundations of his own identity and personality. That rooted identity led him to reach out to others: 'precisely because I was securely anchored in my own belief I have always sought the company of others holding different beliefs so as to exchange ideas and learn from them as they might possibly learn from me' (216). Although he called himself 'a frontiersman', Aronsfeld turned the concept of the border to advantage, regarding it not as a line of separation but as a point of contact between different groups. He described himself as 'living on the border where you can never be one but must be divided [...] between race and religion, home and exile, between our national and our universal vocation'. His reflections end with a vision of a fruitful synthesis between the three elements in his life that had combined to shape his identity:

> I am a Jew, I am also a Briton, and I must not forget (even if I could) that my roots are in Germany where I grew up. I am a citizen of one country and I have an allegiance to a greater citizenship. All these strands of my experience go to make up the tensions of my life in which I must struggle, as best I can, to combine different, even conflicting loyalties into some kind of harmony. (217)

John Izbicki, born as Horst Izbicki in Berlin in November 1930 and twenty years younger than Aronsfeld, belonged to the younger generation of refugees. Although his family had the narrowest of escapes from Germany, arriving in Britain as war was declared, Izbicki, an only child, enjoyed the security of strong and unwavering parental support throughout the difficult early phase of emigration. From the outset, he formed a highly favourable impression of Britain, which was greatly to ease his progress into British society; the image of the British fleet drawn up in preparation for war, viewed from the ship that had brought him from Flushing to Harwich in September 1939, recurs in his memoirs as an emblem of the safety that Britain offered the refugees from Nazism.[7] On that secure basis, Izbicki was able to build a highly successful career as a journalist, becoming the leading education correspondent in Britain. Indeed, his memoirs are structured as the narrative of a success story, described in his introduction as

> the story of a little Jewish refugee boy who came to England on the day the Second World War was declared, unable to speak a single word of English, and who became the education correspondent (editor) of the *Daily Telegraph* and head of its Paris office. (1)

Izbicki's father, Luzer Ber Izbicki, had been a recent immigrant from Russia, a hardworking trader who remained conscious in Germany of his modest origins. Yet, paradoxically, the relatively humble station that they had occupied in Germany helped to smooth the transition of Izbicki's parents into British society; they were grateful for any acts of kindness, acceptance, or recognition shown them in Britain. This attitude of deferential respect to their supposed British social superiors manifested itself in their pride at their son's graduation ceremony at the University of Nottingham or at his passing-out parade as an officer in the British Army. Izbicki's father, though reduced to manual work and forced to move around the country to obtain employment, nevertheless respected the society that had given his family refuge and was thankful for the opportunities that it offered his son. He made every effort to adapt with good humour to the social culture of his British workmates, establishing friendly relations with them, though that entailed converting his original name into Leonard or Len (47).

The description of the family's arrival in Britain (33–34) sets the tone for much of what follows. At first, Britain appears as 'overwhelmingly exciting — and also very frightening, for none of us knew what awaited us, where we would live, *how* we would live and what we would live on' (33). But after being formed into an reassuringly orderly queue, the Izbickis were interviewed by a smiling and courteous immigration officer who did his best to smooth their way into Britain: he spoke German to them, granted them entry as Russian nationals (thus saving them from internment), and gave them a receipt when he had to confiscate their prized camera; six years later, Izbicki's father was to receive a letter from Customs and Excise informing him that his camera was awaiting collection, and it has remained in his son's possession as a memento of their reception in their new homeland. Chapter 3, entitled 'A New Life' (35–49), depicts their first years in Britain. From Harwich, a train took them through 'the beautiful English countryside' to Liverpool Street Station, where the 'mass of [...] strangers in a strange land' (35) were efficiently marshalled by members of the Jewish Refugees Committee and taken to their accommodation, in the case of the Izbickis, the comfortably appointed Bloomsbury Hotel.

The family found the people of London — porters, taxi drivers, or waitresses — friendly and helpful. The only discordant episode was their brief foray into the East End, where they encountered only vermin-infested accommodation and unfriendly British Jews. The image of Anglo-Jewry in Izbicki's memoirs is unflattering, from the East End employer who cynically exploited his father to his own unhappy experiences with Jewish youth associations in Manchester. Izbicki never questioned his Jewishness, but twice married gentile wives and severed his connection with organized Judaism entirely, only observing one High Holy Day each year, out of respect for his parents. The family settled first in a 'garret' in Belsize Park, where

Izbicki attended a Catholic convent school; at first, he was bullied as 'the odd one out' on account of his defective English, but soon belonged to a group of friends (41–42). All their refugee fellow tenants were, however, interned, to the consternation of his mother, whose fears that they would be treated as in Nazi camps were only gradually assuaged by reports to the contrary.

Like many refugees, Izbicki was astonished by the calmness and good humour of the civilian population during the Blitz. But the bombing forced him and his mother to leave London for Steventon, south of Abingdon, Oxfordshire. Arriving late at night (45–46), they were given shelter by a kindly policeman in the police station, where they were comfortably accommodated and treated to a breakfast of eggs, toast, and butter, a veritable feast at a time of wartime rationing. It was at this policeman's prompting that Izbicki adopted the name John, a significant stage in his rejection of the identity of Horstchen from Berlin. He was also to take the middle name Howard, in gratitude to a Quaker who helped the family in Manchester. After several months in Steventon, which they spent as lodgers of a kind lady to whom Izbicki refers as 'dear Mrs Rogers', the family moved to north Wales, where his father's firm had relocated; his mother worked as a cook in a restaurant. Izbicki spent four years in Llandudno, 'a fabulous place' (46), where he began his successful passage through the British education system. His natural ability ensured that he was sent to a grammar school, where he encountered severe and recurrent anti-Semitic bullying.

When his family moved to Manchester, where his father had found work in a munitions factory, Izbicki excelled at North Manchester High School for Boys (North Manchester Grammar School), winning a scholarship to study German and French at the University of Nottingham, chosen because 'it boasted a ratio of four women to each man' (64). Izbicki's English was by now fluent, nurtured by a diet of boys' comics and radio comedy shows, but also by an inspirational English teacher and by a love of acting. Izbicki's new self-confidence manifested itself in his successful stage appearances, at university, during his periods of study in Germany, and during his national service. That self-confidence, founded on a secure sense of his identity as a German-Jewish refugee who had come to consider himself as British, characterized Izbicki intellectually, professionally, in his distinguished career as a journalist, and sexually, as demonstrated by various liaisons.

The high degree of Izbicki's social and cultural integration into British society contributed, together with natural ability and a self-confident personality, to a notable record of success. At university, he threw himself into student activities, as he did during the year of postgraduate study that he spent in Germany. In 1954, he commenced his two years of national service, was commissioned as an officer, and was sent to the Canal Zone in Egypt, where he excelled as a public relations officer. After his demobilization, he started out as a reporter at the *Manchester Evening Chronicle*, part of the Kemsley Group, which then sent him to head up its office in Paris. In 1964, he joined the *Daily Telegraph*, becoming its education correspondent in 1969. For seventeen years, Izbicki was an influential figure, enjoying the confidence of successive Secretaries of State for Education, including Margaret

Thatcher. He twice helped to save the Open University, the brainchild of Labour Prime Minister Harold Wilson, from closure by Conservative governments, and later, as Director of Public Affairs for the Committee of Directors of Polytechnics, played a leading part in the conferral of university status on the polytechnics. Looking back on his younger self as a small Jewish boy, he concludes his memoirs by asking: 'Could that little boy have guessed that he would one day become the education editor of so famous a quality newspaper as *The Daily Telegraph* and even help a nation's polytechnics become recognised as universities?' (343). Izbicki, unlike the older Aronsfeld, had found a place as a journalist and a niche in the British establishment.

The Limits of Integration

For a number of refugees, the adverse effects of forced emigration were so powerful as to make it difficult, if not impossible, for them to establish a secure existence within the framework of British society; this left them painfully aware of their status as outsiders, a marginalization that found expression in a fractured sense of identity and contributed to a deeply felt loss of stability and happiness. This was the case with Ruth Barnett, née Michaelis, who was born in Berlin in January 1935 to a Jewish father and a non-Jewish mother and came to Britain in 1939, aged four, and Annette Saville, née Bankier, who was born in Vienna in November 1923 and came to Britain in December 1938, aged fifteen. As children sent away on Kindertransport trains, both experienced the trauma of separation from their parents and of spending the wartime years in a strange country. Although both sets of parents survived the war — Saville's emigrated to Shanghai, as did Barnett's father, while her non-Jewish mother remained in Germany — the long period of separation had a severe impact on the children and on the development of their lives and personalities; the relationship between parents and children was fractured permanently.

The title of Ruth Barnett's autobiography, *Person of No Nationality: A Story of Childhood Separation, Loss and Recovery*,[8] reflects her long and painful struggle to achieve a stable life in Britain based on a secure identity. She was sent away from Germany in 1939, brought up as an outsider in a series of foster homes in Britain during the war, and obliged to return to Germany by her parents in 1949, only to return again to Britain, where she was eventually granted British citizenship, married a Jewish husband, and converted to Judaism, rediscovering her Jewish origins.[9] Alongside the complexities of this struggle to integrate the Jewish, German, and British dimensions of her identity, she also sought to heal the division that she sensed within herself between 'the child I was', Ruthchen from Berlin, and the 'new Ruth' that she had become in Britain. 'For many years', she explains,

> I felt ashamed of the child I once was. I rejected this child by locking her away in some corner of my mind. [...] By denying the existence of this child that was once my whole self, I did not have a complete adult self.

An important part of her strategy to gain acceptance was to try to 'be more English than the English'; 'desperate to be like everyone else', her status as a stateless minor

Fig. 7.5. Ruth Barnett. Courtesy of Ruth Barnett.

nevertheless marked her out as different. It was for that reason that, having no passport, she loathed the travel paper that she was forced to use, which carried the damning words 'Person of No Nationality' (xiii).

Barnett practised as a psychotherapist; this is reflected in the narrative of her autobiography, which is structured around a process of psychic healing and reintegration. Annette Saville, on the other hand, structures her memoirs around her victimhood, in the sense that she repeatedly blames conditions, events, and other people, starting with her parents, for 'ruining my life' (e.g. 84).[10] The title of her memoirs, *Only a Kindertransportee*, reflects the poor treatment and second-class status meted out to her as a child refugee in Britain. The conditions with which Saville was faced were consistently amongst the worst described in any of the texts analysed here. She had been a gifted and intelligent schoolgirl in Vienna, with musical ambitions. In Britain, however, she switched schools frequently and was deprived of the regular schooling that would have given her the education that her abilities merited; only for brief periods, at Hove County School and especially at the renowned Godolphin and Latymer School, which had been evacuated from west London to Newbury, Berkshire, did she enjoy an education that satisfied her expectations. She consequently harboured a lifelong grievance against both Britain and the refugee organizations for their failure to nurture the talents of refugee children.

Saville was unable to pursue her musical training methodically, leading to the failure of her attempts to gain entry to a college of music or, later, to train as a music teacher. Central to her sense of isolation and dislocation were the frequent and deeply unsettling changes of accommodation that she experienced: she was first accommodated with other Kindertransport children at Pakefield Camp, Lowestoft, then at Dovercourt Camp, Harwich, after which she lived in no fewer than eight placements in British households (not counting short stays), as well as in hostels, before she started work and lived independently. These placements were almost all unsatisfactory, in terms both of their physical conditions and of the care and emotional support that she received; only for the short period that she spent in summer 1940 with the Misses Pickett in Brighton did she experience a caring home, but that was cut short when Brighton was declared a protected area where 'enemy aliens' were not permitted to reside.

Barnett and her older brother Martin were first taken in by a married couple, the Steads, who lived in the rectory at Merston, near Strood in Kent, where she was treated with a harshness that bordered on cruelty. That contributed to the destabilization of her sense of her own selfhood and identity, as she could not understand what it was in her that merited such punishment: 'My life in Merston Rectory was a nightmare of confusion, fear and pain that I can't really remember in any sort of order' (21). After two years there, the children were sent to the Friends' School in Saffron Walden, Essex, 'a paradise for us' (30) thanks to the kindness and understanding shown them by the Quakers. But two and a half years later, and when the Steads would not have them back, they spent three months at a hostel in Richmond, south-west London, where they were allowed to run wild. The hostel housed displaced children, which exacerbated Barnett's insecurity as well as her longing for a settled family life in the framework of which she could also develop a settled identity.

The turning point in Barnett's childhood came when, in October 1943, they were taken in by the Goodrickes, a family with five children who lived in Horsmonden, near Maidstone in Kent. Barnett was overjoyed at finding herself in a family environment again, 'A Real Family at Last', as she puts it in the title of Chapter 7 (40–45). At the Goodrickes', Barnett developed a deep interest in farm life, a process that was enhanced when in autumn 1945 she went to live with the Haltings, another farming family with several children, at East Harting, near Rogate; she was at once enraptured by the beauty of the South Downs in Sussex, which 'never lost their magic for me' (67). Her intimate relationship with the English countryside and its animal life remained with her for life. She 'adored' the Haltings (63); but, however hard she tried to resemble the Haltings' children, she remained aware that they were her guardians, not her real parents. Her new sense of stability was, however, reinforced by her time at Petersfield High School, where her academic talents became clear. She also became integrated into English rural life, attending village fairs, Christmas parties at the local manor house, events at the Women's Institute, and even becoming an active member of the Young Farmers' Club. She had assumed much of the lifestyle and self-image of a young British girl.

That stability faced its greatest crisis when, ten years after her separation from them, her parents made contact with her and demanded her return to Germany, which they eventually enforced by means of a court order. Barnett had been a child of four in 1939 and was now entering adolescence. She barely remembered her parents, having decided as a small child that her mother was long dead; this was the only way in which she had been able to make sense of her situation, as otherwise her mother would surely have come to her rescue. Consequently, her principal reaction to her mother's appearance was to defend her hard-won security within the Halting family against what she experienced as a traumatic threat to her life and being:

> It was an immense shock to be confronted with a strange woman and told that she was my mother. [...] What on earth had this big fat woman to do with me!? She certainly didn't fit the vague image of my mother that I had had in my mind since I was four. She couldn't speak a word of English, I couldn't speak German and I didn't want to talk with her. She wanted to pull me to her and hug me, but I couldn't bear her touching me. [...] I was so full of confused, unmanageable feelings that I feared I would explode. (105)

The gulf in language that divided mother from daughter was emblematic of the division within Barnett between her origins in Germany and her development as a British schoolgirl in a British family. Those feelings were only exacerbated by her very unhappy stay with her parents in a small Bavarian village, which ended when they were forced to concede that she should return to Britain.

Annette Saville's image of Britain is unremittingly negative from the very first lines of her autobiography, and remains so throughout the text. Her first chapter, sarcastically entitled 'What A Welcome!' (1–2), contrasts the friendly reception that the children on her train had received in the Netherlands with its British counterpart:

> Our first shock: instead of friendly welcoming Dutch people all we saw was about five or six sullen-looking, middle-aged English men and women, staring at us with undisguised hostility. Our comments between ourselves were: 'What an unfriendly country!' 'Wish we could have stayed in Holland.' 'Not a smile, not a word of greeting!' 'Oh dear, they don't want us here!' Our hearts sank. (1)

The text is designed to shatter the comfortable illusion that refugee children were treated with hospitality and kindness in Britain, whereas in reality neglect, loneliness, and marginalization were their lot. In her concluding comments, Saville reaches the damning judgement that, for an unaccompanied refugee child, death in a concentration camp or life under the harsh regime of the Japanese occupying forces in Shanghai was preferable to life in Britain:

> Most of us would rather have died with our parents in concentration camps, or, in my case, gone to Shanghai with them. The Jewish belief is that children's lives must be saved, but not at the cost of psychological damage, thank you very much! (323)

This provides the framework within which Saville's account of her life, with its unhappiness, failures, bouts of mental illness, and depression, including an attempt at suicide by gassing, is played out. She records the disastrous course of her first marriage and the long, drawn-out acrimony of the ensuing divorce; the failure of her attempts to build a career as a nurse, a nursery nurse, and a music teacher; her inability to hold down any job for any length of time, which led her to the expedient of taking temporary jobs as a means of earning a living; and the financial problems which condemned her to live in inadequate accommodation in south-east London, distant from the refugee community in the wealthier north-west.

Barnett's life, by contrast, took a happier course. She studied horticulture at the University of Reading, where she met her husband, a British Jew. She had three children and pursued a distinguished career in teaching, rising to the position of deputy head at schools in Acton and Greenford, before her interest in counselling led her to train for her second career as a psychotherapist. A turning point in her life came in June 1989, when she attended the first reunion of Kindertransport children, which opened up to her the possibility of applying her psychotherapeutic techniques to her own life (201–04). She gained a new insight into her situation:

> Up until that conference, it had not occurred to me that any children, other than my brother and I, had come to England as refugees. Suddenly, there were a thousand of us together, and it was only then I learnt there had been 10,000 children rescued by the British Government. I finally saw my place in history. (202)

Having realized 'how much I didn't know because I had not allowed myself to know', Barnett used that new understanding to gain a measure of control over her life. Although the Kindertransport children who had lost their parents in the Holocaust considered her fortunate, she understood that the traumatic separation from her parents had nevertheless left her prey to an apparently irreparable confusion of identity and selfhood:

> I was shocked and saddened by the tragic stories of other Kinder but, in a way, I felt I had lost my parents too. The parents I met after ten years were total strangers, who were completely different to the parents I had known before. My inner world was peopled by two sets of parents and three sets of foster parents. How could I not be confused?

In Barnett's account, the reunion was the catalyst in the healing process that allowed her to reunite the two parts of herself, the German-Jewish child and the British woman that she had become, which she had previously kept apart:

> It was the moment that I let Ruthchen back into my life. It was as if a mask had suddenly vanished from my eyes and ears; a mask that had shut out a part of the world that I couldn't bear to see, hear and know about. Suddenly I saw everything differently. (202)

Confident in her new understanding of her identity, Barnett began to specialize in working with Holocaust survivors, thereby mastering, in a sense, her own troubled past. The integration of 'Ruthchen' with 'Ruth', by providing her with the basis of a stable identity, had enabled her to assert agency over her own life, as well as to assist other victims of Nazism.

Annette Saville experienced no such healing reconciliation. Her attitude to British society around her remained deeply hostile, as in her bitter criticism of the snobbery and class-consciousness of the British middle classes, who deemed the refugee children fit only for domestic service. Yet she was also scathing in her comments on the British working classes, which she dismissed as boorish, drunken, idle, and uncultured; she went so far as to refer to a work colleague from a working-class area of London as a 'slum slut' (279). She discerned a similar vulgarity, illiteracy, and lack of hygiene among lower-class British Jews, including the relatives on her father's side whom she visited in Soho in 1939, as described in the chapter entitled 'Relatives — Who Needs Them?' (23–25).

Saville was the victim of repeated misfortunes, such as a near-fatal bicycle accident in November 1949, or of acts of malice, as when she was expelled from her hostel in Speen, near Newbury, in 1941, on a false charge of theft and could not stay at Godolphin and Latymer School. But her image of herself as a victim led her repeatedly to place the blame for her problems on other people: the teacher at Dovercourt Camp who 'ruined' her musical career by advising her against undertaking musical training (8); her parents, for not taking her to Shanghai, where, she believed, she could have become a professor at the conservatoire; or the Misses Collyer, who took her into their home in Purley, but then, as she put it, 'spoilt my life again' (52) by leaving London for rural Berkshire and obliging her to interrupt her education at Purley County School. Saville's narrative is that of a life unhappy and unfulfilled. Above all, she blames the Smiths, the married couple with whom she lived in Hoddesdon, Hertfordshire, after her stay in Berkshire, for converting her to Christianity. From 1941 until 1955, she was a practising Christian, even undergoing training at the Redcliffe Missionary Training College in Chiswick, until, unable to pay the fees, she was forced to leave. She blamed Christianity, with its strict code of sexual morality, for her failure to find happiness in love: 'Unfortunately I awoke to this fact too late when I realised Christianity had ruined my life' (84).

The image of life in Britain conveyed in Saville's autobiography is conditioned in large measure by her sense of herself as a victim, which left her unable to assert any significant degree of agency over her life; her identity remained that of the outsider: isolated, marginalized, and deprived of the life that she might have led under different circumstances. Barnett, on the other hand, fashions a narrative in which, after her separation from her parents and its acutely painful consequences in her childhood and youth, she is able to assert a degree of control over her own life and, eventually, to arrive at a new identity in which the fractures of her childhood are at least partly healed: the British and German-Jewish elements in her identity are able to coexist.

By the time that the more recent memoirs and autobiographies by Jewish refugees from Nazism covered in this chapter were written, over half a century had passed since their authors had had to leave their native countries and had come to Britain. The great majority of the authors were younger refugees, those who had arrived as young children or teenagers and who had not lived in their countries of birth long enough to acquire a settled identity and predispositions there. Consequently, a central theme lies in their attempts to overcome an initial phase of acute instability and insecurity, and to find a solid foundation and a solid sense of identity on which to build new lives for themselves. Those attempts met with widely differing degrees of success, as shown in this chapter. The distance from the events of the 1930s, which some of the authors recall only hazily, results in far more space in these texts being devoted to conditions in Britain than to conditions in Germany, Austria, or Czechoslovakia. These refugee authors had spent by far the greater part of their lives in Britain, a country which they came to regard, unlike their older counterparts, as their home; some celebrated their successful integration into British society, while others focused more on their struggle to achieve some degree of integration and the obstacles that they encountered in that process. But for all of them it was Britain that formed the background to their lives.

Notes to Chapter 7

1. Irene White, *I Came as a Stranger* (London: Hazelwood, 1991).
2. On this unit, see Ian Dear, *10 Commando* (London: Cooper, 1987).
3. Martha Blend, *A Child Alone* (London: Vallentine Mitchell, 1995).
4. Lisl Klein, *Nobody Said It would Be Easy* (Brighton: The Book Guild, 2012).
5. C. C. Aronsfeld, *Wanderer from My Birth* (London: Janus Publishing, 1997).
6. On the Wiener Library, see Ben Barkow, *Alfred Wiener and the Making of the Holocaust Library* (London: Vallentine Mitchell, 1997).
7. John Izbicki, *Life between the Lines: A Memoir* (London: Umbria Press, 2012).
8. Ruth Barnett, *Person of No Nationality: A Story of Childhood Separation, Loss and Recovery* (London: David Paul, 2010).
9. Since her mother was a gentile, Barnett could not, according to Jewish law (Halacha), be Jewish.
10. Annette Saville, *Only a Kindertransportee* (London: New Millennium, 2002).

AFTERWORD

Over the course of its seven chapters, this book has sought to reveal something of the wealth of literary material created by the Jewish refugees from Nazism who fled to Britain, focusing in particular on their perceptions of the British and their reactions to British society. By analysing a range of texts published between the 1930s and 2012, it has aimed to set the refugees' experience in its historical context, from the pre-war years of their arrival and initial settlement, through the caesura of World War II, which so greatly influenced their attitudes to British society, and on into the more settled decades after 1945. The final three chapters were no longer chronological or historical in structure, but instead analysed three important groups of refugee authors.

As this study has shown, identity and agency are key factors that emerge from an analysis of accounts of the lives of Jewish refugees in Britain; in turn, they play a central role in determining the image of Britain conveyed in the texts. The refugees, especially those who did not arrive in Britain as young children, had already acquired predispositions, attitudes, and values before their emigration. It was then necessary for them to adapt those predispositions to the changed conditions of life in emigration — to the extent that they were able, or wished, to do so. In this respect, the texts discussed have demonstrated a wide range of differing reactions among the refugee writers, from those who resolved to engage actively with the society around them to those who found it almost impossible to do so. At times, in particular during the period of wartime internment, it appeared as if British society was set on marginalizing or excluding the 'alien' refugees; but that was counterbalanced by a stronger long-term trend towards at least a qualified acceptance of the refugees, evident most obviously in their inclusion in the British war effort and their service in the British forces — though not even all those who fought for Britain in the war settled there permanently.

Texts by the younger refugees, who were educated and socialized in Britain and grew into adulthood after 1945, demonstrate the tensions and conflicts that frequently marked the long and difficult process of their adaptation to British conditions; for them, the assumption of a German or Austrian identity was no longer an option. Some of them also abandoned any Jewish identity, though others remained true to Judaism, often against the odds. Over the decades, most of them, though not all, reached a balance of some kind between the conflicting claims of these identities. That is a tribute to them, but also in some measure to the society around them.

BIBLIOGRAPHY

Unpublished Sources

ROSENSTOCK, WERNER, *Memoirs 1941–86*, unpublished typescript, 2 vols (1945, 1986)
WAGNER, LILY, 'Emigrants' Daily Life', unpublished typescript (1940)

Published Sources

AMBROSE, KENNETH, 'The Second Generation', *AJR Information*, February 1949, p. 5, and July 1949, p. 3
—— 'Your Newspaper', *AJR Information*, January 1950, p. 3
—— 'Struwwelpeter', *AJR Information*, February 1954, p. 8
—— 'The Best of Both Worlds', *AJR Information*, June 1960, p. 11
ARONSFELD, C. C., *Wanderer from My Birth* (London: Janus Publishing, 1997)
BARKOW, BEN, *Alfred Wiener and the Making of the Holocaust Library* (London: Vallentine Mitchell, 1997)
BARNETT, RUTH, *Person of No Nationality: A Story of Childhood Separation, Loss and Recovery* (London: David Paul, 2010)
BEARMAN, MARIETTA, and OTHERS, *Wien–London, hin und retour: Das Austrian Centre in London 1939 bis 1947* (Vienna: Czernin, 2004); published in English as *Out of Austria: The Austrian Centre in London in World War II*, trans. by Miha Tavčar (London: Tauris, 2008)
BENTWICH, NORMAN, *I Understand the Risks: The Story of the Refugees from Nazi Oppression Who Fought in the British Forces in the World War* (London: Gollancz, 1950)
BLEND, MARTHA, *A Child Alone* (London: Vallentine Mitchell, 1995)
BONDY, PAUL, 'Internment Notes', in *Civilian Internment in Britain during WW2: Huyton Camp: Eye-Witness Accounts*, ed. by Jennifer Taylor ([London]: Anglo-German Family History Society Publications, 2012), pp. 15–37
BORCHARD, RUTH, *We Are Strangers Here: An 'Enemy Alien' in Prison in 1940*, intro. by Charmian Brinson (London: Vallentine Mitchell, 2008)
BRINSON, CHARMIAN, ANNA MÜLLER-HÄRLIN, and JULIA WINCKLER, *His Majesty's Loyal Internee: Fred Uhlman in Captivity* (London: Vallentine Mitchell, 2009)
Britain's New Citizens: The Story of the Refugees from Germany and Austria: Tenth Anniversary Publication of the Association of Jewish Refugees in Great Britain (London: Association of Jewish Refugees, 1951)
BRUNNHUBER, NICOLE, *The Faces of Janus: English-Language Fiction by German-Speaking Exiles in Great Britain, 1933–1945* (Berne: Lang, 2005)
CASTONIER, ELISABETH, *Stürmisch bis heiter: Memoiren einer Außenseiterin* (Munich: DTV, 1967)
—— *Mill Farm: Menschen und Tiere unter einem Dach* (Reinbek bei Hamburg: Rowohlt, 1976)
CESARANI, DAVID, and TONY KUSHNER, eds, *The Internment of Aliens in Twentieth Century Britain* (London: Cass, 1993)

CRANE, PETER, 'Wir leben nun mal auf einem Vulkan' (Bonn: Weidle, 2005)
DEAR, IAN, 10 Commando (London: Cooper, 1987)
DOVE, RICHARD, Journey of No Return: Five German-Speaking Literary Exiles in Britain, 1933–1945 (London: Libris, 2000)
―― ED., 'Totally Un-English'? Britain's Internment of 'Enemy Aliens' in Two World Wars, Yearbook of the Research Centre for German and Austrian Exile Studies, 7 (Amsterdam: Rodopi, 2005)
EBERSTADT, WALTER ALBERT, Whence We Came, Where We Went: From the Rhine to the Main to the Elbe, from the Thames to the Hudson (New York: W. A. E. Books, 2002)
FEINER, RUTH, Fires in May, trans. by Norman Alexander (Philadelphia: Lippincott, 1936)
FLESCH, CARL F., 'Where Do You Come From?': Hitler Refugees in Great Britain Then and Now: The Happy Compromise (London: Pen Press Publishers, 2001)
FRIEDENTHAL, RICHARD, Die Welt in der Nußschale (Munich: Piper, 1956)
GÁL, HANS, Musik hinter Stacheldraht: Tagebuchblätter aus dem Sommer 1940, ed. by Eva Fox-Gál (Berne: Lang, 2003)
GILLMAN, PETER, and LENI GILLMAN, 'Collar the Lot!': How Britain Interned and Expelled its Wartime Refugees (London: Quartet Books, 1980)
GISSING, VERA, Pearls of Childhood (London: Robson, 1988)
GRENVILLE, ANTHONY, 'German-Jewish Refugees in the British Forces and the Re-Education of German Prisoners of War in Britain: The Case of Herbert Sulzbach', Angermion, 2 (2009), 143–57
―― Jewish Refugees from Germany and Austria in Britain, 1933–1970: Their Image in 'AJR Information' (London: Vallentine Mitchell, 2010)
―― 'Guardians of a Heritage: The Editors of the Association of Jewish Refugees Journal', in Voices from Exile: Essays in Memory of Hamish Ritchie, ed. by Ian Wallace (Leiden: Brill Rodopi, 2015), pp. 162–77
HAGEN, LOUIS, Arnhem Lift: Diary of a Glider Pilot (London: Pilot Press, 1945)
HAMMEL, ANDREA, Everyday Life as Alternative Space in Exile Writing: The Novels of Anna Gmeyner, Selma Kahn, Hilde Spiel, Martina Wied and Hermynia Zur Muehlen (Berne: Lang, 2008)
HANNAM, CHARLES, A Boy in That Situation: An Autobiography (New York: Harper & Row, 1977)
―― Almost an Englishman (London: Deutsch, 1979)
―― Outsider Inside: Volume III of the Hartland Trilogy (Brighton: Alpha Press, 2008)
IZBICKI, JOHN, Life between the Lines: A Memoir (London: Umbria Press, 2012)
JACOBSTHAL, PAUL, 'The Long Vac', in Refugee Scholars: Conversations with Tess Simpson, ed. by R. M. Cooper (Leeds: Moorland Books, 1992), pp. 198–228
JACOBY, INGRID, My Darling Diary, 3 vols (Penzance: United Writers Publications, 1998–2009)
JAGENDORF, ZVI, Wolfy and the Strudelbakers (Stockport: Dewi Lewis, 2001)
KAHN, LEO, Obliging Fellow (London: Nicholson & Watson, 1946)
KAUDERS, RUDOLF, Donauwalzer am Irawadi: Exil in England, Kampf in Burma, Rückkehr nach Wien (Vienna: Mandelbaum, 2011)
KERR, ALFRED, Ich kam nach England: Ein Tagebuch aus dem Nachlaß, ed. by Walter Huder and Thomas Koebner (Bonn: Bouvier, 1979)
KERR, JUDITH, Out of the Hitler Time (London: Collins, 1995)
KLEIN, LISL, Nobody Said It would Be Easy (Brighton: The Book Guild, 2012)
LAFITTE, FRANÇOIS, The Internment of Aliens (London: Penguin, 1940)
LAURENT, LIVIA, A Tale of Internment (London: Allen & Unwin, 1942)
LEIGHTON-LANGER, PETER, The King's Own Loyal Enemy Aliens: German and Austrian

Refugees in Britain's Armed Forces, 1939–45 (London: Vallentine Mitchell, 2006)
LOMNITZ, ALFRED, *'Never Mind, Mr. Lom!'; or, The Uses of Adversity* (London: Macmillan, 1941)
LONDON, LOUISE, *Whitehall and the Jews, 1933–1948: British Immigration Policy, Jewish Refugees and the Holocaust* (Cambridge, Cambridge University Press, 2000)
LYNTON, MARK, *Accidental Journey: A Cambridge Internee's Memoir of World War II* (Woodstock, NY: Overlook Press, 1995)
MESSINGER, IRENE, 'Marriages of Convenience as a Strategy for Escape and Survival', *AJR Journal*, November 2014, pp. 1–2
MIKES, GEORGE, *How To Be an Alien* (London: Allan Wingate, 1946)
MOSSE, WERNER E., ed., *Second Chance: Two Centuries of German-Speaking Jews in the United Kingdom* (Tübingen: Mohr, 1991)
NEUMANN, ROBERT, *By the Waters of Babylon*, trans. by Anthony Dent (London: Dent, 1939)
——*Ein leichtes Leben: Bericht über mich selbst und Zeitgenossen* (Munich: Desch, 1963)
PELICAN, FRED, *From Dachau to Dunkirk* (London: Vallentine Mitchell, 1993)
PERRY, GEOFFREY H., *When Life Becomes History* (London: White Mountain Press, 2002)
PERRY, PETER J. C., *An Extraordinary Commission: The Story of a Journey through Europe's Disaster* (Bristol: published by the author, 1997)
PISTOL, RACHEL, *Internment during the Second World War: A Comparative Study of Great Britain and the USA* (London: Bloomsbury, 2017)
ROSS, VICTOR, *Basic British* (London: Parrish, 1956)
——Letter to the editor, *AJR Journal*, September 2015, p. 6
ROTH, SOPHIE, *Für mein Schurlikind: Tagebuch 1940–1944*, ed. by Evelyn Adunka (Vienna: Theodor Kramer Gesellschaft, 2012)
RUHEMANN, FRITZ, 'Vorfrühling in Swiss Cottage', *AJR Information*, August 1953, p. 5
SANDERS, ERIC, *Emigration ins Leben: Wien–London und nicht mehr retour*, ed. by Peter Pirker (Vienna: Czernin, 2008)
SAVILLE, ANNETTE, *Only a Kindertransportee* (London: New Millennium, 2002)
SEGAL, LORE, *Other People's Houses: A Refugee in England 1938–48* (London: Bodley Head, 1974; original edn New York: Harcourt Brace, 1964)
'Sergeant Louis Edmund Hagen', <http://www.pegasusarchive.org/arnhem/louis_hagen.htm> [accessed on 13 February 2016]
SHERMAN, A. J., *Island Refuge: Britain and Refugees from the Third Reich 1933–1939* (London: Cass, 1994; original edn London: Elek, 1973)
SINSHEIMER, HERMANN, *Shylock: The History of a Character; or, the Myth of the Jew* (London: Gollancz, 1947); published in full as *Shylock: Die Geschichte einer Figur* (Munich: Ner Tamid Verlag, 1960)
——*Gelebt im Paradies: Gestalten und Geschichten* (Berlin: Verlag für Berlin-Brandenburg, 2013; original publication Munich: Pflaum, 1953)
SINSHEIMER, HERMANN, and CHRISTOBEL SINSHEIMER, *Briefe aus England in die Pfalz*, ed. by Hans-Helmut Görtz, Gabriele Giersberg, and Erik Giersberg (Neustadt an der Weinstraße: Selbstverlag der Stiftung zur Förderung der pfälzischen Geschichtsforschung, 2012)
SPIEL, HILDE, *Die hellen und die finsteren Zeiten: Erinnerungen 1911–1946* (Munich: List, 1989)
——*Welche Welt ist meine Welt?: Erinnerungen 1946–1989* (Munich: List, 1990)
SPIER, EUGEN, *The Protecting Power* (London: Skeffington, 1951)
STENT, RONALD, *A Bespattered Page?: The Internment of 'His Majesty's Most Loyal Enemy Aliens'* (London: Deutsch, 1980)
TERGIT, GABRIELE, 'In Memory of a Refugee Artist', *AJR Information*, October 1956, p. 10.
——'Große Generation', *AJR Information*, August 1957, pp. 10–11

—— 'Das Volk des Buches und das Jubilaeum von Martin Breslauer', *AJR Information*, October 1958, p. 12

—— 'Buecher auf Wanderschaft', *AJR Information*, April 1971, p. 8.

—— *Etwas Seltenes überhaupt: Erinnerungen* (Frankfurt a.M.: Ullstein, 1983)

UHLMAN, FRED, *The Making of an Englishman* (London: Gollancz, 1960)

—— *Reunion* (London: Adam Books, 1971; republished London: Collins & Harvill, 1977)

UNGERSON, CLARE, *Four Thousand Lives: The Rescue of German Jewish Men to Britain, 1939* (Stroud, Glous.: History Press, 2014)

VIETOR-ENGLÄNDER, DEBORAH, 'Hermann Sinsheimers deutsch-jüdisches Schicksal', in *Zwischen Rassenhass und Identitätssuche: Deutsch-jüdische literarische Kultur im nationalsozialistischen Deutschland*, ed. by Kerstin Schoor (Göttingen: Wallstein, 2010), pp. 285–303

WAGNER, HANS-ULRICH, 'Über alle Hindernisse hinweg: London-Remigranten in der westdeutschen Rundfunkgeschichte', in *'Stimme der Wahrheit': German-Language Broadcasting by the BBC*, ed. by Charmian Brinson and Richard Dove, Yearbook of the Research Centre for German and Austrian Exile Studies, 5 (Amsterdam: Rodopi, 2003), pp. 139–57

WASSERSTEIN, BERNARD, *Britain and the Jews of Europe, 1939–1945* (Oxford: Oxford University Press, 1988; original edn London: Institute of Jewish Affairs, 1979)

WEBER, REGINA, *Lotte Labowsky (1905–1991): Schülerin Aby Warburgs, Kollegin Raymond Klibanskys: Eine Wissenschaftlerin zwischen Fremd- und Selbstbestimmung im englischen Exil* (Berlin: Reimer, 2012)

WHITE, IRENE, *I Came as a Stranger* (London: Hazelwood, 1991)

Z[EITLIN], L[EON], OBITUARY FOR RUTH FEINER, *AJR Information*, September 1954, p. 4

ZWEIG, STEFAN, *Die Welt von gestern: Erinnerungen eines Europäers* (London: Hamish Hamilton; Stockholm: Bermann-Fischer, 1941)

INDEX

acculturation 31–32, 70, 95, 160
agency 3, 10, 86, 88, 147, 176
  lack of 6, 44, 49, 63, 175
  relationship to identity 106, 139, 142–43, 147, 162, 164, 174, 175
AJR, *see* Association of Jewish Refugees
AJR Information (from 2000, *AJR Journal*) 13, 16, 89 n. 3, 89 n. 15, 149
  publications by refugee writers in 96, 97–100, 122–24
'aliens' 118, 126, 147, 176
  in the British forces 72, 75, 79
  'friendly' 78
  see also 'enemy aliens'; Mikes, George, *How to Be an Alien*
American Guild for German Cultural Freedom 112
Anglo-Jewry 89
  relations of refugees from Nazism with 15–16, 26, 27, 91, 134, 136, 165, 167, 174
Anschluss, *see* Austria: annexation of
anti-Semitism 1, 142, 155
  in Austria 11, 84, 87, 111, 115
  in Britain 19, 32, 79, 87, 106, 124, 127, 142, 145–46, 146, 168
  in Czechoslovakia 137, 138
  in France 131
  in Posen 162
  in Silesia 81
assimilation into British society 5, 15, 124, 131, 136, 153
  difficulties of 26, 108
  generational differences 146, 159
Association of Jewish Refugees (AJR) 13–15, 16, 122
  see also *AJR Information*
Australia, deportation to 43, 52, 54, 55, 97, 141
Austria:
  annexation of (*Anschluss*) 6, 8, 11, 87, 111
  as perceived by refugee writers 29, 30–31, 84–87, 104, 110–11, 113, 115, 155, 156
  Zweig's exile from 6–8
Austrian Centre (London) 16, 89 n. 14
Auxiliary Military Pioneer Corps, *see* Pioneer Corps

Belsize Group 122
Belsize Square Synagogue 16, 122
Berlin:
  attachment to 27
  occupation of 74–75
  pre-emigration life in 93, 117–18
  visited after the war 111, 115
Blitz 63, 123, 152
  impact of civilian response on refugees 16–17, 53, 120–21, 132, 168
  see also London: bombing; 'Manchester Blitz'
Bloomsbury House 12, 86
boarding houses 11–12, 29, 32, 117
  used for internment 41–42, 48
Breslauer, Martin 122–23
Britain, Battle of 34, 49, 52, 58
British citizenship 16, 86, 91, 93, 104, 169
  difference from being English 107
  difficulties acquiring 70, 75, 81
  motivations for acquiring 21–22, 87–88, 95–96
British Union of Fascists 129 n. 19
  see also Mosleyites

Cambridge (city) 12, 91, 131
Cambridge (university and colleges) 77, 93, 131, 132, 140, 142
Canada, deportation to 43, 54, 56, 57, 78, 106, 117
Central Europe 157
  Jewish refugees from 16, 96, 116–17, 123
children, refugee 10, 16, 19–20, 25, 45–46, 48, 92, 98
  accounts by 29–32, 130–48, 153–62, 166–68, 169–75
Christianity:
  competing with Jewish identity 155
  conversion to 32, 77, 105, 160, 173–74
  fear of being converted to 136, 145, 146
  rapprochement with 70, 95, 146, 166
Christian-Jewish Relations 166
Cliveden Set 115
concentration camps 21, 62, 66, 83, 92, 157
  absence from Britain 126
  Bergen-Belsen 80, 138
  Buchenwald 123
  comparison of British internment to 39, 117
  comparison of life in Britain to 113, 173
  Dachau 82, 123
  Neuengamme 84
  'transmigrants' from 69, 89 n. 11
Cosmo (London):
  café 96
  restaurant 152

INDEX

Council of Christians and Jews 166
Czechoslovakia 121, 136–37, 157–59, 161–62

Dachinger, Hugo, *Portrait of a Man* 60 (fig.)
deportation:
    to Australia 43, 52, 54, 55, 97, 141
    British management of 43, 52, 55
    to Canada 43, 54, 56, 57, 78, 106, 117
    threat of 8, 24, 42
diaries 9–10, 19–20, 29–32, 35–43, 100, 102–06
    diary form 66
    difference from later accounts 49–50, 117, 127
    use in later accounts 56, 65, 72, 78
Diaspora Jews 145–46, 164
Doitch, Eric, *The Old Underground Station* 101 (fig.)
Dominican Republic 133, 136

Eastern Europe 15, 16
    Jews from 27, 84, 91
Eastern Jews 16, 143, 145, 146
    see also under Eastern Europe
'enemy aliens' 77, 127, 141, 149, 171
    categories 35, 43, 44, 63 n. 2
    deportation 52
    internment 1, 2, 6, 17, 18–19, 19–20, 34–35, 38, 53, 55, 65, 78, 132
    see also 'aliens'

France, as country of refuge 9, 29, 124, 130
    compared with Britain 128, 131
    potential alternative to Britain 110, 164
Free German League of Culture (FGLC) 16, 126

German-Jewish symbiosis 15
Germany:
    contrasted with Britain 22, 23, 50, 52, 53, 70–71, 140
    cultural legacy among refugees 15, 16, 27, 76, 94, 98, 162–64
    pre-emigration life in 11, 13, 27, 76, 84, 93, 117–18, 121, 122, 164
    refugees' post-war contribution to 73–75, 80
Glasgow 91

Hebrew 142, 146
Holloway Prison 17, 19, 45–47, 48, 48–49
Holocaust:
    and Cäsar (C. C.) Aronsfeld 164, 165
    coming to terms with 92, 115, 138, 156–57, 174
    deaths of relatives in 29, 100, 138, 157, 173
    public awareness of 1, 149

identity 3, 5, 8, 69, 82, 108, 152, 176
    British and past 25–33, 70, 75, 76, 77–78, 86, 91–92, 95–96, 103–06, 108 n. 2, 110–14, 130–43, 153–75

Continental Jewish 15–17, 84, 89, 98, 122–24
    of Eastern Jewish refugees in Britain 145–47
    and internment 38–44, 63
    of refugees in the armed forces 73, 78–79, 81, 84, 87, 88, 132
    relationship to agency 106, 139, 142–43, 147, 162, 164, 174, 175
Institute of Jewish Affairs 165
integration into British society 2, 18, 89 n. 8, 97, 107, 108 n. 2, 138, 149–52, 175
    as alternative to absorption into Anglo-Jewry 15–16, 91
    of assimilated German Jews 15, 50, 70
    difficulties and failures 5, 23, 65, 81, 95, 143, 153–62, 169–75
    generational differences 92, 98–99, 152–53, 159, 160, 162–69
    influence of refugees' original social status 81
    preservation of identity during 15–17, 91–93
    of young refugees 25–32, 100–06, 131–33
internment 2, 6, 17, 34–35, 88, 113, 123, 135, 176
    accounts and depictions 3, 17, 18–19, 20, 35–64, 77–78, 108, 116, 117, 127–28, 129 n. 20, 132, 145
    avoidance 88, 141, 165, 167
    and identity 38–44, 63
    research on 1, 34
    temporary accommodation 36, 40, 56, 127
    see also Holloway Prison; internment camps; transit camps
internment camps 35, 54–56, 57, 61–63, 117
    camp universities 42, 55, 56, 64 n. 12
    Central Promenade Camp (Isle of Man) 41, 42
    Hutchinson Camp (Isle of Man) 41, 42, 59, 127
    Huyton (Merseyside) 20, 40–41, 50, 50–52, 53, 78, 86
    Onchan (Isle of Man) 54
    Port Erin (Isle of Man) 48, 59
    Port St Mary (Isle of Man) 48
    Rushen (Isle of Man) 45, 48
    see also transit camps
Isle of Man, internment on 17, 35, 39, 45, 54, 56, 123
    experiences of 41–44, 48, 59, 59–61, 62, 117, 127
    transfer to 40, 41, 46, 47–48
    see also under internment camps
Italy 87
    country of refuge 118

Jewish Central Information Office, *see* Wiener Library
Jewish Refugees Committee (JRC) 27, 165, 167

Karlsbad (Karlovy Vary) 157, 161–62
Kindertransport children 27, 133, 136, 139, 153, 169
    in later life 92, 173–74
    treatment of 134, 140, 171
    see also reception camps
Kindertransports 1, 130

Kitchener Camp (Kent) 69, 82
Kristallnacht, *see under* pogroms

Leeds 91, 165
letters, as primary sources 25–27, 93, 94–96
London:
　areas of Jewish settlement 16, 26, 84, 91, 110, 123–24, 146, 173
　bombing 9, 10, 52, 62, 72, 152, 168 (*see also* Blitz)
　home to Alfred Kerr 9, 10
　home to Stefan Zweig 6–7, 8
　refugees' perceptions 22, 23, 26, 70–71, 86, 95, 96–97, 112, 114, 115, 126, 147, 151, 167, 174

Manchester 19, 20, 91, 167, 168
'Manchester Blitz' 20
Mikes, George, *How to Be an Alien* 106
Mosleyites, 113, 115
　see also British Union of Fascists
Munich Agreement 7, 10, 118, 159

naturalization, *see* British citizenship
Netherlands 164, 173

Oxford (city) 29, 39, 42, 53, 91, 100–02, 104, 105
Oxford (university and colleges) 36, 63 n. 4, 76, 77, 78, 81, 100, 117, 136

Palestine, emigration to 93, 121, 151, 165
Paris 21, 23
　refugee writers' associations with 7, 117, 122, 124, 126, 167, 168
Patterns of Prejudice 166
PEN Club (London) 112, 122
PEN-Zentrum deutschsprachiger Autoren im Ausland, *see* PEN Club (London)
Pioneer Corps 69–70, 88
　refugee writers in 66, 71–72, 78, 79, 82–83, 86–87, 88, 106, 108
pogroms:
　Kristallnacht (November 1938) 16, 82, 149
　in Poland 145–46
Poland 81, 143, 145–46, 147, 162, 165
Posen 162
Prague 136, 138

reception camps (for Kindertransport children):
　Dovercourt (Harwich) 134, 171, 174
　Pakefield (Lowestoft) 171
refugee children, *see* children, refugee
refugees from Nazism 28 (fig.)
　confused with Nazi Germans 41, 61–62, 63, 120
　Continental cultural heritage 15, 27, 94, 98, 99, 122–24, 164
　relations with Anglo-Jewry 15–16, 26, 27, 91, 134, 136, 165, 167, 174

research on 1, 2, 65, 117
returning to country of origin 25, 27, 89 n. 14, 95, 104, 110, 111, 113, 114–15, 122, 137, 138, 157, 161–62, 168, 169, 172
service in the British forces 13, 65–90, 97, 132, 142, 152, 168 (*see also* Pioneer Corps)
Remarque, Erich Maria 110
　All Quiet on the Western Front 66
repatriation, attempted 91
Rosenbaum, Julius 122
Roth, Joseph, *Radetzkymarsch* 6

schools, British:
　refugee children's experience of 10, 29, 31, 70–71, 76–77, 88, 131, 140–41, 153–55, 168, 171
　refugees' work for 81, 88, 157, 173
Shanghai 82, 169, 173, 174
Struwwelpeter 99
Suschitzky, Joseph 123
Switzerland 116, 117, 130

transit camps:
　Kempton Park racecourse 35, 38, 45, 54, 59, 61, 62, 78
　Prees Heath (Shropshire) 45, 59, 61, 62, 63
　Warth Mill (Bury) 39, 45, 54, 63
'transmigrants' 69, 82, 89 n. 11

United States 16, 34
　destination for writers fleeing Nazism 110
　emigration to 25, 65, 75, 76, 78, 81, 132, 133, 139
universities and colleges, British:
　refugee academics at 36, 39, 42, 100, 143
　and refugee students 76, 77, 78, 131, 136

Vienna 89 n. 14, 118
　affection for 20, 103–04
　conflicted relationships with 84–86, 87–88, 110–11, 113, 114, 114–15, 156, 157
　post-war returns to 88, 111, 114–15, 157
　pre-emigration life in 32, 111, 116, 133, 143, 145, 153, 171
visas 8, 16, 84–86
　domestic service 133, 139
　transit 82, 89 n. 11

Waldheim Affair 111
Wiener, Alfred 165
Wiener Library (earlier the Jewish Central Information Office) 16, 165
Wiener Library Bulletin 165
Woburn House 27, 28 (fig.), 86, 165

xenophobia 32, 34, 69, 87, 131, 141

Yiddish 16, 84, 134, 142, 143, 145, 153, 155

INDEX OF REFUGEE WRITERS

❖

Ambrose, Kenneth 97–100
Aronsfeld, Cäsar (C. C.) 163 (fig.), 169
   Wanderer from my Birth 162–66
Barnett, Ruth 170 (fig.), 175 n. 9
   Person of No Nationality 169–71, 171–72, 173–74
Blend, Martha 154 (fig.), 159, 162
   A Child Alone 153–57
Bondy, Paul, diary 35, 38–39, 40
Borchard, Ruth, *We Are Strangers Here* 17–19, 45, 45–46, 46, 47, 48, 49
Castonier, Elisabeth 117–18, 128
   Eternal Front 119
   Mill Farm 118
   Stürmisch bis heiter 118–21
Eberstadt, Walter 65, 75–76, 80–81, 83, 88, 89 n. 8
   Whence We Came, Where We Went 75, 77–78, 78–79, 81
Feiner, Ruth 20–21, 124
   Fires in May 20–24
   later novels 24
   Young Woman of Europe 21
Friedenthal, Richard, *Die Welt in der Nußschale* 3, 59–63
Gál, Hans 37 (fig.), 39
   diary 36–38, 40–43, 49, 50
   Huyton Suite 41
Gissing, Vera 136–37, 157
   Pearls of Childhood 137–39
Hagen, Louis 66
   Arnhem Lift 66–69, 89 n. 3
Hannam, Charles 69
   A Boy in That Situation (autobiography, I) 139, 140–41, 141
   Almost an Englishman (II) 88, 139, 141, 141–42, 143
   Outside Inside (III) 139, 142
Izbicki, John, memoirs 162, 166–69
Jacobsthal, Paul 42
   diary 36, 39–40, 41–42, 42, 43–44, 49
Jacoby, Ingrid 27–29, 33, 100–02, 103
   My Darling Diary 29–32, 100, 102–06
Jagendorf, Zvi 144 (fig.)
   Wolfy and the Strudelbakers 3, 143–47
Kahn, Leo, *Obliging Fellow* 3, 43, 44, 54–56
Kerr, Alfred 5, 8, 93, 110, 118, 130
   Ich kam nach England 9–10
Kerr, Judith:
   Bombs on Aunt Dainty 8, 130
   The Other Way Round 8, 130, 131–33

   A Small Person Far Away 133
   When Hitler Stole Pink Rabbit 8, 130–31
Klein, Lisl 157–59, 158 (fig.)
   The Meaning of Work 161
   Nobody Said It Would Be Easy 157, 159–62
   Working across the Gap 161
Laurent, Livia (pseud. of Eva Meyerhof) 63 n. 8
   A Tale of Internment 45, 46, 46–47, 47–49, 49
Lomnitz, Alfred:
   Girl behind Barbed Wire 51 (fig.)
   'Never Mind, Mr. Lom!' 50–53
Lynton, Mark 64, 75, 83, 89 n. 7
   Accidental Journey 76–77, 78, 79–80, 80–81, 89 n. 7
Meyerhof, Eva, *see* Laurent, Livia
Neumann, Robert 49, 115–16, 127, 128
   By the Waters of Babylon 117
   Children of Vienna 116
   The Inquest 116
   Ein leichtes Leben 116–17
Ortmann, Sibylle, letters 25–27
Pelican, Fred 81–82, 83–84
   autobiography 82–83
Perry, Geoffrey, and memoirs 70, 71–72, 72–73, 73–74, 75, 80
Perry, Peter, and memoirs 70–71, 72, 73, 74–75, 80, 81
Reifenberg, Elise, *see* Tergit, Gabriele
Rosenstock, Werner 13–15, 14 (fig.)
   memoirs 15, 16–17
Ross, Victor, *Basic British* 106–08
Roth, Sophie, diaries 19–20
Ruhemann, Fritz 96
   'Vorfrühling in Swiss Cottage' 96–97
Sanders, Eric 81, 84, 85 (fig.), 88
   Emigration ins Leben 84–88
Saville, Annette 169, 171
   Only a Kindertransportee 171, 172–73, 174–75
Segal, Lore 133
   Other People's Houses 133–36
Sinsheimer, Hermann 93–94, 118
   letters 93, 94–96
Spiel, Hilde 110–15, 128
   Die hellen und die finsteren Zeiten 110, 111–15
   Welche Welt ist meine Welt 110, 115
Spier, Eugen 56
   The Protecting Power 56–59
Tergit, Gabriele (pseud. of Elise Reifenberg) 110, 121–24
   Das Büchlein vom Bett 121

Effingers 121
   Kaiserkron und Päonien rot 121
   Käsebier erobert den Kurfürstendamm 121
Uhlman, Fred 49, 110, 124, 125 (fig.), 126, 129 n. 20
   The Making of an Englishman 64 n. 15, 124–28
   Reunion 124

Wagner, Lily 11–13
White, Irene 149–51, 150 (fig), 151–52, 153
   I Came as a Stranger 149–53
Zweig, Stefan 5, 6–8, 110
   Die Welt von gestern 6–8

www.ingramcontent.com/pod-product-compliance
Lightning Source LLC
LaVergne TN
LVHW061251060426
835507LV00017B/2022